MULTIDISCIPLINARY PERSPECTIVES
ON POPULATION AND CONFLICT

DATE DUE

JUN 1987		
OCT 25 1991		
MAY 14 1992		
DEC 15 1993		
MAY 20 1994		
APR 9 1997		

DEMCO NO. 38-298

MULTIDISCIPLINARY PERSPECTIVES
ON POPULATION AND CONFLICT

Edited by NAZLI CHOUCRI

SYRACUSE UNIVERSITY PRESS   1984

Part of Chapter 1 appeared earlier in Nazli Choucri, *Population and Conflict: New Dimensions of Population Dynamics,* Policy Development Studies No. 8 (New York: United Nations Fund for Population Activities, 1983).

Library of Congress Cataloging in Publication Data
Main entry under title:

Multidisciplinary perspectives on population and
    conflict.

    Includes bibliographies and index.
    1. Population — Addresses, essays, lectures.
2. Interpersonal conflict — Addresses, essays,
lectures.   3. International relations — Addresses,
essays, lectures.   I. Choucri, Nazli.   II. Title:
Population and conflict.
HB871.M868 1984   304.6   84-2641
ISBN 0-8156-2314-3
ISBN 0-8156-2315-1 (pbk.)

CONTENTS

FOREWORD

The latter part of the twentieth century has been characterized by the emergence of population as a major issue for individual countries and for the world as a whole. Although the causes, consequences, and policy implications of problems related to population growth, fertility, mortality, migration, distribution, and composition are better understood today, knowledge of the relationships between population and conflict is still quite meager. The subject is indeed quite complex and defies simple analysis.

The present volume seeks to highlight the contributions of various fields and provide substantial information and evidence about sources of conflict and the bases for drawing conclusions about the ways in which population variables lead to violence among individuals, groups, regions, and countries. The authors of the various chapters have adopted perspectives that include the theoretical orientation of each discipline as well as empirical findings.

It is hoped that *Multidisciplinary Perspectives on Population and Conflict* will be of interest to social scientists and policy makers alike.

New York
Spring 1984

RAFAEL M. SALAS
Executive Director
United Nations Fund for
Population Activities

CONTRIBUTORS

EDWARD E. AZAR is Director of the Center for International Development at the University of Maryland, College Park, Md.

DAVIS B. BOBROW is Professor of Government and Politics at the University of Maryland, College Park, Md.

NAZLI CHOUCRI is Professor of Political Science and Associate Director of the Technology Adaptation Program at the Massachusetts Institute of Technology, Cambridge, Ma.

MARK N. COHEN is Professor of Anthropology at the State University of New York, Plattsburgh, N.Y.

NADIA E. FARAH is Visiting Professor of Government and Politics and Fellow in the Center for International Development at the University of Maryland, College Park, Md.

OMER R. GALLE is Professor of Sociology and Faculty Research Associate at the Population Research Center at the University of Texas, Austin, Tx.

JOHN R. HARRIS is Professor of Economics and Director of the Center for African Studies at Boston University, Boston, Ma.

WILLIAM R. KELLY is Assistant Professor of Sociology and Faculty Research Associate at the Population Research Center at the University of Texas, Austin, Tx.

ROBERT C. NORTH is Professor of Political Science at Stanford University, Stanford, Ca.

HAROLD M. PROSHANSKY is President of the Graduate School and University Center at the City University of New York.

VIJAYA SAMARAWEERA is Research Associate at the Center for Asian Development Studies at Boston University, Boston, Ma.

PREFACE

This book is the outcome of a conference on Population and Conflict held at the Massachusetts Institute of Technology at the initiation of Dr. R. M. Salas, Executive Director of the United Nations Fund for Population Activities. The chapters in this volume constitute an edited selection from the papers prepared for the conference. I would like to extend my appreciation to Dr. A. Thavarajah, Director of the Policy and Evaluation Division of the United Nations Fund for Population Activities, and his staff for the assistance extended to us in the preparation of this volume. In particular I would like to thank Dr. S. L. N. Rao and Ms. Linda Sherry-Cloonan of the Policy Branch.

Considerable editorial assistance was provided by Dr. Diane Beth Hyman, then research associate for the Technology Adaptation Program at MIT. Ms. Phoebe Green typed numerous drafts of the entire manuscript and should be commended. Finally I would like to thank Dr. Myron Weiner, Professor of Political Science at the Massachusetts Institute of Technology, who reviewed the manuscript.

Cambridge, Massachusetts   NAZLI CHOUCRI
Spring 1984

MULTIDISCIPLINARY PERSPECTIVES ON POPULATION AND CONFLICT

Perspectives on Population and Conflict

NAZLI CHOUCRI

D ESPITE THE INTERNATIONAL COMMUNITY's increasing awareness of population issues, a curious dichotomy continues to prevail between those who reduce population matters strictly to questions of fertility and mortality and those who view population issues within broader social and economic models. Yet among both factions remains a remarkable disregard for the potential political effects of population factors and their possible impact on conflict behavior. More importantly, there is a continued lack of awareness by both policy-making and academic communities of the close links between population and security. At a time when military expenditures are escalating and insecurities abound, challenges mounting in an international environment already fraught with tension and threat, it would be the height of myopia to persist in disregarding the increasing evidence concerning the relationship of population variables to conflict dynamics.

Until recently attention to population issues primarily has focused on the consequences of high fertility in many parts of the world. Rapidly growing numbers of people create social and economic burdens which cannot be ignored.[1] However, evidence suggests that population problems include not only births and deaths, but also demographic change as it affects national and international politics.[2] Conflict is a central feature of all political behavior, at all levels of human interaction, and the prominence of population variables in shaping political behavior places population and conflict in close proximity. When conflict becomes violent it truly threatens the social fabric.

This volume presents both theory and evidence about the relationships of population and conflict from multiple perspectives, disciplines, and orientations. Our purpose is to place demographic variables in a broader socioeconomic and political context and show ways in which they interrelate. Ours is the task of the proverbial blind man and the elephant: describing the parts illuminates the nature of the whole.

To date, the international community's view of population issues seems to confine population variables to their strict demographic context without significant acknowledgment of their pervasive, society-wide implications. The economic consequences of rapid population growth and change have been gradually recognized at both national and international levels when the pressure of added numbers generates added social strains. By contrast, the conflict-producing dynamics imbedded in particular manifestations of population problems and resource constraints are not yet regarded as being a legitimate aspect of the world's population "problems." This omission, or lag in recognition, is a serious mistake. The social, economic, and political influences of population variables cannot be decomposed or segregated from one another. A society's demographic structure is the most basic and essential element defining the parameters within which governments exercise authority.

Population issues, defined by the realities and priorities of the 1960s and 1970s, may no longer be appropriate in the international context of the 1980s. The large-scale economic, social, and political changes that have taken place over the past decades may well have transformed demographic realities and their implications for international adjustment, development, and cooperation. The definition of population problems of the past decades — intimately tied to rapid population growth — correct in its own right, may well be superseded by the very realities that have come into being due to these problems.

Population issues have consequences far greater than previously envisaged by either policy-making or academic circles. Excessive focus on narrowly defined demographic concerns will only heighten unresolved demographic threats in the future and limit the true security of regimes and nations. The prospects for development, if not survival, in many parts of the world are tied to a broader recognition of the complex demographic issues that will define the realities of the 1980s.

The thrust of views on population aid has changed somewhat over time, from a family planning orientation to supporting broader initiatives than fertility regulation, such as measures in the context of maternal and child care service, and has expanded to include support for activities related to other demographic variables. The new underlying concern is for enhancing social viability.

For a nation, security, stability, and social cohesion in the comprehensive sense encompass the ability to adapt to a changing environment and to adapt at costs that are deemed acceptable and affordable by the society. Such adaptation begins most fundamentally with the meeting of social demands. These demands are defined initially, and most critically, by the configuration of the population and its overall characteristics. Thus investments in population-related programs that go beyond immediate interventions in fertility and mortality are, in effect, investments that enhance prospects for social adaptation and, by extension, for national security in its broader, more pervasive sense.

MARX, MALTHUS, AND MODERN VIEWS

The Malthusian, Marxist, and more recent social science views on population all differ significantly in their approach to the population question and social change, and to the implicit, and sometimes explicit, linkages that are made from population to conflict. This is so, if only because their proponents choose to focus on different aspects of the issue and to make different assumptions concerning the underlying dynamics. Similarly, their assumptions regarding the nature of social order, the causes of conflict, and solutions to population problems or to warring tendencies among nationals also differ. In all three cases, the underlying rationales remain largely as working hypotheses. None has yet been submitted to the empirical test.

The Malthusian (1798) thesis, elegant in its simplicity, traces the origins of want, misery, and war to the relationship between population and resources. The simple proposition that population increases in geometrical ratio but subsistence increases only in an arithmetical ratio, and that "the power of population is indefinitely greater than the power in the earth to produce subsistence for man" provides a basis for linking population to war (see also the exposition on Malthus in Peterson 1969, pp. 154–71). The relationship is direct, mediated only through factors related to subsistence needs and wants, not to social, organizational, or political conditions. In these terms, *war is an involuntary act – a necessity – dictated by the dual constraints of population growth and resource limitations.*

In negating the Malthusian premise, Marxists define the problem in terms of distribution: if resources were properly utilized and distributed, the entire population of the world could subsist upon existing resources. The concept of excess population is, in principle, denied, as is the logical necessity of pressures culminating in war. But Marxists accept the Malthusian rationale when it applies to "capitalist" societies. Recent extensions of Marxist arguments trace political conflict and warring outcomes to population variables, but these do not stem directly from the Marxist critique of Malthus. They represent a radical and highly politicized reaction to international politics during the post-World War II era.

On conceptual grounds, however, the emphasis is clear: the dilemma is thought to lie in the convergence of relatively *increased numbers* and relatively *decreased* or *maldistributed resources*. The interactive effect of population and resources defines the nature of the Malthusian thesis, and its critics interject the manipulability factor to modify the nature of this interaction. But much, if not all, of the ensuing implications is mere speculation: the historical record provides both supporting and refuting illustrations, as does the evidence generated by studies in the social sciences. Perhaps the most controversial data come from studies of animal behavior, where arguments for the numbers/violence thesis abound, but the evidence is only suggestive of, and not directly translatable to, human populations.

Only recently have demographers themselves become concerned with the political implications of added population (see Davis 1956 for an early statement; see also Hauser 1960). In part, they have drawn upon the arguments of political scientists and historians and upon the historical record in putting forth their views on population, power, and conflict. As a result, a certain echo pattern exists across the social sciences. In the absence of convincing empirical evidence, it is difficult to distinguish potentially valid from invalid propositions.

Much of what relates to population and war in the demographic literature can be summed up in the once popular "demographic relaxation" thesis: When people feel constrained by space and resources, they tend to spread out (Sauvy 1969). This thesis is presented as an important determinant of international violence, but it has not yet been seriously examined or tested against recorded history. Indeed, there is little agreement concerning the methods by which such a thesis may be examined.

Several demographers have pointed from time to time to the political and possibly conflictual implications of population dynamics. But the arguments have generally been idiosyncratic, situation specific, and largely atheoretical. The only comprehensive synthesis of various themes put forth in the demographic literature is still provided by Alfred Sauvy, past President of the United Nations Commission on Population. Recognizing the importance of mediating factors, particularly economic ones, and considering the need for differentiating between excess population as an excuse rather than an explanation for conflict, Sauvy (1969) defined four types of wars with reference to the effects of population size, excess population, and differentials of population: premeditated war involving the classical *lebensraum* thesis as an excuse, not a reality; premeditated war with overpopulation as a reality; unpremeditated war arising from internal needs and demands; and spontaneous wars resulting from unrecognized demographic pressures.

The closest analogy to the Sauvy synthesis in international relations remains Quincy Wright's classic work, *A Study of War* (1965). Wright has examined the relevance of demographic variables in the context of other factors pertaining to economic, sociological, military, and political considerations, and has argued that "Imperial wars tend to be initiated by countries with the most rapidly rising populations, while balance-of-power wars tend to be initiated by the alliances with the less rapidly rising populations, providing other factors of the military potential are being equally affected by time."

His major conclusion is that population dynamics are less a direct cause of conflict and violence than are other variables. Essentially, Wright maintains that (1) war and expansionist politics are influenced *more* by unsound economic theories than by population change, and (2) there is no direct or necessary causal relation between population size and war: population *may or may not* lead to war. The indeterminant nature of this conclusion necessitates further inquiry into the conditions under which population leads to war versus those in which it does not, assuming a comparable specification of intervening sequences.

The obvious, but important, inference to be drawn from both these syntheses is the following: demographic factors, perceived or otherwise, have different implications within different contexts. The characteristics of neighbors and their demographic profiles are crucial. Relative population size and rates of growth, differentials, and overall demographic contexts are key dimensions along which the population/violence issue must be viewed. These observations find occasional support in the international relations literature.

However sketchy these comments might appear, they point to two important considerations: in each case, population alone may not be the critical variable; and in each case, other factors intervening between population and politics rendered demographic considerations particularly salient. In these terms, at least, the critical elements in any population/conflict calculus might involve less population variables per se than the ways in which population *combines with other factors* to produce conflictual outcomes. What those other factors are, and how they have been thought to interrelate, is what we hope to clarify in the course of this volume.

More substantively, however, these illustrations raise important theoretical problems.

First, the nature of conflict is often difficult to determine.

Second, the role of population variables cannot be readily specified.

Third, while in some cases it is intuitively obvious that population variables are somehow related to a conflict situation, in others the population/conflict relationship is largely inferential.

And fourth, it is not at all clear what methodology would best assist in resolving the above three problems.

The following section discusses some methodological issues for this volume, particularly the problems and procedures involved in examining the relationship between population dynamics and violent conflict.

POPULATION AND CONFLICT

Population Variables

At first glance it might appear that population variables are so clearly defined by demographers as to pose no serious problem for comprehension and understanding. Simple population variables, such as size, composition, distribution, and change, are indeed unambiguous. *Size* pertains to numbers; *composition* refers to population characteristics such as racial, ethnic, tribal, religious, or age divisions; and *distribution* refers to the movement of populations as well as to their concentration and spatial location. (Demographers do not usually employ the term "distribution" as viewed here, but refer only to the location of population over a given territory.) Density and migration can thus be viewed as two distinct manifestations of population distribution. Population *change* involves an increase or decrease in size, composition, or distribution.

The introduction of change complicates considerably the tasks at hand and, further, draws our attention to the complexities introduced by the coincidence of any two or more of these simple population variables. These become even more complicated when relational population variables are introduced, variables that refer, not only to population, but also to social, economic, or political factors. For example, the term *population pressure* clearly must involve some referent against which population is measured. The same may be said with respect to *over*population, *excess* population, population *equilibrium,* or population *differentials*. Population variables such as these call for specification of the referents or context against which population is evaluated.

Conflict and Violence

Definitions of conflict abound, yet they all share common elements: hostility, insecurity, antagonisms, competition, and willingness to exert violence and inflict harm or damage. These elements are operative at all levels — the individual, groups, states, or at the international level. The subsequent chapters of this volume will examine conflict dynamics at these various levels. Here we note their pervasiveness on the global scale.

At the international level, conflict is "an interstate security dispute" that generally involves "specific power-political aims and demands having direct impacts on national behavior" and is "perceived internationally as being focused on political and security affairs" (Butterworth 1978; Farris et al. 1979). This definition includes political disputes that may not be violent in nature as well as violent disputes conventionally characterized as wars.

While scholars do not yet agree as to why conflicts arise, there is an emerging consensus on characterizations of types of overt conflict (Choucri 1974, especially Chapter 9, and Choucri and North 1975). Table 1, drawing upon an earlier study, summarizes the broad characterizations of international conflict. It is generally agreed that conflicts unfold through a predictable and identifiable set of dynamics. Phases of conflict also are categorized from the emergence of political dispute to the overt expression of military hostilities (based on Butterworth 1978, drawing on Bloomfield and Leiss 1979, and re-coded by Choucri). Yet there is the issue of complexity. A conflict that might be initiated by one set of issues may evolve to include additional and very different issues from those present at the outset of the conflict. The complex nature and transformation of conflict parameters are two of the factors most difficult to identify and characterize in international realities.

Following the definition of conflict as an "inter-state dispute" it has been estimated that there have been 307 explicit conflicts between 1945 and 1980 (this is not presented as a comprehensive list of all conflicts during the period); 191 of these were disputes "involving systematic use of military force, over a specific military objective(s), causing casualties and/or destruction of property" (Farris et al. 1979). A profile of these 191 conflicts, well-documented in terms of parties to the dispute, objectives, targets, and overall evolution and

TABLE 1
Characterizations of Conflict

Types	Objectives
Colonial Conflict	To overthrow a colonial power
Wars of National Integration	To consolidate the political order around some legitimate central authority
Wars of National Expansion	Territorial aggrandizement
Domestic Conflicts Generated by Internal Political Instability	Contenders are competing national or native elites
Political Conflicts	
purely political	To establish or maintain a sphere of influence
purely political — ideology	To establish or maintain a predominant ideology
political, drawing upon population factors	To exploit specific population factors
Dynamic Mixed Process Conflicts	Substantial transformation of nature of dispute in the course of the conflict

Source: Choucri (1974). Based on synthesis of prevailing classifications in political analysis. These characterizations were based initially on analysis of conflict in developing countries. They are generalized here to all international conflicts. Cited in Choucri (1983), p. 16.

resolution (if any) is the partial basis for the following account of the conflict record since 1945. Also included is a summary of 116 (Butterworth 1978 and Farris et al. 1979) recorded political disputes that have not involved overt use of military force and conflicts that are largely internal, thus not involving the use of force or the crossing of national borders. These include situations in which domestic violence leads to internal displacement of persons. The following accounting, therefore, must be viewed as a conservative but comprehensive assessment of different categories of conflict in international relations. It demonstrates the extent to which conflict is as complex as it is pervasive.

According to the Violent Conflicts Summary, Table 2, 191 conflicts involving use of military force have been identified as taking place between

TABLE 2
Violent Conflicts Summary by Regions and Time Periods

	1940–49	1950–59	1960–69	1970–79	Total	Percent of Category	Percent of Total
CONFLICT AMONG DEVELOPING COUNTRIES							
Africa	1	2	15	16	34	33.7	17.8
Asia	9	10	13	17	49	48.5	25.7
Latin America and Caribbean	3	10	4	1	18	17.8	9.4
Subtotal	13	22	32	34	101	100.0	52.9
CONFLICT BETWEEN DEVELOPED AND DEVELOPING COUNTRIES							
Africa	4	11	13	2	30	40.0	15.7
Asia	8	11	13	4	36	48.0	18.8
Latin America and Caribbean	0	3	5	1	9	12.0	4.7
Subtotal	12	25	31	7	75	100.0	39.2
CONFLICT AMONG DEVELOPED COUNTRIES							
Asia	0	2	1	0	3	20.0	1.6
Europe	2	5	4	0	11	73.3	5.8
North America	0	0	0	1	1	6.7	.5
Subtotal	2	7	5	1	15	100.0	7.9
TOTAL	27	54	68	42	191	—	100.0

Source: Choucri (1983), p. 18.

1945 and 1980. By far the largest number (101) consisted of hostilities between developing regions (conflict between developing countries). Only 75 of these conflicts can be identified clearly as disputes involving developed and developing countries. The remaining 15 violent conflicts concern hostilities between developed states. Thus the South-South conflict dimension has been the most frequent for international conflict involving military force during this period.

The incidence of conflict involving military force *among* developing regions themselves has increased steadily since 1940, in comparison with the decline in the number of such incidences between developed states. The trend in north-south conflicts was similar to that of developing countries until the decade 1970–79, at which point there was a dramatic decrease in north-south conflicts. The decline in the number of incidences during the past decade corresponds to the emergence of détente between the superpowers. Conflicts among the developing countries themselves have occurred mainly in Asia and Africa, as have conflicts between developed and developing countries. Conflict between developed states only has occurred in Europe.

In terms of types of violent conflict (see Table 3) the majority of the overt conflicts can be characterized as those caused by internal political instability. Colonial conflicts and purely political conflicts rank second and third, respectively, in terms of frequency. Political conflicts with population factors and purely political conflicts with major ideological factors rank fourth and fifth in this characterization of conflict type. National integration conflicts and dynamic–mixed-process conflicts, whose nature changed over time, rank sixth and seventh. National expansion conflicts rank eighth. Less than two percent of all conflicts since World War II have been coded as involving "national expansion" as compared to 40 percent of the conflicts which have involved specific population-related factors such as integration, ideology, population factors, and mixed processes involving a number of issues over time. Data on type, location, and nature of conflicts, as presented in Table 3, should be interpreted with caution since they are based on only the 191 conflicts examined here.

According to the data in Table 4, it has been established that for the period 1945–1980 there have been 116 conflicts *not* involving the use of military force. Of these, 48 were between developed and developing countries; 43 between developing countries; and 25 between developed countries.

Data on types and location of non-violent conflicts, presented in Table 5, indicate that the majority of such conflicts have been purely political in nature. Pure political conflicts involving major ideological factors rank second. Colonial conflicts and political conflicts with population factors rank third and fourth. Conflicts resulting from internal political instability rank fifth. Dynamic mixed process and national integration conflicts are equally ranked as sixth most frequently occurring non-violent conflicts. Na-

TABLE 3
Types of Violent Conflict

	Colonial Conflicts	National Integra-tion	National Expan-sion	Internal Political Insta-bility	Purely Political	Purely Political: Ideology	Political: Popula-tion Factor	Dynamic Mixed Process
CONFLICT AMONG DEVELOPING COUNTRIES								
Africa	1	3	—	10	7	2	11	—
Asia	1	5	1	8	11	4	15	4
Latin America and Caribbean	—	—	—	13	4	—	1	—
Subtotal	2	8	1	31	22	6	27	4
CONFLICT BETWEEN DEVELOPED AND DEVELOPING COUNTRIES								
Africa	20	1	—	4	4	—	—	1
Asia	12	10	2	3	1	5	—	3
Latin America and Caribbean	3	—	—	5	1	—	—	—
Subtotal	35	11	2	12	6	5	—	4
CONFLICT AMONG DEVELOPED COUNTRIES								
Asia	—	—	—	—	—	3	—	—
Europe	1	1	—	—	1	8	—	—
North America	—	—	—	—	—	1	—	—
Subtotal	1	1	—	—	1	12	—	—
TOTAL	38	20	3	43	29	23	27	8

Source: Choucri (1983), p. 19.

tional expansion conflicts, in seventh place, account for fewer than one percent of the total conflicts, while conflicts which are population related account for over one third of the total non-violent conflicts.

Generally, over the past four decades, non-violent disputes among developing regions and among developed and developing countries have tended to increase in number. For the developed states, there has been a marked decrease in non-violent conflict since 1950. These trends are summarized in Tables 4 and 5. Again, we caution the reader to remember that these statistics represent reliable, but small, data sets. They are presented here to indicate trends which may be deduced as the result of the data collection efforts of prominent scholars.

TABLE 4
Nonviolent Conflicts Summary by Regions and Time Periods

	1940–49	1950–59	1960–69	1970–79	Total	Percent of Category	Percent of Total
CONFLICT AMONG DEVELOPING COUNTRIES							
Africa	1	2	4	4	11	25.6	9.5
Asia	6	5	1	5	17	39.5	14.7
Latin America and Caribbean	4	2	5	4	15	34.9	12.9
Subtotal	11	9	10	13	43	100.0	37.1
CONFLICT BETWEEN DEVELOPED AND DEVELOPING COUNTRIES							
Africa	4	6	2	6	18	37.5	15.5
Asia	5	5	4	4	18	37.5	15.5
Europe	1	0	0	1	2	4.2	1.7
Latin America and Caribbean	2	2	6	0	10	20.8	8.6
Subtotal	12	13	12	11	48	100.0	41.4*
CONFLICT AMONG DEVELOPED COUNTRIES							
Asia	0	1	0	0	1	4.0	.9
Europe	8	7	5	0	20	80.0	17.2
North America	0	3	0	1	4	16.0	3.4
Subtotal	8	11	5	1	25	100.0	21.6
TOTAL	31	33	27	25	116	—	100.0*

*Slight inaccuracies caused by rounding.

Source: Choucri (1983), pp.20–21.

THE ROLE OF DEMOGRAPHIC FACTORS IN INTERNATIONAL CONFLICTS

Of these 307 violent and non-violent conflicts, ethnic factors have had an important bearing on the nature and type of dispute involved in 47 percent of the cases. Within the category of non-violent conflicts, 32 (or 27.6 percent) were characterized by major ethnic factors, while 111 violent conflicts (58.1 percent) were similarly characterized. Population composition thus appears to be an important element in international disputes.

More detailed demographic information has been compiled for only

TABLE 5
Types of Nonviolent Conflict

	Colonial Conflicts	National Integra-tion	National Expan-sion	Internal Political Insta-bility	Purely Political	Purely Political: Ideology	Political: Popula-tion Factor	Dynamic Mixed Process
CONFLICT AMONG DEVELOPING COUNTRIES								
Africa	—	1	—	—	3	4	3	—
Asia	—	—	1	—	7	6	1	2
Latin America and Caribbean	—	—	—	6	9	–	—	—
Subtotal	—	1	1	6	19	10	4	2
CONFLICT BETWEEN DEVELOPED AND DEVELOPING COUNTRIES								
Africa	10	1	—	1	2	1	2	1
Asia	5	1	—	—	6	4	2	—
Latin America and Caribbean	—	—	—	—	6	4	—	—
Subtotal	15	2	—	1	14	10	5	1
CONFLICT AMONG DEVELOPED COUNTRIES								
Asia	—	—	—	—	1	–	—	—
Europe	—	—	—	—	7	11	2	—
North America	—	—	—	—	4	–	—	—
Subtotal	—	—	—	—	12	11	2	—
TOTAL	15	3	1	7	45	31	11	3

Source: Choucri (1983), p. 22.

45 of these conflicts, but evidence regarding population-conflict links in international relations emerges from this set (Choucri 1974). Although this analysis was completed in 1974, it continues to represent the only systematic study to date of the relationship between population and conflict. The evidence summarized here points to the possibility of a broader basis of inference to the entire range of conflicts.

The 1974 study—which includes the relationship between population dynamics, resource availability, and technological development, on the one hand, and the behavior of states, on the other—was completed in the year of the 1974 World Population Conference. Its purpose was to trace the international effects of different demographic, economic, and military profiles.

This was the first systematic study of conflicts to determine any demographic connections. It was based on comparisons of the super powers with smaller states, an examination of the actions and attributes of nations over time, and observations of the effects of sharp changes in power-related characteristics and their influence upon national behavior. The variables intervening between population and violence, at the aggregate (macro) level, then became evident and specific linkages were delineated. One major finding of these analyses was that existence of "non-aggressive" and "aggressive" systems can be traced largely to internal demographic structures. The 1974 analysis also considered additional evidence of the internal determinants of external conflict and armament competition, and found that there were theoretical as well as empirical linkages relating population variables to conflict behavior and to violence.

One of the most important features of this study was the determination of the ways in which population variables affected conflict, i.e. the specific roles that population variables can play. There are at least three basic ways that population variables have an impact on conflict: (1) as *parameters,* by shaping the situation itself; (2) as multipliers, by aggravating underlying or existing hostilities; and (3) as *variables,* by serving as critical factors in the conflict, shaping its unfolding and/or determining its outcomes (Choucri 1974, pp. 93–94). The more complex or potent the conflict, the more likely that population variables play more than one role. The demographic profiles of the 45 conflicts were examined in considerable detail (Choucri 1974, p. 92). We found that population variables played a critical role in 38. In only seven of the 45 cases did population variables have no appreciable influence on the development or conduct of the conflict (Choucri 1974, p. 98). Additional evidence regarding the linkage of demographic factors to conflict which emerged as a result of this analysis can be summarized as follows:

> The current population emphasis on population *size* is largely misplaced and invariant over the time perspective of a specific conflict.
>
> Population *composition* and *distribution,* which generally have been ignored in popular, academic, and official circles, were shown to be of great importance in many of the conflicts examined.
>
> Population *change* tends to exacerbate the effects of size.
>
> Population *distribution* appears to be most susceptible to variation over the course of a conflict.
>
> Population *composition* also frequently appears to set the parameters of conflict situations.

In sum, these 45 cases revealed that population size, change, distribution, and composition are all linked in complex ways. Size and change factors seldom have more than background significance, because their effects are long term and indirect; any pressures generated by these two demographic factors are likely to manifest themselves through other population variables (see Choucri 1974, pp. 83–113, for a complete summary).

There is some evidence to disconfirm any relationship between density and conflict (see, for example, Biermer, Singer, and Luterbacher 1973). However, other historical analyses, tracing the usual linkages between population variables on the one hand and international conflict on the other, find a statistically significant causal linkage between population variables and international conflict through a set of intervening variables.

The analysis of 45 cases demonstrated that rapid change in population dynamics — size, composition, distribution, and change — invariably generates problems that go beyond those created by an increase in numbers alone. Assessment of the population issue must be made in quantitative and qualitative terms and placed in the context of the resources available to a society and its level of knowledge and skills (see Choucri 1974, pp. 197–209).

The detailed study of 45 conflicts has shown that population variables affect conflict in the ways presented in Table 6. In conclusion, note the prominent role of demographic variables as *major* factors in conflict. Further information is given on Table 7.

THE CENTRAL PROPOSITION

The multiplicity of issues and linkages between population and conflict raised in the previous section may appear overwhelming, thus obscuring some robust and fundamental relations. For example, population variables affect conflict behavior both directly and indirectly, and conflict processes in turn can have profound impacts on demographic structure. Despite differences in levels of analysis, disciplinary orientation, and methodological approaches, the evidence so far points to some general conclusions. The most important one pertains to the interactive effects linking population, resources, and technology.

The following synthesis captures the most prominent consensus about the relationship between population and conflict, given the evidence at hand. It summarizes the contribution of a distinguished group of scholars from different disciplines, as presented in the subsequent chapters of this volume. The synthesis here is for introductory purposes only, to indicate the pieces of the puzzle and where they might fit together.

We begin with the recognition that man is critically dependent on his physical environment. As biological organisms, human beings have certain basic needs. A growing population results in an increased demand for basic

TABLE 6
Demographics and Different Types of Conflict

Population-Related Factor (%)	Colonization Conflicts and Decolonization Struggles (N = 5)	Problems of National Integration (N = 12)	Wars of National Expansion (N = 3)	Internal Political Instability with Potential External Consequences (N = 6)	Political Conflicts (N = 21)	Dynamic Mixed Process Conflicts (N = 5)
Segmental Divisions	80	100	67	33	19	60
Difference in Technology, Skills	40	42	—	33	—	80
Migration	60	33	—	33	—	60
Rural/Urban Distribution	40	—	—	—	—	—
Location in Relation to Natural Resources	40	25	—	—	14	40
Location in Relation to Borders	—	17	—	—	—	40
Pressure of Numbers on Resources	—	17	67	50	—	60
Rapid Rate of Population Growth	—	—	67	33	—	—
Differential Population Size	—	—	67	—	—	—
Age Structure	—	—	—	—	—	60

Source: Davis B. Bobrow from Choucri (1974), pp. 106–109, 116.

resources. The technology available to acquire such resources and render them serviceable brings about environmental and social change. The more advanced the technology available to a society, the more varied the types and kinds of resources needed. Demands are likely to increase as technological advances change social perceptions of "needs." Technological advances, therefore, alter and influence economic activity, as well as political institutions and processes. Population increases, in conjunction with developments in technology, contribute to the familiar dilemma of rising demands and insufficient resource availability. The following are ten propositions summarizing both theory and evidence at hand.

1. Demographic factors can lead to conflict behavior, which in turn affects population characteristics. There is almost always an interactive and feedback relationship linking conflict to population, not a direct or linear one.

TABLE 7
The Importance of Demographic Factors in Violent Conflicts*

	1 Back- ground Factor	2 Minor Irritant	3 Major Irritant	4 Central Importance	5 Sole Deter- minant	Total Cases	Weighted Average Descrip- tion†
Population Size	3‡	15	1	2	1	23	2.23
Absolute population level	8	4	2	2	–	16	1.89
Pressure of numbers on resources	1	8	7	2	1	19	2.68
Population Change	8	6	5	–	–	19	1.84
Absolute rate of growth	10	10	3	2	–	25	1.88
Differential rates of growth	3	5	1	–	–	9	1.77
Population Distribution	7	10	13	5	–	35	2.46
Rural/urban distribution	3	10	3	–	–	16	2.00
Population density	2	3	2	–	–	7	2.00
Spatial location in relation to resources	3	4	8	3	–	18	2.61
Spatial location in relation to borders	4	5	4	2	–	15	2.27
Population Movement	11	6	8	5	–	30	2.23
Population Composition	1	6	11	13	1	32	3.22
Sex distribution	2	2	–	–	–	4	1.50
Age structure	3	3	4	–	–	10	2.10
Segmental divisions	2	1	10	12	6	31	3.61
Level of knowledge and skills (technology)	4	9	10	3	–	26	2.46

*Entries are the number of cases in which the factor listed on the left played a role of the magnitude listed above.

†These numbers are purely descriptive, since they treat an ordinal scale as if it were a ratio scale. They indicate the average intensity of each factor's influence. The weighted average descriptor (WA) is a function of the frequency of cases times the intensity of influence of demographic factors in a conflict situation, divided by the number of cases in question. Thus WA = Σ/(number of cases of particular intensity $\times$ level of intensity) / total number of cases. The WA range = 0.0–5.0.

‡The number of cases listed for specific variables within each population category does not add up to the number of cases listed for each general factor (size, change, distribution, composition) because general factors may be composed of several specific variables. The decision rule was to obtain a case-specific coding before undertaking a cross-national comparison. The alternative procedure, to obtain a general factor coding from the sum of specific variable codes, would have produced an inflationary effect by overemphasizing the role of demographic factors in conflict situations.

Source: Choucri (1974), p. 102.

2. Population size and growth, crowding and density, alone do not lead to violence. Population increase is not in itself the source of crowding, stress, and conflict (see Chapter 3). Although there is some relationship between crowding and pathological conditions, there initially must be a critical

mass, i.e., a population "at risk," amenable to violence or using violence as a preferred strategy (see Chapter 4).

3. Differential growth rates in population (size, composition, and distribution), access to resources, and access to technology contribute to the potential for conflict and to overt violence (see Chapters 4 and 8). Differentials in power variables and in demographic characteristics, such as the rate of growth of different ethnic groups, politicize population factors and make them conducive to conflict. Differential rates of growth are central to the evolution of the conflict spiral. The dynamics of conflict are imbedded in such differentials (see Chapters 5, 6, 7, and 8).

4. Conflict behavior can influence demographic structure, creating changes in population variables. The existence of the conflict can itself politicize population variables. Demographic characteristics under these conditions are, or become, construed as political ones and, for all practical purposes, enter as political variables in the calculations of the antagonists. Coercive displacement of people can occur as a result of violent conflict.

5. The age composition of a population is a powerful element in its tendencies to violence. Some evidence suggests that the younger the population and the higher the level of unemployment, the greater the propensities for violence (see Chapter 4). In a prolonged conflict, advantage is with the younger population (see Chapter 7). Age structure directly affects the political process, the political agenda, and the way in which social demands are articulated.

6. Ethnic differences by themselves are not a direct source of conflict but ethnicity can heighten the importance of numbers in the conduct of conflict. Numerous overt conflicts since World War II have had a strong ethnic character and have involved resource scarcity (Choucri 1974). Segmental divisions accentuate perceptions of conflict (Choucri 1974). Demands for social and political equality can be based on the reality of inequality compounded by the existence of ethnic differences (see Chapter 6). The ethnic composition of ruling elites can create differential access to power for different ethnic groups (see Chapters 4, 6, and 7), and differences among ethnic or national groups can impede national cohesion.

7. Large-scale migration across national borders is often induced by political problems in sending countries and/or by economic incentives in receiving countries. The scale of such migration may have profound effects on relations among nations (Choucri 1974).

8. Social institutions can act as powerful inhibiters or absorbers of conflict. Institutions capable of adjusting to changing environments can cushion the effects of demographic changes. When institutions become outmoded, there may be an upsurge of conflict. A lag in institutional adaptation can accentuate conflict potentials (see Chapter 2). Delays in management

of the changes in a physical setting can exacerbate conflict (see Chapter 3).

9. Population-regulating policies in themselves can create conflict. This is a phenomenon too often overlooked. For example, policies that encourage selective immigration or, alternatively, discourage mobility across national borders often create conflict. Paradoxically, such policies, which are often advocated as a means of reducing conflict or as an outcome of existing conflict, can in themselves create new population-related conflicts.

10. Despite the importance of perceptions in assigning meaning to conflict situations, the realities of scarcities and pressures are the most powerful determinants of conflict.

These propositions are in the nature of conditions. But what triggers a situation? What can bring about conflict in unforeseen ways? What are the signals or guideposts to the occurrence of conflict?

CRISIS FACTORS

The evidence in this volume highlights conditions propitious for conflict. The crisis factors listed below are associated with high probabilities of overt conflict. They are clear harbingers of violence. Without presupposing an ordering in salience or importance, elements conducive to conflict are the following:

- pressure of population on resources;
- spatial location of population in strategic areas;
- pronounced segmental divisions, whether or not they are represented in the political process;
- politicization of population at risk, as distinct from the incidence or prevalence of such populations;
- unequal access to power and/or resources, where the stress is on the inequality of access rather than the inequality of basic conditions;
- existence of an officially sanctioned belief system that stresses population segmentation and legitimizes barriers to integration and assimilation;
- changes in the power structure created by changes in demographic characteristics;
- conjunction of strategic issues and military alliances with population characteristics (or differences) across or within nations.

These crisis factors are among the most salient and most commonly referred to in the available evidence. They are necessary but not sufficient conditions for mobilizing population factors and engendering a conflict spiral. In the broader international context, however, certain crisis conditions exist that place everyone at risk. For example, antagonistic relations between North and South, remnants of colonial conditions, expansion of great power hegemony, and existence of great power alignments all contribute to world insecurity. Demographic factors enter directly into such configurations, for they contribute to defining relative power, numerical strength, casualty burdens, and other indicators of military capabilities. The births and deaths of today form the basis of tomorrow's power calculations, viewed as central to every nation's security.

In addition to these eight crisis factors, and the broader conditions of world insecurity noted above, there are some specific crisis conditions of a global nature that may trigger international political or diplomatic crises. At least three such specific conditions bear noting.

First is the collision of spheres of influence when, for instance, the market economies come to a direct clash with the centrally planned economies. The population located in areas where such intersections occur becomes a target of the collision as well as a strategic element in the calculations of the antagonists.

Second are the stresses that arise as countries find it necessary to defend their trade networks. When trade becomes politicized, whether because of a chronic surplus or because of impending or chronic deficits, the political antennas rise and politicization of even the most benign issues can take place.

Third, as a result of these two conditions, the potentials for activation of the action/reaction phenomena — the antagonizing processes — are great. Arms races are the clearest manifestation of such processes, but there are others as well. When action and reaction take hold between antagonists, all their capabilities enter into their calculations and demographic factors loom large.

THE LINKAGE FACTORS

The evidence in this volume indicates that there is a direct link between population variables and conflict behavior. However, we must stress the importance of intermediary factors: the elements and processes that relate and link conflictual outcomes to demographic factors, or the ways in which population-related pressures manifest themselves in political or conflictual outcomes. Three sets of intermediary factors stand out. One bears upon the role of technology, the second on the role of the state, and the third pertains to perceptions, images, and ideology.

The role of technology is an essential factor in the conflict process. The higher the level of technology, the greater are the demands for resources. This conjunction increases the propensities for conflict. Technology serves as a critical countervailing variable in the sense that it serves as an impetus to increase the demand for resources as well as the tool which can expand the availability of resources. Irrespective of the disposition of populations, technological advantage in a conflict situation can, for all practical purposes, be decisive in determining the outcome. Thus a state with a strong numerical advantage will be at a disadvantage if its level of knowledge and skills is inferior to that of its adversary, even if the adversary's population is but a fraction of its own. By the same token, the extent to which population is a "problem" is almost directly related to the distribution of knowledge and skills. Thus numbers in the international arena take on different significances politically depending on the society's level of technology. The combined effects of demographic factors, resource availability and demand, and technological capability determine the true significance of population as a factor (see Chapter 8). Technological development in itself engenders economic and social demands which lead societies to increase their interactions internationally, exerting what is now conventionally termed "lateral pressure." In some cases this leads to conflict (Choucri and North 1975). Population figures are one element in this equation, and technology is a critical intervening factor.

The capacity of institutions to mediate conflict is intimately tied to the resources available to the various institutions and to the legitimacy of those institutions. If perceived as non-legitimate, intervention by the state to deflect conflict processes can, in actuality, accentuate them. Political analysts have argued that the cognizance of views, values, and institutional mechanisms throughout a society is essential to maintain cohesion and integration. Disjunctions of institutions hinder social cohesion and may, in effect, aggravate any latent tensions. In societies where the marketplace is the major allocator of resources, a supporting political structure is essential for the functioning of the market. In such societies, the political process is continually confronted with the task of deflecting conflicts arising from the allocations. In cases where factor availability creates conflict, the marketplace is the generator of conflict and the political process is the means of conflict containment or regulation. Thus the state itself is often a direct actor in this process, relating demographic factors to political ones or to conflictual outcomes. How the state performs may in itself be the key to determining whether population factors realize their conflict potential.

The third set of intermediary factors, namely images and perceptions, is more elusive. Perceptions are hard to elucidate and do not lend themselves to any definitive assessment. Perceptions are not simply there, they are learned, they can be manipulated, and they can engender a desired outcome. Political imagery, created by representatives of the state, is among the most critical in determining behavior. Thus the creation and manipulation of symbols, in addition to whatever predispositions exist, can add an additional layer of uncertainty to processes that might link population factors to conflict. The manipulation of an old or new ideology to gain political support often entails population-related statements or symbols. Demographic characteristics are almost always central features of political ideology.

SOME CONNECTING INSIGHTS

The foregoing is elucidated further by insights gleaned from advances in the social sciences. This volume depicts theory and evidence from different disciplines. Each discipline adopts its favored paradigm or paradigms. Together, they contribute to the vision of the elephant characterized by the proverbial blind men.

From psychology comes the view that the roots of conflict are twofold: first, the crossing of individual personal space boundaries by others, and second, violation of the individual psychological integrity. This violation provokes responses aimed at preventing further violations. Therefore culture is a mediator between conflict behavior and the effects of density because stress due to crowding, which may elicit violence, is also culture-bound.

From sociology comes the insight that the relationships between population and conflict can be described differently, depending on the measures utilized. Nonetheless, mounting evidence shows a positive relationship between crowding and some rate of pathological behavior. Rapid social change has been associated with higher rates of violence in some contexts.

From anthropology, and some evidence from archaeology, comes the insight that congestion, loss of control, and information overload determine human responses to density. The form of that response, however, is powerfully sharpened by institutional arrangements.

Economic theory and evidence provide important reminders that scarcity is determined not by numbers alone but by the relationship of people to assets and to the technology needed to employ those assets. Violence is a sign of institutional failure. Markets can be powerful forces in regulating institutional features only if all actors agree implicitly to respond to impersonal forces and accept market allocation outcomes. Market failures can lead to profound social conflicts.

From political analysis and historical inquiry comes the now self-evident consideration that wars occur at the point where prevailing methods of governance and agreements on the issues of "who gets what, when, and how" are no longer decided by accommodative bargaining, peaceful negotiation, or even the exchange of coercive threats, but by overt military activity. This conjunction, then, places causes of conflict and paths to peace in close proximity.

PATHS TO SECURITY AND PEACE

Increasingly, everywhere, demographic issues are becoming political issues. The politicization of population is one new significant development since the World Population Conference in 1974. Governments almost everywhere have assumed a role, and a posture, on population issues. This development has placed government in the forefront of population issues.

One conventional function of government is to articulate priorities and establish these by influencing allocations of technology, resources, and labor, thus shaping national capabilities. Governments directly influence social activities by the spending of monies and by establishing systems of incentives and disincentives. What population demands are and how they are met, or proposed to be met, depends on the level of technology and the resources that are directly available within national boundaries. Conflict and competition arise, both domestically and internationally, when efforts to meet demands are frustrated or constrained by existing capabilities or by the actions of others. In the entire calculus, the structure of a society's demographic characteristics provides the most basic constraints within which governments operate.

This volume stresses the role of the population factor, in relation to other essential elements of social interaction, in the dynamic processes that result in overt conflict—it is not a study of peace and security, yet one inescapable conclusion is that the attention to the demographic elements is essential for any strategy.

The paths to security—in terms of absence of war and improvement of the quality of life on this earth—are many. At least three strategies are well articulated on an international level. The first is the approach tied to arms control and disarmament that is generally the most well known. There the focus is on deterrence, intents, and military hardware. Its advantages lie in highlighting the role of weapon systems and the assessment of parties in conflict. Its disadvantages lie in its almost total divorce from the broader social context of deterrence. Social pressures toward conflict are ignored, thereby limiting the usefulness of this particular "path to peace."

The second approach to security is the path proposed by the findings on peace research, a growing field of inquiry with an international representation of scholars and scholarship. Here the emphasis is on processes leading to conflicts and arms races, and on conflict-reducing processes. The central focus is on overt manifestations of conflict, with an emerging focus on roots of conflict. Again, as with the arms control and disarmament path, but perhaps to a lesser degree, the deeper social and demographic underpinnings of security are not addressed.

A third approach to security is the diplomatic approach, which focuses on direct talks between national leaders and representatives of hostile parties. Diplomacy, by definition, is an attempt to manage difficult situations at the point of official level of representation. This path to peace — through discussion and attempts to find common grounds to avert conflict and war — by definition ignores the social basis and roots of conflict. It suffers from the same narrow perspective adopted by the arms control and disarmament path. The reluctance of diplomacy to address demographic issues is precisely the factor that limits the usefulness of this approach as a comprehensive path to peace.

Each of these paths to security is fundamentally flawed by ignoring the base of social interaction, namely people. The demographic underpinnings of conflict and violence must be understood in order to develop viable strategies for reducing prospects of war, averting hostile stances, and reducing probabilities of violence. Unless the causal dynamics of interactions that lead to conflict are fully understood, the strategies for peace will continue to be flawed.

The complexity of population dynamics — population size, composition, distribution, and change — are paralleled by the complexity of conflict dynamics in terms of the various levels of conflict and ways in which hostilities can be manifested.

Conflict between individuals reflects processes that are intensely interpersonal and psychological in nature, involving a sense of personal space and concern for protecting personal security.

Conflict between groups reflects social interactions when social security is threatened and overt hostility is regarded as a necessary means of restabilizing the security of the group.

Conflict in marketplaces or economic competitions are designed to protect or increase the group's (or state's) access to scarce commodities.

Political conflict entails competition over power or fears of threats to security. Any conception of security — the absence of overt conflict, peace, enhancing the quality of life — must always focus on people. An explicit recognition of the centrality of demographic variables is the critical dimension in any strategy for security.

At a global level, the evidence in this volume suggests a strategy for peace that recognizes, incorporates, and relates to the most basic element in the conflict spiral—the population factor. A viable strategy for security must, by necessity, begin with demographic variables and acknowledge their critical role in contributing to conflict. If we begin with the correct premises, the prospects of devising and adopting an appropriate strategy for security are greatly enhanced.

NOTES

1. The United Nations Fund for Population Activities (1982) shows the world population to be growing at a current rate of 1.70 percent per year, or a "doubling time" of 41 years. This decline from the 1975-80 level of 1.94 signals a trend toward moderation in the rate of world population growth, but does not indicate a lessening of annual increments of absolute numbers.

2. The first major review and assessment of the problems associated with rapid population growth was included in the United States National Academy of Sciences (1971). A fairly comprehensive review of refugee issues today is found in Stein and Thomas (1981).

REFERENCES

Biermer, S., J. D. Singer, and U. Luterbacher. "The Population Density and War Proneness of European Nations, 1816-1965." *Comparative Political Studies* (October 1973).

Bloomfield, L. P., and A. C. Leiss. *Controlling Small Wars: A Strategy for the 1970s.* New York: Knopf, 1979.

Butterworth, R. L. *Moderation from Management: International Organizations and Peace.* Pittsburgh, Pa.: University of Pittsburgh, Center for International Studies, 1978.

Choucri, N. *Population and Conflict: New Dimensions of Population Dynamics.* Policy Development Studies, No. 8. New York: UNFPA, 1983.

_____. *Population Dynamics and International Violence: Propositions, Insights, and Evidence.* Lexington, Ma.: Lexington Books, 1974.

_____ and R. C. North. *Nations in Conflict: National Growth and International Violence.* San Francisco, Ca.: Freeman, 1975.

Davis, K. "The Political Impact of New Population Trends." *Foreign Affairs* 36 (1956): 293-301.

Farris, L., H. R. Alker, Jr., K. Carley, and F. L. Sherman. "Phase/Actor Disaggregated Butterworth-Scranton Codebook." Working paper. Cambridge, Ma.: MIT, Center for International Studies, 1979.

Hauser, P. M. "Demographic Dimensions of World Politics." *Science* 131 (1960): 1641–46.

Malthus, T. R. *Population: The First Essay,* 1798. Ann Arbor: University of Michigan Press, 1959.

Peterson, W. *Population.* 2nd ed. New York: Macmillan, 1969.

Sauvy, A. *General Theory of Population.* New York: Basic Books, 1969.

Stein, B. N., and S. L. Thomas. "Refugees Today." *International Migration Review* 15 (1981).

United Nations Fund for Population Activities. "Population Facts at a Glance." New York: UNFPA, 1 November 1982.

United States National Academy of Sciences. "Rapid Population Growth: Consequences and Policy Implications." Baltimore, Md.: Johns Hopkins University Press, 1971.

"World Population Growth and Global Security." Briefing Paper No. 13. Washington, D.C.: Population Crisis Committee, September 1983.

Wright, Q. *A Study of War.* 2nd ed., with a commentary on war since 1942. Chicago: University of Chicago Press, 1965.

2

Population Growth, Interpersonal Conflict, and Organizational Response in Human History

MARK N. COHEN

IN HIS CELEBRATED AND INFLUENTIAL ESSAYS on population written at the beginning of the nineteenth century, Thomas Malthus (1798) took an unwar-
ranted, pessimistic view of the future of the human species. He argued that
our reproductive capacity would lead inevitably to a crisis of overpopulation
from which would emanate not only widespread starvation but also poverty,
misery, disease, and "vice." The latter, rephrased in modern terms, is roughly
synonymous with what social psychologists have referred to as "social pathology." In keeping with the title of this volume it might also be considered
roughly synonymous with, or at least one component of, conflict among individuals within a society.

In assessing the prospects for starvation (the central part of his pre-
diction and that most commonly cited), Malthus clearly underestimated at
least the short-run potential of human technology to feed increasing numbers.
More important, he also clearly underestimated the role which population
growth has played through human history (and might still play) in stimulating the expansion of the food supply.[1] Previous works have argued that growing population has in fact been instrumental in stimulating and directing the
evolution of the human food economy (Cohen 1977). The growth of population beyond the "carrying capacity" of existing resource-procuring strategies
has resulted not in Malthusian starvation but in redefinition of those strategies. Faced with overpopulation, we have occasionally invented or adopted
new technologies to increase production, but we have also accepted a wider
range of foods as "edible" and accepted altered and often increased labor inputs in production while settling for declining nutritional quality. In short,
the human food supply has been elastic in the face of increasing demand, although this elasticity has often been bought at the cost of declining quality
in return on investment.

In predicting the degeneration into "vice" or social pathology as an

27

inevitable consequence of crowding, it seems clear that Malthus also under-estimated the ability of human social institutions to integrate and organize increasing numbers of people. It also seems clear that he underestimated the degree to which population growth has worked in the past (and might still work) to stimulate social reorganization of a type appropriate to offset the stressful effects of increased population density. This chapter will argue that psychological stresses associated with increasing population — so-called crowd-ing effects — have in the past been instrumental in stimulating the evolution of new social-cultural systems which function to organize increasing num-bers of people and to reduce the stress. In short, as populations have out-grown the organizational capacity of existing social systems, they have stimu-lated the development of new organizational systems in much the same man-ner that they have promoted new food procurement strategies.[2]

This argument has considerable importance for modern population studies. Malthus' error was important not only because of its historical in-accuracy but also because his perceptions have continued to influence the thinking of scholars and politicians. Malthus and his disciples have assumed that the problem of human misery and conflict was rooted in the reproduc-tive capacity of the poor. One result of this assumption, of course, has been to focus responsibility for poverty, conflict, and social pathology on the poor themselves rather than raising questions about the behavior of elites. An equally important result of the Malthusian bias has been to focus attention on solutions that preserve the status quo by limiting population growth rather than on the ways in which systems might better adjust to cope with growth — or on the institutional barriers, such as class interests and bureaucratic struc-tures that may impede appropriate adjustment.[3] Yet, a long-term perspective on human history suggests that overpopulation is a relative matter to be mea-sured against existing but potentially alterable standards of food production and social organization. This perspective suggests that, *to the extent popula-tion growth is in any way associated with social pathology and conflict,[4] it is not population growth per se that is important but rather the lag between such growth and the appropriate institutional response.*

The implication of this criticism of Malthus is not, of course, that we should forego efforts to quell population growth. The historical record sug-gests that diminishing economic returns as well as a compromising of exist-ing social values have, in the past, accompanied many phases of the adjus-tive process. We may expect that the type of adjustment now required to cope with further population growth may necessitate further compromising of both economic and social values. But the argument presented here suggests that governments might focus more actively on the analysis of the kinds of institu-tional adjustments that can and must be made to increasing density so long as populations continue to grow.

A careful reading of the literature on human (and animal) crowding, as well as a detailed look at how human societies have already evolved to mitigate the effects of increasing numbers, might provide some important clues as to the nature of the proper contemporary institutional response. The key to understanding the role that population growth has played in stimulating social reorganization lies in recognizing the relationship that exists between theories of crowding recently developed by social psychologists and the structure of societies of increasing size and scale as they have been described by anthropologists. The relationship suggests that human societies have in the past adjusted to increased crowding and that they have done so by employing a number of techniques which, properly translated into modern contexts, could serve as a guide for future action.

RECENT ADVANCES IN THE THEORY OF CROWDING

Research in the relationship between population density and social pathology was rekindled in the early 1960s by a series of widely publicized experiments demonstrating the pathological effects of crowding on caged rodents. John Calhoun (1962) demonstrated that if a population of rats was allowed to grow in a confined space without the constraints of disease, predation, or food shortage, the growth of the population eventually ceased amid a variety of symptoms of generalized "stress" syndrome. Many of the symptoms appeared to mimic antisocial or psychotic behavior among human beings: infant mortality increased as the quality of parental care and nurture declined; sexual aberrations developed; growth was inhibited; fertility was reduced; there was partial failure of normal maturational processes; aggression and conflict became common as did various forms of social withdrawal.

More recent experiments have demonstrated similar effects of high density (as well as others such as immune system failure) in a variety of caged and wild animal species (see Christian 1980; Terman 1980; Lloyd 1980; Packard and Mech 1980). The nature of the glandular processes underlying these symptoms has now been partially mapped, and the basic system of glandular reactions is known to be shared at least in part by people as well as other animals (Christian 1980). Thus both laboratory and naturalistic observations on animal populations suggest a chain of events potentially significant for people as well as other animals, which is as follows: population growth with no commensurate expansion of occupied territory leads to high density; density can lead to glandular reaction (stress); stress can result in reproductive failure, disease, and antisocial behaviors; and the latter can lead to the cessation of further population growth. A key point to be emphasized is that effects are most likely to be felt if population growth is combined with constraints on territorial expansion. Such constraints might take the form of physical barriers to movement such as the walls of a cage or the shores of an island. They might take the form of competition from neighboring groups or of abrupt or gradual decline in resources or other parameters of environmental quality as organisms attempt to move away from the core of occupied territory; they might even take the form of social — or, for human beings, cultural — constraints on emigration.

Recent experiments with animals also suggest, however, that the relationship between high density and social pathology (and for that matter the relationship between density and the cessation of population growth) is not as simple as was once thought. On the one hand, numerical density per se does not appear to be a good predictor of the onset of social pathology even though it is one ingredient in its emergence: symptoms of pathology often occur at very different density levels even among repeated experiments with genetically similar organisms in identical environments. On the other hand, there are hints that social factors help regulate the onset of pathology: symptoms are commonly most prominent among subordinate members of the population; individuals display differing stress-inducing effects on one another; the removal of particular individuals may trigger relaxation of stressful relations and a resumption of population growth to new higher levels; conversely, an increase in the space available to a population (and hence a decrease in density) without any alteration of group membership does not always result in new growth (see Lloyd 1980; Terman 1980). Despite such hints about the role of social factors in instigating stress, however, the animal studies have not yet progressed very far in the direction of defining the nature of the factors involved. We know that reactions to high density are complex and are affected by social factors, but we do not know what these factors are.

Attempts to interpret the significance of Calhoun's results in human terms have also proved difficult despite the known similarities of glandular function. It has been repeatedly asserted that there is relatively little evidence of correlation between absolute population densities among human beings and any of the kinds of social pathology which extrapolation from the Calhoun experiments might predict (Freedman 1975, 1980). In fact studies attempting to show a correlation between human population size or density and various measures of pathology have produced inconsistent results (compare Freedman 1980; Karlin 1980; Epstein 1980).

The human studies, however, have some important advantages over those conducted on animals with respect to the kinds of data that can be obtained. Human subjects, of course, are able to report on their own perceptions of test situations. Moreover experimenters and observers are in a position to be fairly certain they understand the significance of the environmental cues to which participants respond — a condition which is rarely met in animal studies. As a result it has been possible to arrange experiments and observations in a manner that permits us to tease out particular social themes that appear to be involved in mediating between density and the stressful perception of crowding among human beings.

These studies suggest that the factors that govern an organism's response to high density can be described by references to five density-related conditions: *resource scarcity, congestion, loss of control, loss of privacy,* and *information overload.* A sixth measure, actual physical proximity and physical jostling, is significant in some human settings, such as mass transit, and in non-human settings such as lemming hordes, but is not otherwise of great interest here (Epstein 1980; Karlin 1980).

Of these major conditions, *resource scarcity* is probably the factor most often considered by animal and human ecologists when they discuss the negative implications of high population density. High density is clearly stressful, if, as a result, there is not enough of a desired resource to go around. Resource scarcity (in combination with *congestion*) is a commonly perceived basis for intergroup as well as interpersonal conflict in the modern world, and it looms large as well in anthropological explanations of conflict in small-scale societies (Vayda 1968 and references cited). But, for people, at least, scarcity may not be so much a function of population density vis-à-vis fixed and immutable resources as it is a function of socially defined demand against technologically augmented supply. As argued earlier, the human food supply is elastic, dependent on cultural definition of what is desirable to eat, on prevailing standards about how hard to work, and on the choice to apply or not apply existing technology or develop new technology. (A similar argument could be made about energy in the modern world.) Conflict occurs in the name of resource scarcity, therefore, primarily because conflict is perceived as an easier — or culturally more acceptable — solution than alternative activities to adjust supplies.

One other point that should be made in this context is that resource scarcity can refer to social resources (such as jobs, roles, or partners) as well as to natural resources, but the supply of such social resources, too, is elastic, dependent on social choices about the definition of tasks and settings.[5]

Congestion refers to the tendency of organisms to interfere with one another's attempts to use a resource within the same limited space or time-span (when for example there is plenty of water but only room for a few people or animals to drink at the same time). Congestion clearly is most significant when population density is high and resources are limited. But congestion can be relieved without altering these basic conditions by any mechanism such as a schedule of actions that organizes the behavior of competing organisms to maximize individual access to resources and to minimize mutual interference.

Much intergroup as well as interindividual conflict overtly directed at resource scarcity is, in fact, directed at congestion, but the distinction should be maintained because the latter concept emphasizes the potential role of organizational factors in affecting the size of apparent supplies.

The other conditions, *loss of control, loss of privacy,* and *information overload,* are less commonly recognized as problems of crowding, at least by laymen, and they are less likely to be considered by legislators and social engineers; yet they are important and have played an important role in defining the social responses that human groups historically have made to crowding. There is even some evidence to suggest that *loss of control,* in particular, may be a more immediately compelling stress — and more instrumental in promoting conflict — than either scarcity or congestion.

Control refers to an organism's competence in achieving desired ends through its own actions (Baron and Rodin 1978). In order for control to exist, outcomes must be contingent, at least in part, on actions taken: the organism must be able to effect specific outcomes by its choice of behavior. To some degree, of course, all successful organisms must have many spheres of behavior in which they are competent, in which they exert some real control over important outcomes (such as getting food, escaping predators, mating, and the like). However, it is important to emphasize here that the organism must not only *be* effective to some degree, but must also *perceive* itself as effective in order to retain its motivation to act appropriately. Perception that outcomes are completely random relative to actions — that one exerts *no* control — may lead to "learned helplessness" and inaction on the part of both human beings and other animals (Seligman 1972). In fact, although some level of real competence is obviously essential to survival, *perceived* control may be the more important quality for an organism's psychological and social well-being. The importance of perceived control presumably accounts for the elaborate magical and supernatural systems which people of all cultures have developed to manipulate aspects of the natural and social environments which they cannot otherwise effectively control — and for the ability people display to maintain their faith in the efficacy of their magical systems in the face of what must often be extremely low correlations between magical acts and desired outcomes. The importance of loss of control — and perhaps its greater immediacy than resource scarcity as a source of stress and conflict — is also suggested by the observation that instability and uncertainty may be more stressful — and may more often lead to outright conflict — than actual deprivation (see, for example, Gellner 1978).

Control theory implies that high population density is stressful to an organism if the presence of other organisms impedes it in pursuing its goal or affects its perception of its ability to manage outcomes. This, in turn, implies that a number of factors can help to reduce the negative effects of crowding even when absolute density is high. These include (1) social definition and allotment of manageable tasks and facilitation of those tasks; (2) organization of the group to provide positive interdependence and role complementarity — cooperative rather than competitive or individualistic orientation; (3) social spacing or scheduling mechanisms that provide the individual with time or space for unimpeded action; (4) provision of leverage such that an individual can shape the behavior of others that would impinge on him or her;[6] and (5) system stability such that successful actions are replicable. The theory also implies that social factors such as religion that give the *illusion* of control can reduce stress.

Control is apparently an important mediator of density and stress even among animals. A number of studies on laboratory and free-ranging populations of various species have shown that stress-related symptoms are more pronounced in low-ranking animals than in those of higher rank, presumably because stress is greater on those organisms that must constantly give way to others (be deflected from their own goals) than it is for those to whom they show such deference. Analogous observations can be made on human populations. Various anthropological studies have suggested that individuals of low status report feelings of stress and anxiety (such as feeling themselves bewitched) more often than do individuals of high status (see, for example, Kluckhohn 1962). Various studies have also suggested that individuals of low status, and particularly women, make more use of compensatory supernatural mechanisms (such as witchcraft) to control other members of their societies than do individuals who wield more real political and economic power (see, for example, Lewis 1971).

Privacy refers to a particular kind of control, the ability of an organism to retain control over access to other organisms and their access to it. Privacy in this sense is again a major part of the privilege and control that high-ranking individuals display in various species, perhaps helping to explain their low levels of stress. It is also a universal need of human beings, one essential for individual and cultural survival, and one to which all cultures address themselves (Altman 1975, 1977; see also Baron 1980; Rapoport 1975, Proshansky et al. 1976). Different human groups meet these needs in different ways or combinations of ways, but comparative analysis suggests that known mechanisms to provide privacy fall into one of several categories: (1) erection of physical barriers to movement; (2) social definition of private space and erection of social barriers to movement; (3) use of clothing as a barrier to interpersonal communication; (4) provision of mechanisms of social withdrawal, isolation, or physical dispersal; (5) restriction of behavior through codes of etiquette, decorum, formal protocol, and avoidance; (6) generation of barriers to communication through hostility.

Information load refers to the assertion that the significant parameter of "density" that may be stressful to an organism is not the number of organisms per se but the total amount of "information" (the number of variables and contingencies) that the organism must process (Rapoport 1975). The greater the number of other organisms present in the environment, of course, the greater the information load will tend to be. A greater number of organisms generates more inputs, creating the need for increasing awareness and consideration of the actions of others. But this load can be reduced by means of organizational strategies that limit the range of variables which must be considered for each organism and limit the "noise" levels produced by other aspects of the environment.

In general, information load can be reduced for the organism (1) if other organisms are similar to it and therefore predictable in their behavior (a solution which, however, can lead to increased competition for both natural and social resources); (2) if they are clearly labeled and categorized ("stereotyped") and abide by the category boundaries on their behavior; or (3) if they are easily dismissed as inconsequential or of consequence only in specified kinds of interactions.[7] Among animals, and presumably among people, stable hierarchies resulting in predictable outcomes to individual encounters help reduce information load and hence tension. For both people and animals, of course, physical barriers to interaction and information transfer (such as walls) also reduce stress. In short, although information load is in part a function of population size and density, the load can be reduced and the potential for stress and conflict minimized, if the behavior of other organisms is properly organized and properly patterned.

APPLICATION TO HUMAN POPULATION HISTORY
AND CULTURAL EVOLUTION

It is apparent from this list of factors that social organization can and does mediate between organisms and the stressful perception of high population density and that it does so by (1) organizing and guaranteeing access to scarce or concentrated resources, (2) organizing interactions to minimize congestion and to provide control and privacy for organisms, and (3) organizing perceptual inputs from other organisms in such a way as to reduce the total information load. It stands to reason that *as long as a population can adjust its behavior and social organization appropriately,* increased density need not result in social pathology, and growth need not be limited.

Most animal species, however, lack the ability to make major social or behavioral changes. They also lack the ability, purposefully, to make major adjustments in the margins of their biological niches, to eliminate environmental hazards, or to increase the supply of necessary resources. As a result, although enjoying relatively high fecundity (potentially high reproductive rates), populations of most species tend to "stabilize" (achieve rough equilibria) or to fluctuate in size rather than grow continuously. Such "stability" is a function of two patterns. First, crowding effects and social pathology limit fertility and force emigration of excess individuals, thus limiting population density at the core of a species range (whenever other environmental hazards fail to restrict growth). Second, these emigrants are themselves usually eliminated at the margins of the range where environmental hazards are particularly severe.

Among human beings, however, the pattern of population growth is slightly different. Our population has expanded fairly continuously, although at varying rates, through prehistory and history.[8] This expansion has occurred because human beings, like other organisms, enjoy high fecundity but also because, unlike other organisms, we are able partly to offset negative feedback systems that might otherwise curtail growth. First, human beings enjoy the behavioral and dietary plasticity necessary to adapt successfully to conditions at the margins of their range. Emigrants from prehistoric human groups were thus able, at least occasionally, to expand the occupied range rather than simply dying out. Second, human groups have the ability, when deprived of room for geographical expansion, to enlarge the local supply of needed resources by redefining their diets and intensifying their efforts so that resources are augmented rather than exhausted. Third, and most important in this context, human beings have the ability, when crowded and unable to expand, to restructure society in ways necessary to minimize crowding effects and stress. In short, high fecundity and the potential to adjust to adverse consequences have resulted in fairly continuous growth, and, indeed, many of the patterns of human cultural history reflect our adjustment to the potentially adverse effects of increasing population density.

The evolutionary record of changing human social organization, like the record of changing food economy, displays a history of such adjustments. In order to pursue this point, it will be necessary to develop and defend two propositions: (1) that structural differences widely recognized by anthropologists as characterizing societies of different sizes appear to address problems of control, privacy, and information load, as well as of resource scarcity and congestion, generated by increasing population size and density, and (2) that the archaeological, historical, and ethnographic record provides evidence that the transition from one form of social structure to the next occurred in a context of increasing population size and, at least in part, as a function of that increase.

The intent here, however, is *not* to argue that the institutional changes in question are designed *only* to mitigate the effects of crowding or to suggest that these changes occurred as a simple and direct result of crowding stress.

Clearly, many of the social institutions which will be discussed have multiple
purposes—and for this reason there is likely to be a lag or lack of precise
fit between the problems generated by population growth and the institutional
response. The point is, rather, that needs generated by increasing population
densities and the perception of crowding act as one set of factors instigating
institutional change in societies and guiding the direction of that change. The
common need to organize increasing numbers accounts for general parallels
in the evolution of various sociocultural systems.

The observations that follow will be confined to a comparative discussion of types of *nonindustrial* societies which are the anthropologist's traditional area of expertise. These observations are necessarily fairly crude and
preliminary, designed to generate discussion of the nature of institutional
changes rather than to provide a finished or polished interpretation.

Levels of Social Organization

There is a large literature in anthropology on the relationship between
the scale or size of human aggregates and the nature of their organization.
This literature can be divided into two major streams, each slightly tangen-
tial to my purpose. One stream has been explicitly concerned with the evolution of human culture and society and with related increases in population
size and social scale through human history (Morgan 1877; White 1959; Service 1966, 1975; Steward 1955; Fried 1967; Childe 1951). But this group has
tended to focus on changing relationships between culture and environment
or on major features of the organization of whole groups; it has been relatively unconcerned with the impact of changing scale on individuals or with
the potential of individual actors and interactions as an aggregate to affect
social forms. The second stream is more concerned with the impact of group
size or scale on individual function. (Wilson and Wilson 1945; Redfield 1941,
1953; Barth 1972; Barth ed. 1978; Berreman 1978). Moreover, members of this
tradition tend to perceive social organization, at least in part, as the aggregate outcome of individual encounters between actors. Since this approach
builds upward from the individual actor to the larger system, it opens the way
for analysis of the effects of aggregate individual needs and behavior on the
evolution of society as a whole. Much of the work in this tradition, however,
is nonevolutionary, dealing with differences in social scale not in terms of
progressive increase in group size through history, but rather in terms of the
confrontation of large and small contemporary societies or in terms of the
functioning of the hierarchical or concentric levels of integration within particular modern societies. Many of the studies in this stream involve a level of
detail about particular modern societies that cannot easily be applied to gen-

eralized reconstructions of prehistory. Moreover, much of this work may combine (and even confuse) certain contemporary particulars (such as the impact of European colonial regimes on smaller African societies) with the analysis of difference in group size per se. What follows is therefore an attempt to combine the two approaches, to integrate some of the insights of the latter stream into the evolutionary perspective.

For this purpose this chapter builds upon the classification of societies offered by evolutionist Morton Fried, a largely arbitrary choice conditioned by two factors: first, Fried's threefold division of human societies can be readily matched against features of the archaeological record which continue to be of major interest to archaeologists, and, second, the terms of his classification are more explicitly directed at social and political factors than are the classifications of many other evolutionists.[9]

According to this scheme, nonindustrial societies were classified into three types based on differing levels of complexity, the "egalitarian," "rank," and "state" levels of organization. While this classification addresses itself to contemporary societies and is based primarily on differences in the manner in which these societies are organized and run, it also includes two other major properties. First, the categories also reflect differences in group size; the three levels of organization are associated with increasing size and density of incorporated populations. Second, as evidenced by the archaeological record, the three types of societies represent an historical sequence as well as a synchronic classification. Early archaeological human societies appear invariably to have been of the small "egalitarian" type although only a few examples of this type now remain. Most egalitarian societies evolved into (or were replaced, displaced, or absorbed by) first "rank" and then "state" level societies within approximately the last 10,000 and 5000 years, respectively. In short, as human population has grown through history, the prevailing type of organization has changed.

Egalitarian Societies

Egalitarian bands are small groups of people: they typically contain between about fifteen and fifty persons who subsist by hunting and gathering of wild foods (see Lee and Devore eds. 1968; Bicchieri 1972; Cohen 1977; Service 1979; Hassan 1981; Barth 1972). Groups are generally de facto aggregates of friends and kin which move periodically to areas where new seasonal resources are available but which also split and reunite or realign with other groups periodically in response to the changing distribution of resources and in response to interpersonal tensions and attractions. As long as population density remains low and high mobility is possible (and outside of extreme environments), such groups can apparently feed themselves reliably and well with relatively little effort and with little prior investment in the productivity of their resources.

Problems associated with crowding are clearly at a minimum, and, as might be expected, elaborate social mechanisms to regulate interactions and reduce stress are also at a minimum. Egalitarian societies are largely defined by the absence of a number of formal structural principles shared by other societies. What they lack (or minimize) quite simply are the formal mechanisms that other societies use to organize and distribute scarce resources, to eliminate congestion, and to resolve problems of privacy, control, and information load.

Privacy needs, which might otherwise be threatened by the level of intimacy or visibility, are met because there are few "others" with whom to deal, because those others tend to be friends and kin, and because, in any case, one can easily withdraw temporarily or permanently from their company. Possibly in consequence, egalitarian campsites typically have relatively few physical barriers to movement. Shelters are commonly less substantial and are utilized for fewer activities than are the shelters of more complex groups in comparable environments. Clothing, too, tends to be less developed as a source of privacy than in many larger societies. Moreover egalitarian groups have relatively few of the formal rules of etiquette and protocol that create social barriers to unlimited interaction in other groups.

Information load similarly is minimized by the small number of others and their similarity to one's self; relatively few efforts are made to simplify the load by classifying and stereotyping other members of the local group or prescribing their behavior with formal rules. Although kinship may be used as a means of recognizing responsibilities to others and may, as in the case of the Australians, be highly elaborate, kinship does not appear to serve the more formal classifying function *within the local community* that it does in larger groups. Individuals may be united by bonds of kinship, but kinship per se (at least in comparison to rank societies) seems secondary to the positive (and negative) feelings which proximity and kinship generate. Few specialized statuses other than age and sex roles are defined, and even the latter are informally drawn.

Control in the sense used here is provided by the direct access each individual has to resources and by the immediacy of rewards for labor, by the small number of others likely to impede that access, by the largely cooperative basis for interaction among members, by the direct access that each individual has to others and to their goods, and by the ability that each individual has to modify the behavior of others through personal contact and influence. Ultimately, of course, an individual exerts control in exercising ability to leave the group.[10] The result is that such groups need few rules to keep individuals out of each other's way; have few rules that formally direct, schedule, or co-ordinate activities; and have no formal or permanent leadership or formal mechanisms for enforcing behavioral limits. Even trade tends to be informal reciprocity among friends, lacking the organizational structures necessary in larger groups to provide knowledge of, and access to, resources.

The system seems to work reasonably well as long as groups remain within the size limits discussed. But, for lack of appropriate organizational principles, such groups are largely unable to cope with group sizes that represent even a relatively modest increase over the numbers described. Groups of much over fifty people appear unstable. Larger aggregates, of as many as a few hundred people, which occasionally form as a result of seasonal concentrations of resource or centripetal social forces regularly fission back into smaller groups amid increasing social tension.[11] Where tensions cannot be resolved by dispersal, and where no mechanisms have evolved to provide order, conflict is likely to erupt.[12]

In a few historic cases where egalitarian bands regularly gathered in large seasonal aggregates, as for example, among certain plains Indian groups, more complex social organization (paralleling that of rank societies) emerged temporarily, only to disappear again when groups dispersed. In such cases the level of social organization appears to respond in an elastic manner to the demands of increasing group size (Carneiro 1967).

Rank Societies

In contrast to egalitarian societies, rank societies are characterized by the emergence of a number of institutions appropriate to increasing size, density, and permanence of social units.[13] New technologies and new food sources (farming of domestic plants and animals, or in a few cases the intensive harvesting of particularly productive wild resources such as acorns or migratory fish) permit more people to be fed from each unit of land. These same resources, however, necessitate permanent settlement (except where domestic animals alone are exploited) because they demand long-term prior investment in fixed resources and seasonal storage. Such an investment removes one major avenue of individual control, the ability to move away from stress (although the same inability to move can strengthen one's ability to influence the behavior of others who must remain within reach of social sanctions). In addition such investment diminishes control in another sense by greatly increasing the risk that other individuals will intrude between initial investment and final consumption. Moreover increasing social scale means that individuals increasingly come to lack personal knowledge of, and personal influence on, all others with whom they must interact locally.

To offset the potential for increased "crowding" stress, rank societies must therefore employ a number of organizational mechanisms. First, they *differentiate* their membership through a number of classificatory mechanisms (formal extension of kinship systems, age grades, membership in sodalities, specialization, prestige ranking) which substitute social separation for the spatial separation which is no longer possible. Such differentiation serves primarily to eliminate some members of the society from competition and consideration by other members; and where it does not separate individuals completely, it at least simplifies individual interactions and makes their outcomes predictable by making statements about predetermined, group-related rights of prior access to particular natural and social resources at particular times and places.

Second, rank societies also *stereotype* their members. The various systems of differentiation all have the common attribute of reducing some other people to "faceless" group- or class-members about whom one need know only their group or class attributes; from whom one need receive only specific kinds of information; and toward whom one need give only automatic, stereotyped responses.

Third, rank societies *announce* group membership through cues (primarily visual, such as styles of clothing and badges of status) that permit rapid evaluation of the status of others.

Fourth, rank societies *solidify* and *stabilize* categories in such a way that the various bases for differentiation need not be renegotiated between individuals. This is accomplished primarily through the increase in the importance of ascribed as opposed to achieved status and through the establishment of permanent institutionalized leadership, both of which create predictable and reliable patterns of interaction with "others" too numerous to evaluate through personal interaction and negotiation.

Fifth, rank societies *coordinate action by creating nested hierarchies of administration* that permit society as a whole to be administered as a cluster of groups rather than as an aggregate of individuals and that simultaneously create defined lines of information flow between individuals and the central administration.

Sixth, rank societies *reinforce* group membership and proper action through a number of mechanisms. These include formal instruction in the proper limits to individual behavior and the elaboration of ritual behavior. Participation in rituals serves to reinforce group membership and appropriate behavior by reminding the individual of the rationale for membership. The reminder takes a particular form, I think — a kind of reassurance about personal "control" (in the sense defined above) through social mediation. Ritual is, after all, basically the repetition of actions for which the proper contingent responses are more or less assured by social contract. Thus, participation in rituals allows individuals to rehearse "control" (i.e., to perform actions with reliable contingent outcomes) and thus to be reassured; but *group* ritual also conveys the message that it is group membership and social rules that provide control. In short, the control or competence that egalitarian group members can more easily practice through direct action on other individuals or on resources is provided for members of more complex societies by social convention; and rituals serve to remind them of this fact.

State Societies

The preindustrial state provides means for organizing and coordinating even larger aggregates of people. An increasing number of people dependent for their livelihood on the resources of a particular region increases the potential for congestion and competition of individuals engaged in extraction activities. It also increases the potential for real resource scarcity either long-term, resulting from an imbalance between population and extractive techniques, or short-term, resulting from temporary fluctuations in the environment, the potential consequences of which increase in severity as population density increases (see Cohen 1981 and references cited).

In consequence, major functions of state organization appear to include: (1) the management of trade and distribution networks and storage facilities which act to buffer particular locations against shortage, thus helping to prevent both real scarcity and real or anticipated loss of control over food supplies; (2) the investment (including mobilization of massed labor) in productive activities such as irrigation which expand productive capacity and help buffer levels of output against natural disaster; (3) the protection of the group against competition from without and the policing of the group against competition from within; (4) the organization of access to resources; and (5) the maintenance of a complex system of complementary activities or specializations. In organizing access to resources, states tend to maintain relatively rigid spatial boundaries and rules of group membership as well as formal rules governing access; in fact, they regularly involve systems of class stratification which first limit access to strategic resources, such as land or water, to elites and then permit limited and controlled access to other members of society. The state's maintenance of complementary activities or specializations not only increases the efficiency of production and expands the range of available goods but also helps to reduce congestion by organizing segments of the large group into separate activity patterns, scheduling their activities to minimize conflict, and creating a need for cooperative interaction among strangers who might otherwise view their interaction as competitive.[14]

But large population (and particularly the aggregation of population into urban centers where many of the specialized functions of the new organization occur) creates other problems of crowding. Individuals are exposed to, and must deal with, a large number of others who are unlikely to be similar to them, about whom they can know only a little, and over whom they can exert relatively little influence. The problem of maintaining personal control is also exacerbated by the very nature of state organization as a system of specialists and as a system of interregional economic buffers which force the individual to rely on and interact with persons and institutions well beyond their personal influence (see Berreman 1978 and discussion appended thereto). The problem of information load, too, is heightened, not just by increased numbers and heterogeneity in the population, but also by the likelihood of increasing rapid innovation and change as the number of innovators and the potential for creative juxtaposition of new combinations of ideas increases (Burnett 1953).

The formal institutional response to these problems on the part of the state apparatus itself is to define appropriate codes of behavior in increasingly formal and explicit terms and to take new steps to enforce compliance. States are defined by the sanctioned use of force to maintain social order and by the maintenance of professional groups whose prime function is to enforce compliance. In addition law may be codified and depersonalized. Its application within the state tends to lack the kind of sensitivity to individuals which adds a personal element to the legal proceedings of small societies, but this same application adds predictability to the actions of strangers. By such law economic exchange and other forms of interaction are given standardized and relatively impersonal form, and the potential for innovation is reduced and channeled.

On a less formal level participants in state systems (and particularly in cities) appear to adopt a number of common adaptive strategies (Barth ed. 1978, especially contributions of Colson, Jacobson, Barth, and Schwartz). The basic intent of these strategies appears to be for each individual to gather around himself one or more small communities from within the larger group to serve the positive personal needs of interaction and then deliberately to minimize the importance, except in strictly functional terms, of all others. As in rank society social isolation is substituted for spatial isolation, but a more powerful set of mechanisms of discrimination is now put into play. Ethnic diversity and craft specialization force individuals to deal with many different persons, but at the same time these badges of status permit individuals to perceive others (and react to them) as less than whole — as having only the special group membership or function, not a full range of human needs. Craft specialization and ethnicity thus become mechanisms whereby individuals can minimize their share of the ever-increasing aggregate of information load that must be stored and processed by the society as a whole.[15]

One other tentative suggestion has to do with physical barriers promoting privacy and further reducing information flow. Within states, communities (and particularly the urban centers where specialized functions concentrate) should be found to contain relatively large numbers of physical impediments to movement. Dwellings should be relatively substantial and private, housing more activities than do the dwellings of smaller groups, and clothing should be relatively elaborate both as a sign of role and status and as a barrier to communication. Moreover, formal protocols or automatic formulas governing personal interactions should be relatively elaborate — or at least should govern a higher percentage of interactions than they do in smaller groups.

In sum, preindustrial states offset the potential effects of crowding by augmenting and buffering supplies of resources, by defining access to resources very precisely and even excluding some members from immediate access, by subdividing the population into behavioral categories, by defining relatively narrow and specialized spheres of activity for each segment of the population, by making the segments readily identifiable, by establishing strict formal rules for carrying out each specialization and for performing the more general acts of participants in the system, and by enforcing such rules uniformly and rigidly. Individuals further adapt by creating social and physical barriers to interaction with all but relatively few people. Those outside the narrow circle are dealt with only for narrowly defined purposes and in a fairly stereotyped or mechanical manner.

POPULATION GROWTH AND THE EVOLUTION OF SOCIETY

Although the preceding review is necessarily brief and highly generalized, it should serve to make clear that the progression from egalitarian to rank and state societies involves a number of changes that are directly responsive to the problem of organizing ever-larger population aggregates to minimize the stressful effects of crowding. As the number of people competing for local resources increases, techniques for augmenting those resources also increase, but in addition rules scheduling and restricting access to those resources become more detailed, more formal, more restrictive, and more powerful. As the number of "others" increases, formal categories emerge to reduce information load by simplifying anticipation of their behavior, and rules of etiquette as well as barriers of clothing and architecture emerge to limit the range and extent of behavioral interactions. As the increasing number of people threatens to impede individuals in pursuit of their goals, and as the ability to depart is lost, rules increasingly define private spaces for personal action and limit the range of potential intrusion by others.

It remains now to defend the second of the two propositions: that these social transformations were not simply new "inventions" which fortuitously reorganized society, but rather new directions in cultural evolution which were necessitated (or "selected for" in the Darwinian sense) by growing population and the problems it generated.

The Transition from Egalitarian to Rank Society

The argument that hunter-gatherers adopted agriculture in various parts of the world, beginning about 10,000 years ago, as a response to the pressure of population on resources has been developed elsewhere (Cohen 1977). Briefly, ethnographic analogies suggest that hunter-gatherers are unlikely to adopt agriculture by choice without such compelling circumstances. Hunter-gatherers appear generally to be better nourished and more reliably provisioned than are farmers; they work as little or less than farmers do. The only advantage to farming seems to be that it can support denser populations.

The archaeological record, in fact, indicates that farming was adopted independently in a number of regions of the world in a context of growing population; that it was adopted as one of a long series of steps taken in each region to broaden the range of foods eaten and increase the food supply; that it occurred at the culmination of a long period of geographical expansion and infiltration of new niches; and *that it occurred at the time when space available to each group was increasingly limited by the presence of others, so that geographical expansion was ceasing to be possible as a means of resolving further population growth.* The archaeological record also shows that the transition was accompanied (in many areas of the world where comparative skeletal analyses are reported) by a decline in health and longevity and an increase in episodes of biological stress and/or a decline in stature, all suggesting that the transition was an episode of stress, not progress. The decline in health has previously been interpreted as an indication of increasing infection or malnutrition, but it is interesting to note that similar symptoms could also be accounted for by increasing social pathology (which affects both growth and disease resistance) alone, or in synergistic interaction with biological factors. This new interpretation may be supported by the fact that in some well-studied regions such as the Nile Valley and Central Illinois this period was also marked by relatively high levels of interpersonal violence. In both regions skeletons of this transition period display a high incidence of skeletal traumata of a type and pattern suggestive of human agency. Available data do not yet permit us to assess how widespread this pattern is.[16]

Of more immediate interest for purposes of this chapter, indications of rank society begin to appear in the archaeological record in various parts of the world at a time roughly synchronous with the emergence of agriculture (but in some cases shortly before and in others shortly after the economic transition). Communities appear that are now more formally organized with central foci; personal ornament indicative of status and group differentiation begins to appear; houses are more substantial; and larger and deeper areas of refuse indicate more permanent habitation by larger groups. Whereas in the earlier era hunter-gatherers may temporarily have adopted rank organization as a function of temporary aggregation, the shift now appears to be largely irreversible, suggesting that it is no longer a function of seasonal economic choices or temporary economic necessity but rather reflects a general and permanent shift in the size of groups and in the space available to them. But most important, rank society appears independently in so many regions of the world that its emergence cannot have been coincidental, nor can it have been an "invention" that diffused. The need for a new type of organization was presumably in part generated by increasing ecological and political vulnerability which sedentism along with prior investment in resources created and which some degree of centralized administration could help relieve.[17] But the need was also presumably generated in part by the problem of increasing density and permanence and the concomitant potential for increased social pathology when crowding effects could no longer so easily be relieved by emigration. The preferred solution to crowding is to move apart, but when there is no space for emigration the problem can be met by reorganization (see Colson 1978).

The Transition to Statehood

The case for the transition from rank to state societies is similar, but perhaps not as strong. Beginning about 5000 years ago, archaeological remains in a number of world regions begin to show evidence of the transition; massive construction projects appear that demonstrate the coercive powers and large-scale organizational capabilities of elites; class distinctions are evidenced in the scale of housing, the treatment of the dead, and even the health and stature of neighboring groups; specialization is evident in the spatial distribution of activities at sites and in the quality of artifacts produced; communities are built on a scale not previously in evidence; systems of codification and recording are found.

The most important point to be made in this context is that, like rank societies before them, states appear to have emerged repeatedly and independently in various parts of the world. The scattered distribution of the first states indicates clearly that they do not owe their common structure to diffusion. Yet the number of cases and the relatively brief period of human history in which they all first occur defies coincidence. Emergent statehood is at least in part a common adaptation to common circumstances.[18]

Increasing population within rank societies is clearly one of the conditions underlying this emergence. The emergence of early states in the archaeological record is commonly, if not always directly, preceded by evidence of population growth. Recognizing this fact, scholars have put forward a number of theories of state formation that emphasize the role of population growth in their emergence (compare Boserup 1965; Carneiro 1970; Fried 1967; Sanders and Price 1968; Sanders and Webster 1978; Smith and Young 1972). However, these theories largely ignore several of the consequences of crowding — lack of control and privacy, information load, and congestion — and focus heavily on the state as an apparatus developed to compete for, or organize access to, scarce resources or to assure control over resources that could not otherwise provide reliably for growing numbers of people.

A number of scholars also see evidence that, amid increasing competition for resources, conflict and warfare play a role in state formation, and a number of theories have been offered to explain both the conflict itself and its role in political evolution. There is considerable debate, however, as to whether warfare was indeed more prevalent in this period of incipient state formation than in earlier times; whether it simply played a new political role, substituting conquest and class stratification for mere raiding; or whether indeed it played an essential role in statehood at all (compare Fried 1967; Carneiro 1970; Webster 1975; Lewis 1978; Service 1975; Flannery 1972).

Perhaps the most influential and ambitious modern proponent of the role of population growth and resulting conflict in stimulating the development of early states is Robert Carneiro. Carneiro (1978) has argued that the first states were stimulated by the competition, conflict, and conquest of dense populations in particularly confined or "circumscribed" areas where spatial adjustments to growth were particularly limited. Carneiro's model of growth and circumscription is attractive in the context of the arguments presented here, although he stresses the political and economic consequences of crowding without considering some of the other problems involved. But the model he proposes does not seem totally defensible. Various critics have pointed out that, while the areas of the world under consideration are "circumscribed," they are not uniquely so. They have also pointed out that, although high population density and population growth correlate in a loose or general way with state formation, population growth at the critical stage of political transformation cannot always be demonstrated (compare Service 1975; Wright and Johnson 1975; Flannery 1972; Cohen 1981). The correlation is not as close as Carneiro would suggest.

Two improvements can be offered to the Carneiro model. The first is to add consideration of the problems of information load, privacy, and control to problems of resource scarcity and competition in explaining the role of population growth in stimulating state formation and in molding the emergent institutions. The second is to suggest that, while population growth, circumscription, and the resulting problems contribute or help to *stimulate* state formation, they do not *determine* it to quite the degree he implies. The reason is simply that a whole host of local variables, particularly the idiosyncrasies of local interest groups and local institutions, interceded between this general stimulus and the emergence of statehood (see Cohen 1981).

A comparison between the emergence of rank society and that of state society is instructive in this context and contains an interesting insight on our contemporary problems. In the earlier transition population growth and increasing spatial confinement of egalitarian hunter-gatherers may have been followed fairly widely and regularly by the onset of farming and rank organization because there were few conflicting institutional needs. Each member of an egalitarian group exerted one unit of demand for food, so, as population grew, the food supply was expanded fairly evenly. Similarly, each member of an egalitarian group exerted a unit of demand for organization. Therefore, as individuals began to perceive crowding, they were motivated to adjust the systems in which they participated. They undoubtedly experienced inertia geared to existing values and some desire to maintain the status quo, but the very informality of the system meant that there were few institutional barriers to change and the homogeneity of the group minimized conflict of interest.

Once authoritarian ranking, differential status, and group subdivisions emerged, however, and particularly once these began to evolve toward true power and economic privilege, the aggregate demand of individuals, whether for food or for organization, had to be balanced against the needs and wishes of those with power and authority and against the institutional needs and inertia of organizational systems already in place. This chapter suggests that the origin of the state was generally but not specifically correlated with increasing density precisely because of these conflicting needs which might delay, accelerate, or conceivably prevent adaptive change. The same problem is one of the keys to our modern dilemma; individuals do not generate demand for change which can effectively offset the inertia of institutions.

In sum, it seems clear that, as human population has grown, human societies have adjusted to the potential for adverse crowding effects in a number of ways: (1) they have invested increasing effort in expanding the supply of essential resources; (2) they have invested increasingly in mechanisms to buffer local groups against shortage; (3) they have exercised increasing central control over the allotment of scarce resources; (4) they have scheduled access to those resources with increasing care; (5) they have differentiated groups of individuals, thereby reducing the ratio of actual to potential social contacts in order to reduce information load, and differentiated spheres of activity to reduce congestion and assure cooperative interaction; (6) they have established increasingly well-defined and powerful central control over individual behavior, helping to offset in part the reduction of effective interpersonal control. On an individual level people have responded by developing a series of social and physical mechanisms to reduce the potential overload of information by limiting the social sphere in which they interact as a whole person and by defining others as unimportant, relegating most others to "bit parts" or to another theater altogether (see Colson 1978).

It would also appear that population growth itself has played a major role in stimulating these shifts. There is some evidence, particularly in the descriptions of over-large egalitarian groups, that population growth beyond organizational capacity can produce social pathology and conflict. Indeed, the archaeological record suggests that new forms of organization were repeatedly developed by human societies in various parts of the world when population growth was combined with geographical limits to spatial expansion. The record also suggests, however, that, as societies become more complex, the aggregate needs of individuals came increasingly to be balanced against (possibly conflicting) needs of the bureaucracy or power structure itself.

IMPLICATIONS FOR CONTEMPORARY SOCIETY

It seems apparent that modern industrial societies generate their own peculiar problems of crowding which cannot be completely explained by further increases in scale. One major factor distinguishing industrial from preindustrial society is the rate of change. It has been argued, for example, that, because modern society changes so fast, individuals can no longer prepare singlemindedly for particular familial specializations as they could in many preindustrial societies (Gellner 1978). As a result, although most individuals ultimately specialize and, in fact, engage in narrower and more finely coordinated specialties than in preindustrial societies, they must first be *generally* prepared by the formal educational institution of their societies. The effect is that the social and cultural distance between specialists is minimized. Society is homogenized, reducing in part the information load as people become similar. Yet at the same time congestion and competition for scarce social (and even some natural) resources are exacerbated. Moreover, homogenization and mobility seem to undercut the mechanisms that individuals use to partition their social worlds, while the rate of change itself as well as the potential for long-distance transport and communication offset whatever reduction in information load may occur through homogenization. Rapid change also contributes to a sense of loss of control. In the end, the potential for social pathology and interpersonal conflict is high, and perhaps we are witnessing more than just the potential for such conflict in our cities.

The problems of crowding are likely to be particularly acute in developing countries where problems of scale are exacerbated by patterns of rapid, recent change. Members of these societies are moving rapidly through a series of changes in social scale which have commonly unfolded over many generations, or even many centuries, in the developed countries. The populations of developing countries are often being pressured to abandon old modes of organization and adopt new ones based on the experience of the developed countries, instead of making new and culturally appropriate organizational responses of their own. In fact the people of developing countries are often put through a series of organizational changes more as a matter of style — mimicking the structures of advanced societies — than as a matter of real need, even though change itself adds to levels of stress.

We know, however, that the potential for stress and conflict can be at least partially offset by good social design. It is therefore incumbent on governments to examine and initiate, or at least facilitate efforts at, reorganization and redesign, efforts to quell further population growth notwithstanding. The direction of necessary social change is clearly pointed out by the direction of earlier changes, and the detail of that design can be elucidated by comparative study (in far greater detail than is possible here) of the organization of simpler societies. The task for contemporary research is first to elucidate with greater precision the dimensions of loss of control, information overload, or the other stressful aspects of crowding; and second to explore more fully the various cultural systems of the world for clues as to how these stresses have traditionally been offset. The comparative analysis of cultural systems should facilitate cross-fertilization, the chance for cultures to learn from one another techniques that can successfully offset the negative effects of crowding. (Our own culture might do well, for example, to study alternative modes of classifying people as a means of eliminating unjust and socially costly racial and sexual stereotypes without losing the organizational benefits which such stereotypes provide.) Comparisons among societies should also enhance our appreciation of the need for different cultures to deal with common problems in different ways in accordance with their own values. For example, it is essential that the value of traditional structures in developing countries be recognized and that cultural relativism be employed in their selective adoption of organizational techniques borrowed from the developed nations.

But the research necessary to translate the principles of social psychology theory and comparative ethnographic analysis into workable modern design is only one step. A more challenging step is to make good choices.

A reduction in stress and conflict levels may have to be bought at the price of sacrificing some professed modern (particularly Western) values which are perhaps more appropriate to small egalitarian bands or to societies with open frontiers.[19] The basic problem is to balance priorities and seek new organizational forms that will not violate the more important of these values.

A further problem is that we must anticipate. The lesson of the past is that growing population can forge new principles of organization, at least very slowly (provided governments and special interests do not interfere), but only *after* the pressure of population on the old system is felt. The modern challenge is to use that lesson to foresee stress and circumvent it by design *before* the stress becomes acute. Such anticipation involves not only sophisticated research but also enlightened and forceful leadership.

Possibly most difficult is the challenge of overcoming the self-interest of elites and interest groups and the inertia of existing institutions. The problem is that today industrial states like their nonindustrial counterparts must pay disproportionate attention to the interests of the powerful and must balance complex institutional demands. The needs of individuals at the level discussed here are unlikely to be a major priority for study, let alone for implementation; but it is in this fact, and not simply in the fact of population growth alone, that the problem resides.

NOTES

1. See Boserup (1965) for a historical-evolutionary perspective opposing that of Malthus. See Simon (1980) for a critique of Malthusian thinking about the modern population "crisis."

2. One interesting piece of evidence in support of this contention, which, however, does not explain how new organizational forms emerge or exactly what they accomplish, is the demonstration by Carneiro (1967) of a surprisingly regular (logarithmic) crosscultural relationship between the size (number of people) of various contemporary or historic autonomous sociopolitical units and the number of organizing units the systems employ. Such a correlation does not, of course, show the direction of the cause and effect relationships between population and organization so much as it suggests the existence of a fairly fine-tuned equilibrium between the two. Carneiro argues, as I do, for the role of population growth in stimulating the transformation of social organizations.

3. The continued attraction of the Malthus model to scholars and politicians may be due in part to the manner in which it feeds their professional and class self-interests. See Kleinman (1980).

4. In challenging the Malthusian assumptions about population growth and its negative effects, I am concerned primarily with the effects that such growth and crowding play in generating social pathology and conflict by raising levels of stress *in individuals*. I make no claim

that crowding is the source of all such stress and conflict, or even the dominant portion thereof, although I think that it is one important factor. I also make no claim that at least in modern societies such stress is associated with conflict on a large scale (war), although it may contribute to conflict at the local level. Anthropologists — see Fried et al. 1968, especially papers by Vayda and Lesser — often distinguish between conflict in small stateless societies and in larger modern states. In the former, intergroup conflict is poorly organized but often intensely personal. Much conflict occurs in competition for resources, but conflict may also be directed at the redress of personal or familial grievances. Conflict between groups may even be motivated by the need to direct outward aggression generated by personal interactions within one of the groups. In this case linkages to crowding and stress are plausible. In state societies, in contrast, intergroup conflict is often highly organized and largely impersonal. The link to crowding and stress is far more tenuous, except perhaps in the sense that personal frustrations can make a populace malleable for its leaders.

5. Wicker (1979) describes the relationship between population size and the supply of available social roles in terms of the "over-" and "undermanning" of specific, culturally defined behavior settings. He considers the consequences to individuals of participating in over- and undermanned settings.

6. Compare the discussion by Jacobson (1978) of social control in human societies. Social control — roughly the ability to affect the actions of others — is not identical with control of the outcomes of one's own actions or *competence* in the sense used here, but it is one important aspect of such competence.

7. Compare the discussion of Colson (1978) of the mechanisms people use — and must use — to limit the size of their social networks and the number of their interactions to tolerable, manageable levels as the number of potential contacts goes up.

8. For opposing points of view concerning this and other aspects of the population-pressure model, see Hassan (1979, 1981); Hayden (1975, 1981); Cowgill (1975). One of the major points of controversy concerns whether or not human populations are effectively self-regulating through cultural means. Many anthropologists argue that human populations not only limit fertility through cultural means, including infanticide and abortion, but do that regularly and effectively so that population growth beyond the capacity of existing production systems cannot occur. I agree that most cultures within our experience employ some mechanisms to limit births, but I would argue that such mechanisms are likely to be something less than completely effective. As Hayden (1975) himself has pointed out, such fertility regulation is costly (takes effort) to keep up. It is therefore not likely to be strictly enforced unless the rate of population growth (like the rate of inflation in modern terms) is high enough to force a change in life style which is perceptible in the short run. Very slow growth would not be so perceived; hence regulatory systems, although they keep growth rates well below those theoretically possible, are unlikely to achieve true zero growth. Moreover, even if strictly and consistently enforced, it would be very difficult for such a regulatory system to achieve accurate zero growth since, in order to do so, the system would have to anticipate (among other things) accidental deaths and even the possible failure of neighboring populations. The likely result is that population will creep upward, fueled by high human fertility, despite attempts at regulation. And this is what the archaeological record suggests has occurred.

Another issue concerns why, if population growth can occur at all, growth was so slow (less than 0.003 percent per year in contrast to 1 to 2 percent per year for many modern groups) during the early, preagricultural phases of human history. One possible answer is that the fertility of hunter-gatherers was (and in some cases still is) lower than that of farmers. Hunter-gatherers, though qualitatively well-nourished and healthy, get little starch in their diets and are therefore very lean. Also, for want of easily prepared weaning foods they may generally nurse for prolonged periods. Both low bodily fat levels and prolonged nursing are considered likely to dampen female fertility. Modern hunter-gatherers such as the !Kung Bushmen are apparently relatively infertile for these or other reasons, although even they are fertile enough to permit some population growth. Another reason for low growth rates among hunter-gatherers is that the marginal utility of additional children is low, the marginal cost high, and regulation by infanticide therefore *relatively* strictly enforced. Once farming is adopted, the labor of each child more surely offsets the costs of feeding it, so cultural regulation is relaxed. For a fuller discussion of these issues, see Cohen et al. (1980), particularly chapters by Cohen, Lee, Hassan, and Ripley.

9. Fried (1967). In addition to the three stages discussed, Fried also recognizes a fourth hypothetical state which, however, he admits has few empirical examples.

10. Compare the observation by various experimenters cited in Epstein (1980), suggesting that modern experimental subjects are less stressed by crowding when they are given (or believe they have been given) the ability to depart or to terminate the experiment.

11. See, for example, the discussion by Lee (1972) of an aggregation of Kalahari Bushmen.

12. Chagnon (1968) provides a particularly graphic description of this process among Yanomamo Indians of South America, who, although they now farm, retain an essentially egalitarian social organization and live in groups not much larger than most hunter-gatherers. The population is growing, and on the peripheries of their territory, where space is available, groups split apart before they reach a hundred people. However, when surrounded by other (often hostile) groups and prevented for reasons of security from splitting into smaller units, villages grow to unmanageable size amid increasing tensions and ultimately erupt in intragroup conflict which becomes intergroup conflict after fission is completed.

13. A modification of Fried (1967). Compare Service (1962, 1975), who offers a slightly different division of the evolutionary continuum. Service's description of tribes and chiefdoms as two separate stages roughly equivalent to rank society underlies my modifications.

14. See Cohen (1981). In this definition of state functions I depart from Fried and others who see state apparatus as primarily exploitative in defense of the economic privilege of elites. I side with others, like Service, who assume that the state apparatus is at first managerial and only secondarily exploitative.

15. Barth (1969) makes an interesting argument about the persistence and function of ethnic groups in state societies which parallels and elaborates this point. See also Rapoport (1975) and his discussion of this article by Barth.

16. For summaries of the paleopathology, see Cohen (1980); Buikstra and Cook (1980); for evidence of violence in the Nile Valley, see Clark (1970); in Illinois, see Buikstra (1977).

17. One of the puzzles to be solved, if crowding is indeed stressful, is to explain why in many regions farmers compounded their already high population density by further clustering in nucleated settlements rather than remaining as dispersed as the new economy would permit. A major answer is probably political vulnerability. Unlike hunter-gatherers, farmers can be located by their enemies, and the food in which they have invested can be expropriated or destroyed. But there is safety in numbers, a fact which may well offset the stresses of group living. Chagnon (1968) provides an example of this effect. Hassan (1981) also suggests that certain economies of scale and cooperation entice farmers into aggregates.

18. Peru, Mexico, Mesopotamia, Egypt, India, and China are most commonly mentioned as early independent centers of state formation, although the complete independence of some cases, such as Egypt vis-à-vis Mesopotamia, is disputed. See Carneiro (1970); Flannery (1972); Fried (1967); Service (1975); Claessen and Skalnick eds. (1978). Identification of the loca-

tion of the first, or pristine, states, however, is less important than recognizing that the attributes of statehood which were unknown in the world more than about 5000 years ago become increasingly important, beginning in many geographic locations thereafter, suggesting that these attributes, whether invented or diffused to each location, had newly acquired adaptive value. Even more striking is the fact that the earliest states seem to have been only part of a truly worldwide trend, at about this time, toward the increasing formality and centralization of political organizations. In many regions other than those listed here, complex chieftainships, having some attributes of statehood but lacking others, emerged at about the same time as the early states.

19. Hardin (1968), in his article "The Tragedy of the Commons," discusses the necessity of relating values and morals to their social context and suggests that certain of our values may be inappropriate for our present circumstances. The whole thrust of his argument in that article is very similar to the one presented here if one reads "commons" as a metaphor not just for various kinds of shared economic resources but also for shared space in which individuals interact. I am arguing, in effect, that through social evolution individual access to "the commons" in the latter sense has been increasingly governed, scheduled, and circumscribed as population density has increased.

REFERENCES

Altman, I. *The Environment and Social Behavior: Privacy, Personal Space, Territory, and Crowding.* Monterey, Ca.: Brooks/Cole, 1975.

_____. "Privacy Regulation: Culturally Universal or Culturally Specific?" *Journal of Social Issues* 33 (1977): 66–84.

Barnett, H. G. *Innovation: The Basis of Cultural Change.* New York: McGraw-Hill, 1953.

Baron, R. M. "The Case for Differences in the Responses of Human and Other Animals to High Density." In *Biosocial Mechanisms of Population Regulation,* edited by M. N. Cohen et al. New Haven: Yale University Press, 1980, pp. 247–73.

Baron, R. M., and J. Rodin. "Personal Control as a Mediation of Crowding." In *Advances in Environmental Psychology,* vol. 1, edited by A. Baum, J. Singer, and S. Valins. Hillsdale, N.J.: Erlbaum Associates, 1978, pp. 145–90.

Barth, F., ed. *Ethnic Groups and Boundaries.* London: Allen and Unwin, 1969.

Barth, F. "Analytical Dimensions in the Comparison of Social Organizations." *American Anthropologist* 74 (1972): 207–20.

Barth, F., ed. *Scale and Social Organization.* Oslo: Universitetsforlaget, 1978.

Berreman, G. D. "Scale and Social Relations." *Current Anthropology* 19 (1978): 225–45.

Bicchieri, M. *Hunters and Gatherers Today.* New York: Holt Rinehart, 1972.

Boserup, E. *The Conditions of Agricultural Growth.* Chicago: Aldine, 1965.

Buikstra, J. "Biocultural Dimensions of Archaeological Study: A Regional Perspective." In *Biocultural Adaptations in Prehistoric America,* edited by R. Blakely. Athens: University of Georgia Press, 1977, pp. 67–84.

———, and D. Cook. "Paleopathology: An American Account." *Annual Review of Anthropology* 9 (1980): 433–70.

Calhoun, J. B. "Population Density and Social Pathology." *Scientific American* 206 (1962): 139–48.

Carneiro, R. "Slash and Burn Cultivation Among the Kuikuru and its Implications for Cultural Development in the Amazon Basin." *Anthropologica,* Supplementary Publication 2 (1961): 47–67.

———. "On the Relationship between Size of Population and Complexity of Social Organization." *Southwestern Journal of Anthropology* 23 (1967): 234–43.

———. "A Theory of the Origin of the State." *Science* 169 (1970): 733–38.

Chagnon, N. "Yanomamo Social Organization and Warfare." In *War: The Anthropology of Armed Conflict and Aggression,* edited by M. Fried et al. Garden City, N.J.: Natural History Press, 1968, pp. 109–59.

Childe, V. G. *Man Makes Himself.* New York: Mentor, 1951.

Christian, J. "Endocrine Factors in Population Regulation." In *Biosocial Mechanisms of Population Regulation,* edited by M. N. Cohen, R. S. Malpass, and H. G. Klein. New Haven: Yale University Press, 1980, pp. 55–115.

Claessen, H. J., and P. M. Skalnick, eds. *The Early State.* The Hague: Mouton, 1978.

Clark, J. D. *The Prehistory of Africa.* New York: Praeger, 1970.

Cohen, M. N. *The Food Crisis in Prehistory.* New Haven: Yale University Press, 1977.

———. "Population Growth and Parallel Trends in Cultural Evolution." Presented to the annual meeting of the American Anthropological Association. Washington, D.C., 1980.

———. "The Ecological Basis of the New World State Formation: General and Local Model Building." In *The Transition to Statehood in the New World,* edited by G. D. Jones and R. Kautz. London: Cambridge University Press, 1981, pp. 105–22.

———. R. S. Malpass, and H. G. Klein, eds. *Biosocial Mechanisms of Population Regulation.* New Haven: Yale University Press, 1980.

Colson, E. "A Redundancy of Actors." In *Scale and Social Organization,* edited by F. Barth. Oslo: Universitetsforlaget, 1978, pp. 150–62.

Cowgill, G. "Population Pressure as a Non-Explanation." In *Population Studies in Archaeology and Biological Anthropology: A Symposium,* edited by A. Swedlund. *American Antiquity* 40 (1975): 127–31.

Epstein, Y. "Physiological Effects of Crowding on Humans." In *Biosocial Mechanisms of Population Regulation,* edited by M. N. Cohen, R. S. Malpass, and H. G. Klein. New Haven: Yale University Press, 1980, pp. 209–24.

Flannery, K. V. "The Cultural Evolution of Civilizations." *Annual Review Ecology and Systematics* 3 (1977): 399–426.

Freedman, J. *Crowding and Behavior.* San Francisco: Freeman, 1975.

_____. "Human Reactions to Population Density." In *Biosocial Mechanisms of Population Regulation,* edited by M. N. Cohen, R. S. Malpass, and H. G. Klein. New Haven: Yale University Press, 1980, pp. 189–208.

Fried, M. *The Evolution of Political Society.* New York: Random House, 1967.

_____, M. Harris, and R. Murphy eds. *War: The Anthropology of Armed Conflict and Aggression.* Garden City, N.J.: Natural History Press, 1968.

Gellner, E. "Scale and Nation." In *Scale and Social Organization,* edited by F. Barth. Oslo: Universitetsforlaget, 1978, pp. 133–84.

Gulick, J. "Urban Anthropology." In *Handbook of Social and Cultural Anthropology,* edited by J. Honigmann. Chicago: Rand McNally, 1973, pp. 979–1030.

Hardin, G. "The Tragedy of the Commons." *Science* 162 (1968): 1243–48.

Hassan, F. "Demography and Archaeology." *Annual Review of Anthropology* 8 (1979): 137–61.

_____. *Demographic Archaeology.* New York: Academic Press, 1981.

Hayden, B. "The Carrying Capacity Dilemma." In *Population Studies in Archaeology and Biological Anthropology,* edited by S. Swedlund. *American Antiquity* 40 (1975): 11–21.

_____. "Research and Development in the Stone Age: Technological Transitions among Hunter-Gatherers." *Current Anthropology* 22 (1981): 519–48.

Jacobson, D. "Scale and Social Control." In *Scale and Social Organization,* edited by F. Barth. Oslo: Universitetsforlaget, 1978, pp. 184–93.

Karlin, R. "Social Effects of Crowding on Humans." In *Biosocial Mechanisms of Population Regulation,* edited by M. N. Cohen, R. S. Malpass, and H. G. Klein. New Haven: Yale University Press, 1980, pp. 225–46.

Kleinman, D. S. *Human Adaptation and Population Growth.* Montclair: Allanheld, Osmun, 1980.

Kluckhohn, C. *Navaho Witchcraft.* Boston: Beacon Press, 1962.

Lee, R. B. "The Intensification of Social Life among the !Kung Bushmen." In *Population Growth: Anthropological Implications,* edited by B. Spooner. Cambridge: MIT Press, 1972, pp. 343–50.

_____, and J. Devore, eds. *Man the Hunter.* Chicago: Aldine, 1968.

Lesser, Alexander. "War and the State." in *War: The Anthropology of Armed Conflict and Aggression,* edited by M. Fried, M. Harris, and R. Murphy. Garden City, N.J.: Natural History Press, 1968, pp. 92–96.

Lewis, H. S. "Warfare and the Origin of the State: Another Formulation." Presented to Tenth International Congress of Anthropological and Ethnological Sciences. New Delhi, India, 1978.

Lewis, I. M. *Ecstatic Religion.* London: Penguin, 1971.

Lloyd, J. "Interactions of Social Structure and Reproduction in Populations of Mice." In *Biosocial Mechanisms of Population Regulation,* edited by M. N. Cohen, R. S. Malpass, and H. G. Klein. New Haven: Yale University Press, 1980, pp. 3–22.

Malthus, T. *On Population.* 1798. New York: Modern Library, 1960.

Morgan, L. H. *Ancient Society.* New York: Holt, 1877.

Packard, J. M., and D. Mech. "Population Regulation in Wolves." In *Biosocial Mechanisms of Population Regulation,* edited by M. N. Cohen, R. S. Malpass, and H. G. Klein. New Haven: Yale University Press, 1980, pp. 135–50.

Proshansky, H. M., W. H. Ittelson, and L. G. Rivlin, eds. *Environmental Psychology: People and Their Physical Settings,* 2nd ed. New York: Holt Rinehart, 1976.

Rapoport, A. "Toward a Redefinition of Density." *Environment and Behavior* 7 (1975): 133–57.

Redfield, R. *The Folk Culture of Yucatan.* Chicago: University of Chicago Press, 1941.

_____. *The Primitive World and its Transformations.* Ithaca, N.Y.: Cornell University Press, 1953.

Sanders, W. T., and B. Price. *Mesoamerica.* New York: Random House, 1968.

Sanders, W. T., and D. Webster. "Unilinealism, Multilinealism, and the Evolution of Complex Societies." In *Social Archaeology,* edited by C. L. Redman, M. J. Berman, E. Curtin, W. Langhorne, Jr., N. Versaggi, and J. Wanser. New York: Academic Press, 1978, pp. 249–302.

Schwartz, T. "The Size and Shape of a Culture." In *Scale and Social Organization,* edited by F. Barth. Oslo: Universitetsforlaget, 1978, pp. 215–52.

Seligman, M. E. P. *Helplessness.* San Francisco: Freeman, 1972.

Service, E. *Origins of the State and Civilization.* New York: Norton, 1975.

_____. *The Hunters,* 2nd ed. Englewood Cliffs, N.J.: Prentice-Hall, 1979.

Simon, J. L. "Resources, Population, Environment: An Oversupply of False Bad News." *Science* 208 (1980): 1431–37.

Smith, P. E. L., and T. C. Young. "The Evolution of Early Agriculture and Culture in Greater Mesopotamia." In *Population Growth: Anthropological Implications,* edited by B. Spooner. Cambridge: MIT Press, 1972, pp. 1–59.

Stevenson, R. F. *Population and Political Systems in Tropical Africa.* New York: Columbia University Press, 1968.

Steward, J. *Theory of Culture Change.* Urbana: University of Illinois Press, 1955.

Steward, J., and L. C. Faron. *Native Peoples of South America.* New York: McGraw-Hill, 1959.

Terman, C. R. "Behavior and Regulation of Growth in Laboratory Populations of Prairie Deermice." In *Biosocial Mechanisms of Population Regulation,* edited by M. N. Cohen, R. S. Malpass, and H. G. Klein. New Haven: Yale University Press, 1980, pp. 23–36.

Vayda, A. "Hypotheses about Functions of War." In *War: The Anthropology of Armed Conflict and Aggression,* edited by M. Fried, M. Harris, and R. Murphy. Garden City, N.J.: Natural History Press, 1968, pp. 85–91.

Webster, D. "Warfare and the Origin of the State: A Reconsideration." *American Antiquity* 40 (1975): 464–70.

White, L. *The Evolution of Culture.* New York: McGraw-Hill, 1959.

Wicker, A. *An Introduction to Ecological Psychology.* Monterey, Ca.: Brooks/Cole, 1979.

Wilson, G., and M. Wilson. *The Analysis of Social Change.* Cambridge: Cambridge University Press, 1945.

Wright, H. T., and G. Johnson. "Population Exchange and Early State Formation in Southwestern Iran." *American Anthropologist* 77 (1975): 267–89.

3

Population Change and Human Conflict
The Individual Level of Analysis

HAROLD M. PROSHANSKY

T HE PROBLEM OF POPULATION change and human conflict from the perspective of the environmental psychologist is rooted to a large extent in the concepts of "crowding" and "stress." However, the significance and meaning of these concepts, indeed of the concepts of "population change" and "conflict" as well, require precise classification of this perspective. Two essential properties of the approach of the environmental psychologist deserve special attention. First, the focus of analysis is at the level of individual psychological process and function. In effect, the problem of population change in creating human conflict becomes a question of conflicts experienced by the person as a psychological and social being because of crowding and the attendant psychological stress.

No less important in the approach of the environmental psychologist is that substantive concern at the individual level of analysis is not just a matter of the influence of other people, but of *places* or *physical settings* as well. The search then is for systematic relationships between the behavior and experience of the person and the physical properties of contextualized settings. Settings are contextualized by social, cultural, and personal meanings which interact with, and are modified by, their physical properties. Psychological explanations emerge from these searches that help to clarify the nature of the influences of population change on human conflict as revealed in the studies of aggregates by anthropologists, sociologists, economists, and political scientists.

Stated more simply, the focus of the environmental psychologist is on person-physical setting relationships. The first section begins by taking note of some essential ones such as *personal space, human privacy,* and *human territoriality.* Yet it should be evident that these person-physical setting relationships necessarily involve people as well as places. Every one of these concepts implies not only controlling and using physical settings effectively but also managing and influencing other people in these settings. The need for human privacy for a given individual, for example, must not only be achieved but also maintained. In both instances, the requisite properties of spaces and places for achieving such privacy are inextricably tied to the behaviors, attitudes, and values of other people in these spaces and places.

Two implications immediately follow from this conception of person-physical setting relationships. The first is that the individual's ability to achieve and therefore satisfy particular physical environment relationships will depend on his or her capacity to master a relevant physical setting. To use and derive benefit from a physical setting requires that the person understand it, be behaviorally competent in it, and feel secure and in control of it. Environmental skills are necessary attributes in satisfying territorial needs, minimizing stress and more generally in making adaptive responses to crowding.

The second implication can be stated simply and directly: there is no physical setting that is not also a social setting. Of course, the social character of a physical setting in turn implies far more than the presence of other people. The nature of the physical setting itself, its activities, the individuals involved, and thus its meaning and purpose are all rooted in social and cultural processes. These processes are defined by and expressed in the socialization of the person, the group context of individual existence and higher-order social organizations. The social environment then, conceived of as a sociocultural system at various interlocking levels of social organization, such as family, neighborhood, community, and city, plays a critical role in determining the meaning of spaces and places, how they are used, and their effects on the individual.

Of particular importance in this respect is the small face-to-face primary group, such as the family, work group, and friendship groups. Such groups must not only relate to and use physical settings as social entities in themselves, but they must also, through their influence on individual group members, ensure that the environmental skills of the members and the established norms for person-physical setting relationships will support and maximize the possibilities of achieving the group's goals. The second section of this chapter considers the nature and function of small face-to-face groups in establishing person-physical setting relationships. Such an analysis can only be meaningful if the sociocultural contexts of different groups within a given society and between those in different societies are considered. Some attention to cross-cultural comparison is given in our review of the research literature in the final section of this chapter.

The first two sections of this chapter present an analytic scheme attempting to link population change conceptually within human conflict. As we have already suggested, crowding and stress in relation to such individual needs as personal space, privacy, and territoriality help us to understand how conflict either within the person or between individuals may emerge. But what are the relationships between crowding and stress and population change? Here it is critical to emphasize that population change as a source of crowding and stress is by no means to be construed in the simplistic terms of increasing numbers of people leading to social or spatial density and the psychological consequences of crowding and stress. Population change or dynamics is more than a matter of population increases. Significantly, when demographic factors, such as group composition or distribution, are viewed, even if the number of people remains constant, they too may result in crowding and stress effects and may become a source of conflict. The causes and consequences of crowding are not solely a function of increasing numbers of individuals in given spaces or places. Where crowding ensues as a result of one or more dimensions of population dynamics, its negative consequences in the form of stress and conflict may in fact be vitiated by other psychological and social conditions.

After the analytic framework used to establish conceptual linkages between population dynamics and human conflict is laid out in the first two sections, a series of tentative generalizations on principles derived from this framework is presented in the third section. The implications that follow from this conceptual scheme, along with the relevant data from systematic research that support and illustrate these implications, are presented; the significance of the physical setting in creating human conflict is established. By the same token, it is important to note limiting or conditional factors involved in arriving at this significance.

Clearly the principles or generalizations derived can only be considered as tentative, and unquestionably far more research needs to be done before the concepts formulated and their interrelationships as well as the data supporting the theoretical structure can become part of a cumulative body of knowledge. In the matter of physical settings and their relationships to the behavior and experience of people, the importance of societal and cultural norms, traditions, and practices both past and present cannot be stressed too strongly. Yet much of the thinking and research presented here not only represents the context of highly developed Western societies, but most of it by far is based on the efforts of American researchers studying Americans as individuals or in groups. We do note and point up the meager cross-cultural thinking and research that exists. From Asia, Africa, and South America, with many undeveloped nations and groups, the available data and theory are almost nonexistent.

Finally, we must alert the reader to a distortion in our presentation. Speaking of the effects of population dynamics on human conflict — say, crowding and stress in the family household on parent-child interactions — is to suggest an overly simplified cause and effect relationship between these phenomena. Human conflicts emerging from a host of factors other than population dynamics may indeed have effects on population changes in terms of demographic changes, group composition, and group distribution. The complex patterning of influences that underline human behavior and experience, whether at the individual, group, or societal level (patterning as a set of interrelationships among a variety of variables in which causes and effects are interchangeable depending on the nature and scope of the problem defined, how it is being studied, and for what purpose), must approximate the integrity of the complex human social phenomena being studied. Environmental psychologists recognize and accept the unassailable assumption that social conflicts within and between individuals and groups are just as likely to result in experiences of crowding and stress in the person, who is the basis for human conflict.

The final section of the chapter considers our theoretical framework and its attendant supporting data from two points of view: first, implications for additional research, and second, given the derivations from our framework in terms of concepts, data, and tentative principles or conclusions, policy implications for practitioners, government officials, and community groups and leaders.

ENVIRONMENTAL CONCEPTIONS
IN PERSON-PHYSICAL SETTING RELATIONSHIPS

Whatever the complexities and elaborations of existing theoretical modes of human behavior and experience, each begins with the recognition of the person as a cognizing, goal-directed, affectively responding organism. This is true whether the concern of the model is with enduring dispositions, that is the personality structure of the individuals, or with the behavior and experience of the person in given situations as a function of the interaction of personality structure tendencies with an array of environmental or situational determinants. The environmental psychologist gives far more emphasis to the latter orientation: the problem focus is not simply on how the person characteristically relates to physical settings, but far more on how he or she relates in any given setting as a function not just of personality dispositions, but of sociocultural influences, social context properties, the momentary behavior of other people, past experiences, and so forth.

In considering particular environmental needs, or person-physical setting relationships, environmental psychologists make two critical, unassailable assumptions, although seldom explicitly. The first is that the person — for all of his or her "human" qualities — exists in the physical world as a tangible object as well as an actor who influences and uses, and is in turn influenced and used by this world. However, the object characteristic by itself is self-evident, if for example we see the person in a crowded situation who can be pushed, squeezed, prevented from moving, or used (the person behind pushes him so a path is cleared). It is the second assumption made by environmental psychologists (indeed all psychologists) which gives us insight into the meaning and significance of this object characteristic of the person. It is assumed not only that the person can feel, experience, and respond, but that more significantly, at the core of these response capacities and abilities is the essential and persistent need to preserve, maintain, and enhance the value and integrity of the individual's *self-identity*. Birth and the socialization process that follows establish the individual with a distinct and separate identity as a person, with continuity over time. This "identity" is a valued object to the person himself and to others, and therefore must be protected, maintained, and enhanced in its own right. Any alternative involving the end of the person as a separate and distinct identity is neither conceivable nor acceptable to the person.

Part of the self-identity of every individual is the perception of oneself as a physical entity with a host of specific physical attributes involving shape, size, weight, color, and so on. Just this aspect of self-identity requires that the person occupy a given physical space so that the uniquely defined physical self can be maintained and indeed enhanced. The concept of *personal space,* therefore, emerges as an important first-step analytical tool for understanding person-physical setting relationships. Human beings, as we have said, are physical entities as well as social beings. Since no two of them can occupy the exact same physical locus at the same time, the attempt of one person to do so necessarily violates the well-being and integrity of the other. The concept of personal space is defined as that minimal circumscribed imaginary bubble or real space around each person that is perceived of by the person and others at any given moment as his or her *personal* space. If others were to cross this personal space boundary, it would not only be seen as violating the physical and psychological integrity of the person, but would also evoke responses and strategies to prevent such transgressions. Therein lie the roots of conflict.

The human need for *privacy* goes well beyond this fundamental requirement of distance from others. At issue is the psychological integrity or autonomy of an individual, which is rooted in the person's desire to order the physical world so that he is free to behave and experience himself without the restraints of the presence of others: for example, learning new roles; overcoming shame and the loss of self-esteem; carrying out socially unacceptable behaviors; engaging freely in verbal fantasy; attempting to be creative in solving personal problems (Westin 1967). Privacy then is the desire to be free from the observations of others whether directly or indirectly (directly seen or heard or via written documents, tapes, pictures, etc.), but above all to be able to *achieve* this state and *maintain* it in ways consistent with other needs and desires of the person that have to be satisfied.

Human territoriality is still another critical person-physical setting analytical tool that is conceptually related both to personal space and the human need for privacy. It refers to the need of the individual to define and establish a given physical space or place as his own, and to maintain this ownership and *control* over it in relation to others. Territorial behaviors represent the manifest expressions of whatever personal space and privacy needs the person seeks to satisfy. These needs, of course, serve as instrumental achievements for the satisfaction of a host of other human needs. The existence of one's place is an empirical reality that can be observed by others; it not only helps to define and maintain the physical and psychological integrity of the individual, but it clearly extends and enhances both. In one's place, the person can choose whether to be private or not and can determine what activities go on, who will or will not be involved, and more generally how to conduct his life in his personally controlled territory.

Protecting and maintaining a personal space, or achieving privacy, or satisfying territorial desires are not simply a matter of satisfactions there for the asking. Physical settings are complex systems in which there are always competing and sometimes hostile others, a plethora of socially regulated and determined human activities, and a vast system of technology known as the built environment that both supports and reflects the values and essential goals of the system. Person-environment relationships, that is, the person coming to terms with physical settings, depend on acquired environmental skills. Quite crucial is the person's ability to achieve *environmental understanding.* Physical settings, whether a city, school, or hospital, are socially defined in terms of how, when, and who shall use them. One grasps their size, boundaries, and the specific meanings they convey after orientation and navigation through them. To be able to understand a given physical setting is the first requirement for being able to use it effectively, including changing and manipulating it so that other social and personal goals can be satisfied.

But knowledge is not enough. Effective use of a space or place also requires *environmental competence,* the ability of the individual to make the appropriate responses to a physical setting whose properties are ever-changing and dynamic in character. Most familiar physical settings are smaller units of larger settings and thus are predictable and often stable systems to which individuals learn to respond routinely on a day-to-day basis. However, the larger physical settings of which they are a part are given to change, to the unexpected behaviors and activities of others, and as a result an individual's environmental competence is challenged to some degree quite frequently in mundane settings, although not always in obvious ways.

The ability to understand a physical setting and to be competent in using it depends thus on the *environmental security* of the individual. A lack of appropriate environmental skills for responding to the physical world in the past can only lead to a corresponding lack of environmental security which, of course, makes it difficult to develop environmental understanding or competence. Nevertheless, even individuals highly skilled in their responses to their day-to-day physical settings are not necessarily environmentally secure at all times in all physical settings, and very complex or dangerous settings may lower the individual's environmental security considerably.

Person-physical setting relationships expressed by the human search for personal space, privacy, and territoriality are rooted in the fundamental, underlying need of each person to maintain and protect his or her physical and psychological integrity. Each person strives to be a distinct self and to maintain and enhance that particular *self-identity*. By the self-identity we mean the individual's beliefs, ideas, memories, expectations, attitudes, and values about one's self, both conscious and unconscious, whose substantive context invariably involves self-evaluation.

The critical assumption here is that the person's conception of self-identity evolves out of both physical setting and social setting experiences. It follows that part of self-identity has some constellation of ideas, conceptions, memories, beliefs, feelings, and attitudes about characteristics of spaces, places, and objects which separately and in their relationships define at a given moment and over time who and what the person is. We have chosen to identify that cognitive structure in the system as the person's *place-identity*. Places and spaces and their attributes as well as social groups, roles, and defined relationships serve to establish the self-identity of each person (Proshansky and Kaminoff 1981).

The meaning and implications of person-physical setting concepts for understanding the psychological consequences of population dynamics are rooted in the unassailable fact that the relationships of each person to his or her physical setting often depend on his or her relationship to other individuals. The following section examines the nature and function of small, face-to-face groups. It is primarily within these groups that the definition of the individual, both in relation to others and to the physical settings they occupy, occurs. Yet in any consideration of small group influences on their various physical settings it is critical to compare such influences across groups in a given society and between groups in different sociocultural contexts. Wherever possible the critical issue of cross-cultural comparisons in the nature and use of space and place can and should be addressed.

FACE-TO-FACE GROUPS:
THE CONTEXT OF PERSON-PHYSICAL SETTING RELATIONSHIPS

That physical settings are also social settings can be conceived of in a number of ways. The physical setting for any individual, for example, is often a shared setting; it involves the presence of other individuals. Social interaction and social process characterize such settings far more often than individual behavior. The fact that the characteristics, objects, activities, and purposes of all physical settings are defined and identified in sociocultural terms, language and meaning, suggests the inextricable relationships between social and physical environments.

The concept of small face-to-face groups best organizes the physical and social relationship between the person and an ongoing physical setting of purposes and activities. Such groups consist of individuals in defined roles and structured relationships; they engage in a variety of activities to satisfy not only the needs of each member, but also the goals and purposes of the group itself. The members of such groups behave, think, and function in terms of their given *roles,* the *norms* of the group, and more generally in terms of the basic values and *commitment* of such groups.

Although face-to-face groups can be found in an infinite variety, and may come and go in very brief periods of time, the primary group is of special concern to the environmental psychologist. Those of a relatively long enduring nature, such as the family, school groups, or neighborhood friendship groups, provide definitive social and physical contexts in which the socialization of the individual begins and continues to develop during the formative years.

In these contexts person-physical setting relationships are shaped by the unique, normative group experiences the person has in learning to understand and use his physical setting, to behave appropriately in it in the pursuit of ends and satisfactions, and in learning to manage and control it in its variations from one event to the next and over time. In small group settings, the use and management of space are related generally to the structures and purposes of a given social group and, more specifically, to the expressed values of the group, the status of its various members and subgroups, the roles played by each member, and the traditional norms and beliefs of the group. The self-identity of the individual socialized by various primary group experiences must necessarily reflect learned person-physical setting relationships and experiences as revealed in the place-identity aspects of self, as well as interpersonal and social interactions that define day-to-day existence in the group.

Both the dynamic nature of individual behavior and the broader social systems of which small groups are a part subject the course of human relationships in those groups to stresses and strains. This will be no less true in regard to the use of spaces and places by group members than it will regarding human relationships. Such stresses and strains can and often do express conflicts within the individual; for example, a person's strong, positive place-identity feelings about the setting he or she grew up in and the need to leave it in order to achieve economic security and social status. Surely the person forced to live in a physical setting that is less than what he aspires to but as much as he can afford experiences both frustration and conflict. Intraindividual conflict of this kind, however, is only a part of the problem of conflict and population dynamics.

If the individual in the group experiences conflict with other members of the group over the use of space, the resulting interaction between individual and the group is termed *interindividual conflict*. This is a problem of great concern to the environmental psychologist because the behavior, activities, and attitudes and beliefs of *others* present obstacles to need satisfaction and goal achievement for the group member.

Interindividual conflicts need not simply be between individuals in the same face-to-face group. They may, in fact, reflect the hostilities between face-to-face groups called *intergroup conflict,* such as between families or neighborhoods. Intergroup conflict may go well beyond the level of personal-physical setting relationships in small face-to-face groups and involve large numbers of such groups: neighborhood versus neighborhood, community versus community, and beyond, to the level of national, religious, ethnic, or political groups.

Environmental formulations concerning matters of privacy, environmental security, territoriality, personal space, and perhaps place-identity of these social groups have a conceptual validity at the individual level of analysis. Groups, too, by virtue of their values, norms, purposes, and activities, all of which are reflected in the behavior, beliefs, and attitudes of their members, express goals involving environmental formulations. The history of modern community life is rife with accounts of intergroup conflicts turning on these very issues.

Our theoretical framework up to this point has sought to establish conceptual linkages between population changes and human conflict by interposing the conception that such changes have effects not only on aggregate groups of varying demographic properties but in turn on the small, primary face-to-face groups which characterize these larger sociocultural aggregates. It is in the context of these primary groups both at the level of the single person and the group that the nature and purposes of person-physical environment relationships are established. If we can assume that population changes may, and indeed do have negative consequences for primary group life in any broader sociocultural setting, then conflict within the person and between individuals and/or different social groups are inevitable consequences.

But as we have already indicated, at least at the level of the individual and the interaction between individuals, the final conceptual linkages are to be found in the phenomena of *crowding* and *stress*. Composition and distribution changes as a result of population changes may indeed result in actual or perceived crowding or in particular social aggregates at the primary group level. Both generally and for the individual members of these groups such crowding is usually accompanied by psychological stress. There can be little question that individuals and groups may adapt to these conditions. But before and after such adaptation occurs, conflict is often involved at the various individual, interactional, and intergroup levels.

Although crowding has long been studied by sociologists, social psychologists, and environmental psychologists, there is by no means agreement on how to define this widespread problem. Some scholars make a distinction between social overload models of crowding and those emphasizing behavioral constraint (Saegert 1973; Stokols 1976). The former, which is rooted in the early sociological work of eminent scholars (Simmel 1950; Wirth 1939; Altman 1975; Baum and Valins 1977; Desor 1972; Milgram 1970; Saegert 1973), conceptualizes crowding in negative terms because it creates excessive or unwanted levels of social stimulation. On the other hand, the behavioral constraint models proposed more recently (Freedman 1975; Proshansky, Ittelson, and Rivlin 1970; Stokols 1972; Wohlwill and Kohn 1973) are related to the conceptualization of personal space invasion (Sommer 1969). In these models crowding is experienced when the presence of others restricts the individual's freedom of choice in a setting. Crowding has also been defined as a subjective experience in which the individual's demand for space exceeds the available supply (Stokols 1972).

Upon reflection, it becomes clear that the "constraint" and "stimulation" models of crowding are not in any real sense contrasting theoretical orientations. They simply focus on different aspects or components of crowding or density. High levels of *social density* have been defined as the total number of people present in a setting (Saegert 1973, 1978). Under these circumstances individuals are more likely to experience a state of social overload (excessive stimulation) rather than behavioral constraint. Conversely, high levels of *spatial density,* the amount of space available per person, are more likely to result in behavioral constraint than in social overload.

The point is that both forms of crowding—large numbers of people in large spaces and small numbers of people in small spaces—induce *stress* in the individual. Stress is that pattern of psychological, behavioral, and physiological responses of the individual to the demands of the physical and social environment that exceed his capacity to cope effectively, that is, carry out activities, realize goals, and experience satisfactions. If crowding, both social and spatial, engenders stress in the individual, it is not simply a matter of "excessive stimulation" or "behavioral restraint." At issue here is the potential for interindividual conflict, which in turn contributes to the amount of stress a person experiences in a crowded situation.

Of course, crowding—the conditions under which it is experienced and how and by what means adaptation occurs—is tied not only to the normative requirements of face-to-face group life but in turn reflect the values, attitudes, and beliefs of the larger sociocultural setting of which these groups are a part. Scholarly research has revealed the significance of cultural differences in the use of space in relation to such person-physical setting relationships as personal space, territoriality, and privacy, and of course cultural differences with respect to the nature and meaning of crowding and the adaptive responses made to crowding in physical settings (Hall 1966; Rapoport 1975).

POPULATION CHANGE AND HUMAN CONFLICT: DERIVATIONS FROM ENVIRONMENTAL PSYCHOLOGY

The theoretical framework outlined above and actual findings reported in the empirical research literature provide important insights into the analysis of the problem of population growth and human conflict. At best these conclusions and principles are tentative, given the "state of the art" and the lack of a systematically derived cumulative body of scientific knowledge. The approach here is at the level of *individual* psychological analysis as it pertains to the interaction between the individual and those immediate physical settings that define his day-to-day existence. These consequences for the individual are derived from and should be viewed as the end result of a long and complex set of theoretical relationships or linkages in which population growth has social, economic, political, and cultural effects at the regional and national levels of social organization. These in turn have consequences for large and small socially defined groups, and ultimately these effects act on the individual because of his or her memberships in a variety of face-to-face primary groups.

Population Change: Crowding as Overstimulation and Behavioral Constraint

Crowding as a characteristic of a society is most often related to population growth, particularly to accelerated growth. It is viewed negatively (see Chapters 2 and 4) because of its implications for food shortages, economic strains, unplanned developments in the society, social upheavals, and the like. Crowding is negatively conceived by some environmental psychologists because in large settings with increasingly large numbers of individuals there are excessive levels of social stimulation, sometimes referred to as "social overload." In effect, crowding is psychologically stressful. Both systematic research and anecdotal evidence lend credence to this view. But there are a number of modifying factors, as revealed in investigations of high levels of environmental stimulation, on the degree of stress experienced by the person.

1. Knowledge of the high level of a particular form of stimulation, for example, the sound of other people, "noise," or density, is not enough to predict whether or not that stimulation will produce stress for any given person. High noise levels have frequently been associated with lowered task performance (Boggs and Simon 1968), reduced helping behavior (Matthews and Cannon 1975), as well as various health problems ranging from nervousness, sleep difficulties, and headaches (Koksha 1973), to increased blood pressure (Parvizpoor 1976), elevated cholesterol levels (Khomuls, Rodinova, and Rusinova 1967), and cardiac arrest (Capellini and Moroni 1974). However, other investigators have not found these significant effects of noise on such variables (Brunetti 1972; Gattoni and Tarnpolsky 1973; Stevens, 1972). Similarly, although the majority of studies investigating the effects of high concentrations of people have found crowding to be associated with either one or more measures of physiological arousal (D'Atri 1975), social withdrawal (Bickman et al. 1973), and various physical, psychological and social pathologies (Dean, Pugh, and Gunderson 1975), others have not reported such density effects.

2. The contradictory findings noted clearly suggest that environmental or social stimulation per se does not induce human stress and therefore the potential for conflict, but the *interaction* of various physical, social, cultural, and individual factors. For each potential stressor, such as the numbers of people, it is thus necessary to distinguish between the objective levels of physical and social stimulation that are impinging on the individual and the person's subjective experience of that stimulation (Cohen and Weinstein 1980; Kryter 1970). Whether or not a given level of "sound" is experienced as "noise" or a particular density level is perceived as "crowding" depends upon other characteristics of the stimulus situation, as well as characteristics of the individual, the social system, and the setting (Lazarus 1966; Rapoport 1975, Stokols 1978).

3. The degree to which environmental stimulation is perceived to be predictable and controllable influences the extent to which it induces stress in the person and therefore the potential for conflict (Averill 1973; Cohen, Glass, and Philips 1979). Noise that is unpredictable and uncontrollable has been found to produce poorer task performance and lower frustration tolerance (Glass and Singer 1972), as well as less helping behavior (Sherrod and Downs 1974), and more aggression (Donnerstein and Wilson 1976) than noise

that is predictable and controllable. In the case of both predictability and the ability to control stimuli, the environmental skill of the person may help to determine whether or not stress is experienced. Environmental understanding, that is, knowing why increased social density in a given setting is occurring, is a factor that contributes to the "predictability" of such social stimulation. Without such skill, we can expect a decrease in environmental security. Of course, even with such skill, the person must have the environmental competence to control such stimulation.

4. The *meanings* communicated by potential stressors, including crowds or high social density situations, have implications for whether or not stress is experienced (Cohen 1978; Lazarus 1966). The extent to which *social* meanings are communicated appears to be particularly important. Thus office workers consistently report being bothered more by noise generated by people conversing with one another than they are by noise emanating from office machinery and equipment (Brooks and Kaplan 1972; Harris 1978). High population densities are particularly taxing to the individual's information processing because of the social nature of the information provided by the other people involved (Saegert 1978). The behavior of other people is generally less predictable and more socially meaningful than the patterns generated by strictly physical sources of stimulation.

5. The actor in a social density or crowded situation, in addition to choosing and carrying out an individual course of action, must coordinate his or her behavior with others. It is for this reason that the composition and normative structure of the group, particularly the small face-to-face group, may mediate the perception and the effects of crowding in high density situations (Epstein 1981). Being with familiar and/or homogeneous others renders their behavior and physical characteristics more predictable (Rapoport 1975). A study of extremely high-density households in Hong Kong found few adverse effects when only kin shared the apartment, but many such effects were found when unrelated people shared the same dwelling unit (Mitchell 1971). Being with people whom one trusts in face-to-face physical settings reduces the need to be constantly vigilant in the situation (Saegert 1978). This not only directly obviates stress in the situation by reducing the threat of social encounters and conflict, but requires less monitoring of others and therefore of having to be involved in the experiences and consequences of excessive cognitive activity. Furthermore the problems of personal space, privacy, or territoriality can be more quickly resolved with known and trusted others than with strangers.

If being with familiar and homogeneous others renders the physical and social setting more predictable, less threatening and demanding, then it is also more likely to lead to more cooperative and better-coordinated behavior than being with unfamiliar and heterogeneous others. Groups that adopt a cooperative orientation have been found to experience less crowding stress than those who adopt a competitive one, because they are better able to pool their resources and coordinate their behaviors to try to achieve the greatest good for the greatest number (Baum, Harpin, and Valins 1972; Epstein 1981). Stress is not only affected by the orientation of the group but may itself influence the orientation that is adopted by the group. Students living in a crowded dormitory have been found to act more competitively on an interactive laboratory task than students who experienced less crowding in their dorms (Valins and Baum 1973). Floormates who were able to develop cooperative strategies experienced less crowding stress than those who did not, despite comparable social and spatial densities (Baum, Harpin, and Valins 1975).

6. Members of different cultures vary in their personal space habits and requirements (Hall 1966). This implies that members of different cultures will also differ in response to crowding and other environmental stressors. Members of different cultures show a range of sensitivities to environmental stimulation, such as desired and required levels of privacy. They also vary in the mechanisms employed for controlling such stimulation, that is, in their ways of achieving privacy (Altman 1975; Rapoport 1975). These strategies range from physical distancing and the use of physical barriers to the reliance upon social rules which establish manners, status hierarchies, avoidance behavior, and/or time-space scheduling, to the extreme of psychological withdrawal when the physical presence of others is unavoidable. Thus it is reported that in the Chinese culture privacy for the family is considered more important than for the individual, and therefore it is considered desirable for large numbers of relatives to share housing units (Anderson 1972). There are also strict rules governing the timing, location, and nature of social interactions, which allow the Chinese a fair degree of tolerance for and control over environmental stimulation despite extremely high household densities (Mitchell 1971).

The cross-culture literature supports the view that crowding per se does not cause stress, social deviance, or psychological pathology. The focus is on *culture* as a mediator of density by way of behavioral strategies, spatial planning, and so on. Of the studies included here, those that approximate Western culture show deleterious effects of high density; those cultures most different from Western tradition show the least negative effects.

Density in Japan has been seen as contributing to the vitality of nodal towns and villages (Canter and Canter 1971). The positive aspects of a society with many members can be seen in the variety of its people and spaces. Japanese society has late night street activity although there is relatively little violence or vandalism. Residences are low-rise and high density; communities are small and closely bound. Privacy within the home is accomplished through house design which sacrifices outdoor open space and a view to private interior courts. In planning, the emphasis is on small interchangeable units in order to meet changes in larger contextual environments. Research on crowding in Japanese communities confirms these findings (Michelson 1970).

7. A study of working-class families in an industrial society found that crowding contributed to social pathology, with children more susceptible than adults (Chombard de Lauwes cited in Hall 1962). A study of a similar kind involving men in Filipino families living in a highly populated municipal district in one Asian city also found that the degree of crowdedness was related to the development of patterns of mental disorder (Marsella, Escudero, and Gordon 1971). The interpretation was that the greater the number of people in the dwelling the greater the interpersonal demands, thus the greater the experienced stress. In studies on the effects of density on criminal behavior of adults and juveniles and on pathology the results clearly tend to confirm the crowding-stress-social pathology relationships reported in other studies (Schmitt 1957, 1966).

8. Among more primitive societies, a study of crowding among the !Kung Bushmen (hunters and gatherers) found that although camp settlements had very high densities, there were no biological signs of stress, such as high blood pressure, and high serum cholesterol levels (Draper 1973). On the other hand, it was found that in three rural East African societies those living in crowded residences evaluated family roles as stressful, and the general quality of social interactions in the family engendered stress (Munroe and Munroe 1972).

Within a given society or culture we also find norms for particular subgroups or social systems that govern the degree of control members of these groups or systems may exert over environmental stimulation. For example, in the business or corporate setting different management styles allow employees varying degrees of privacy in an office setting (Steele 1973). Within a single organization management may permit privacy in certain situations while prohibiting it in others. In one corporation norms were formed that allowed employees to close their doors when having confidential meetings with others but not when they were working alone on a task (Justa and Cohen 1977). Similarly, different families allow varying amounts of privacy to their members and for different purposes that depend on their concept of what it means to be "family" (Kantor and Lehr 1975).

Crowding and the Personality: Past Experience of the Individual

Taking the findings and "principles" related to the effects of crowding on person-physical setting relationships, particularly on the classes of factors that mitigate such effects, this section considers mitigating factors such as the characteristics of the person, personality attributes and past experiences. The crowding and related stress experiences of the person that through conceptual interrelationships can be linked to population changes depend in part on the specific individual, his or her disposition, and past experiences.

1. Individuals differ both in the amount of environmental stimulation they seek and the amount they can tolerate (Mehrabian and Russell 1973; Zuckerman 1971). These differences include varying sensitivities to crowding stress. Some studies have found that individuals who desired greater amounts of personal space had lower thresholds to crowding stress than those needing less personal space (Cozby 1973; Dooley 1974). Others found that individuals who were high in the trait of "internal locus of control," that is, the person rather than the environment determining outcomes, experienced less crowding stress than those who were high in "external locus of control" (Schopler and Walton 1974). The more the person perceives he or she has control of the physical setting, the less the crowding stress.

2. Crowding experiences may influence over time the individual's degree of "locus of control," the degree to which the person perceives that he or she has control over physical settings. One study found that children from high-density households exerted less control in an experimental situation than did children from lower density households (Rodin 1976). This finding was attributed to a *learned helplessness* effect, whereby the child tends to perceive situations as uncontrollable physical settings. Such learned helplessness implies that not only does the child have difficulty in establishing and maintaining personal space, privacy, or territoriality but that the "helplessness" itself was and continues to be derived from a lack of environmental skills.

3. Research into adaptation to crowding stress, as revealed by using repeated measures over time, frequently shows the opposite of adaptation to occur. One study found measures of physiological arousal to increase over time (Aiello et al. 1975). Another, a study of responses to high density conditions aboard a ship, found greater stress to be experienced during the second half of a twenty-one day period (Smith and Haythorn 1972). However, studies investigating the influence of previous living experiences on current thresholds to crowding do frequently lend support to the notion of adaptation (Sundstrom 1978). In other words, people who have a history of exposure to crowded situations have a high tolerance to crowding stress (Wohlwill and Kohn 1973). However, the converse effect was found in a report on tolerance to crowding for inmates who had a longer history of imprisonment in high-density cells (Paulus et al. 1975).

Some scholars have attempted to sort through the various linkages among background density experiences, personality factors, and current responses to highly dense settings (Saegert and Kaminoff 1981). Those individuals growing up in large cities as compared to those from small cities or suburban areas were less able to offset stimulus distractions in an embedded figures test, that is, they were more field dependent. In effect, it may be that once again it is a case of "learned helplessness": individuals growing up in large cities experience confusing arrays of environmental stimuli and as a result give up quickly when it comes to discrimination of a figure within a complex visual context. However, when another measure of background density is used, the density of the household one lived in before age twelve, those growing up in high-density households have a greater ability to screen stimulation than those who experienced low household densities during their formative years.

4. Status, the characteristic of the individual that links him or her to a social system, has direct consequences for the extent to which privacy and territoriality are achieved. Individuals occupying low-status roles are permitted less privacy than are high-status members of a given social structure. This has been observed for clerical workers in the office setting (Steele 1973), inmates of residential psychiatric facilities (Wolfensberger 1977), and children in household settings (Baldassare 1977). That the lack of control over environmental stimulation and interaction translates to greater stress for low-status members of a social system is evidenced by the findings of studies comparing the responses of children of high-density households with those of their parents (Stokols 1978). The children are more apt to experience increased nervousness (Gasparini 1973), suffer greater decrements in intellectual development (Booth and Johnson 1975), have their social interactions curtailed, and are more apt to be blamed for household problems than are children in high-density residences (Clausen and Clausen 1973).

Crowding and the Boundedness of Physical Settings

Having identified by means of research findings and theoretical analysis the factors in individuals, small groups, large organizations, and the broader culture or society that influence crowding, stress, and their effects on person-physical setting relationships, we turn to the influences of space organization, in particular the "boundedness of space." The term "boundedness" refers to properties of physical settings that serve to distinguish and separate spatial areas from each other, including sound, light, and other stimulation such as a person's access to and egress from one spatial area to another.

Spatial boundaries can and do determine the control that individuals and groups have over environmental stimulation and social interaction. Boundaries, for example, walls, can be too permeable, causing invasions of privacy and the problems that follow from incompatible activities, both of which may end in interpersonal conflict. Boundaries that are not permeable enough may create problems of access and contact among isolated individuals and groups who require greater degrees of communication. *Territory* refers to a unit of space — a room, house, hallway, a block, a train seat, a hospital ward, a bed in a hospital ward — the outer limits of which are defined by a *boundary*. Territories may be under the exclusive control of specific individuals or groups, or may be open to competition among different persons or groups.

1. The creation of boundaries to establish clearly demarcated territories can help to mitigate the perceptions and effects of high social densities. In a doll-placement simulation study, it was found that when the dollhouse was partitioned subjects placed more human figures in it before it was seen as crowded, than when the room was not partitioned and left open (Desor 1972). In a real-world analog, another study compared social interaction levels of army personnel housed in barracks of either an open or a partitioned design (Blake et al. 1956). Although each of the barracks housed sixty recruits, one of them used partitions to create ten fairly separate groups, while the other was left completely open. Although there were a potentially greater number of social interactions in the open barrack, more social interaction was reported in the partitioned barrack. What these findings suggest is that, given the undifferentiated social stimulation due to the lack of boundaries which could serve to distinguish individuals and groups from each other, the recruits in the open barracks were more likely to perceive the setting as crowded than those in the partitioned barracks.

Studies conducted in other residential settings, such as college dormitories, point more directly to the role of boundaries in influencing the ability to predict and control social interaction. In comparing the behavior and experience of freshman in a double-loaded corridor design (rooms on each side of corridor) with those in suite-designed rooms, it was found that freshman in the former experienced more crowding stress, less social interaction, and more competitive behavior than those in the latter, although the two dormitories had comparable spatial densities in area per resident (Baum and Valins 1977). Of course, the different arrangement of spaces created different levels of social density. Studies carried out in institutional settings underscore the importance of boundaries in allowing freedom of choice in determining when and where social interactions will take place (Ittelson, Proshansky, and Rivlin 1970). For example, the behavior of residents of a psychiatric ward was found to be a function of the number of patients assigned per room. As this number increased, the amount of both isolated active behaviors and social interactions decreased dramatically. Patients assigned to private rooms were not only more active and socially interactive than those sharing bedrooms, but they also exhibited the widest range of activities.

These various studies suggest that the provision of clearly bounded spaces affords people greater freedom of choice to pursue desired activities as well as greater control over the physical and social environment (Holahan and Saegert 1973; Knight et al. 1973; Paulus et al. 1978). When interaction is not desired, the person can retreat and pursue other activities with a minimum of distractions and maximum confidentiality. When such boundedness is missing, the individual sacrifices choice and control. Faced with excessive levels of stimulation, especially when such excessive stimulation transcends environmental skills for overcoming them, the individual withdraws from social activity and is more likely to engage in isolated passive behavior.

2. Within the family household the degree of boundedness influences the extent to which conflict occurs in the activities of family members, how much time they spend together as a unit, and how much privacy is allowed for different family members for different purposes (Crowhurst 1974). A study of apartment living reported conflicts over internal space use as the most salient issue when children are involved, particularly when the conflicts arise out of television viewing (Becker and Friedburg 1974). Three major ways of dealing with such conflicts involved *time territory* (family members using the same space at different times), *space territory* (family members engaging in different activities at the same time but in different places), and *cooperation-capitulation* (all family members engage in one activity that is determined by dominant members of the group). Since high-density households frequently reveal boundedness problems, studies of such households reveal that the high densities, first, increase both the extent to which parents hit their children and the number of verbal quarrels and, second, negatively affect the perceived quality of relationships with spouses. Lack of perceived privacy was emphasized as a factor interfering in sexual relationships.

Culture clearly appears to be an important mediator of the degree of boundedness required to minimize stress in family functioning. Research reveals that despite high-density households in certain cultures, families living in these cultures exhibited minimal levels of stress (Canter and Canter 1971; Schmitt 1963). These findings are not only the result of cultural differences in the amount of personal space and privacy required by individuals, but can also be attributed to the variations in the mechanisms different cultures employ to obtain privacy when it is required (Altman 1975; Hall 1966; Rapoport 1969). Americans frequently require closed doors to achieve their privacy, whereas members of other cultures often rely on more subtle strategies such as speaking in a polite, reserved manner and posturing themselves in a way that signals the desire to be alone (Hall 1966). The fact that Americans often need boundaries that enable them to withdraw physically from social interaction may help us understand why American families who are financially able make every attempt to provide separate rooms for each family member.

3. Children have very different boundary requirements at different stages of development. In infancy boundaries that separate parents and child can evoke anxiety and stress in both (Pollowy 1977). In early stages of infancy visual contact with the parent seems necessary, since the child cannot perceive the existence of an apparently absent object or person (Piaget 1971). By the end of the second year, however, the sound of "mother" may suffice if the infant is in familiar surroundings (Pollowy 1977). As the child progresses from one developmental stage to the next, his or her requirements for privacy become more pronounced (Wolfe 1978). These privacy requirements reach their maximum in adolescence when increased autonomy, surges in physical maturation, and concentrated intellectual activity, as well as experimentation with social and sexual intimacy, combine to create privacy needs that previously existed in a more primitive, less distinctive form. Children's use of physical barriers to obtain privacy does, in fact, increase with age, with the greatest jump occurring in early adolescence (Sawin, Parke, and Dimicelli 1975).

4. There is evidence suggesting that many settings which characterize daily living are becoming more open, or less bounded, such as household settings (Cooper-Marcus 1975), offices (Brookes and Kaplan 1972), and schools (Rivlin and Rothenberg 1976). Open-plan offices are said to result in greater communication among employees, increased cohesion within workgroups, greater flexibility in the use of space, and financial savings (Brookes and Kaplan 1972). Yet there is a great deal of evidence that employees suffer from visual and auditory distractions as well as lack of conversational privacy. Similarly, some teachers and students have complained about the noise, increased disruptions, lack of display and storage space, and lack of territoriality they experienced in their open-plan classrooms (Kyzar 1971). There is much evidence, however, to suggest that teachers whose educational philosophies conflict with the physical configuration of the classrooms experience more difficulty than those whose orientations match such arrangements (Durlak et al. 1972; Rivlin and Rothenberg 1976). Research suggests that for teachers committed to an open style of teaching the provision of large, unbounded spaces actually allow for *more* privacy and less noise than did the conventional classrooms consisting of fixed-row seating (Brunetti 1972).

Crowding and Physical Setting Size

This discussion of "principles" and findings from environmental psychology deals with the question of size or scale of physical settings, with particular emphasis on family residence. Somewhat dramatic increases in population levels, particularly in urban settings, have led to the construction of large-scale buildings to contain large numbers of people and the machinery and equipment needed to support the living styles of a complex industrial society.

1. Both anecdotal and systematic research evidence suggest that large-scale physical settings may have negative impacts on the individuals who inhabit or use them, ranging from disorientation in airports (Kilday 1979), government buildings (Berkeley 1973), and health care facilities (Izumi 1970; Spivak 1967) to alienation, social withdrawal, and fear of crime by people living in high-rise apartment complexes (Newman 1972), and finally to a sense of neglect because of poorer quality of care in day-care facilities and psychiatric facilities (Ullman 1967). Many studies comparing the behavior and satisfaction of residents living in single family, low-rise, and high-rise structures found the latter to be associated with a number of stressful events, including crimes in semi-public areas (Becker and Friedberg 1974), social isolation and loneliness (Conway 1974), as well as less perceived privacy, friendliness, and helping behavior (McCarthy and Saegert 1978). Such findings have led many to suggest that high-rise structures are inherently an inadequate form of housing which has resulted in a ban on the construction of such structures in Denmark and Toronto, Canada.

Many of the studies have been criticized on methodological grounds. It has been suggested, for example, that building height is often confounded with such variables as social class, physical mobility, residential choice, financial cost, and household composition as well as neighborhood density (Cooperman 1977). Moreover, high-rise housing may be satisfactory and even desirable for some groups while it is inappropriate for others (Adams and Conway 1974; Homenuck 1973; Michelson 1973).

In determining housing satisfaction and preferences, studies investigating the role of a family's stage in the life cycle have consistently found families with young children to be least satisfied with high-rise housing. Parents of young children frequently complain that it is difficult, if not impossible, to supervise children's outdoor play activities while they themselves remain in the apartment (Adams and Conway 1974). There are numerous consequences related to this complaint, such as anxieties and worries of parents increasing with floor height and very young children living in high-rise buildings who play outdoors less frequently than those living in low-rise buildings (Morville 1969). The play activities of children living in high-rise housing are often restricted to the apartment interior, creating tension and conflict among family members (Becker and Friedberg 1974).

Another problem clearly identified with high-rise living is the lack of perceived control over the environment, especially control over the entry of nonresidents and social interactions with neighbors and friends (Becker and Friedberg 1974; McCarthy and Saegert 1978; Newman 1972). Multiple entry points, numerous stairwells, length of corridors, other semipublic spaces, inability to recognize other residents because of high densities, and still other factors lead to this lack of perceived control over the environment. Reinforcing this perception is the high crime rate in the semi-public areas of high-rises located in moderate or high-crime neighborhoods (Becker and Friedberg 1974; Newman 1972). Clearly, these same factors have implications for an evolving place-identity, in this instance one characterized by low environmental security that may in turn interfere with a strong sense of belonging and identification with one's home or residence.

RESEARCH AND POLICY IMPLICATIONS

The findings and principles presented above can only be regarded as tentative at best. The field of environmental psychology is both inchoate and lacking in any definite cumulative body of knowledge. By the same token the findings and principles not only have heuristic value but for those concerned with population changes and human conflict they provide both the concepts and preliminary data for making sense out of this broad problem insofar as the role of the physical setting is concerned. Furthermore, the present state of knowledge has both research implications and policy implications, and it is these implications that we consider in the final section of this chapter.

Research Implications

What implications for further research follow from existing theory and data on population changes and social conflict? That more research is needed is almost axiomatic. Research on crowding and stress in general, and particularly in relation to physical setting properties in the generation of conflicts between and among individuals and groups, is sparse to say the least. In the last two decades a concern with the relationships between the behavior and experience of individuals and the nature of physical settings has indeed accelerated at a very rapid rate. Yet our knowledge concerning personal space, territoriality, the development of place identity, privacy, and still other person-physical setting relationships is still at a formative stage. Since it is assumed here that each of these types of relationships is basic to problems of crowding and stress, our knowledge of the latter remains fragmentary and inconclusive. Nor can we ignore the significant and conspicuous fact that in many instances research findings over time and place are by no means consistent even where consistency is expected.

In spite of all these difficulties, however, some tentative but meaningful generalizations have emerged, suggesting the important research issues. While it can be clearly demonstrated that there are many such issues, three need special note. The task of cross-cultural research stands as a critical means with respect to still other issues. Clearly much of what exists as tentative knowledge concerning population change, crowding and stress as a basis of human conflict is derived from studies of Western societies, and even many Western subcultures or societies have not been included. The need for such research in developing countries and particularly in Eastern and Far Eastern countries looms as a critical problem deserving attention. The crux of such research, and this emerges even with so much of it yet to be done, lies in the importance of cross-cultural comparisons. For what reason? Apart from scientific considerations, the fact is that in many societies unlike the U.S., population change that leads to crowding has not and does not result in stress and/or human conflict. There is much to learn not only about adaptation to crowding and stress as a consequence of demographic and composition changes in population, but also with respect to cultural configurations where such population changes in some societies or cultures may lead to other consequences rather than individual or intergroup conflict, such as population migrations.

Changes in demography, number of people, or population composition may indeed initiate problems of crowding and stress that have as their consequence conflicts between individuals and groups. But who are the protagonists in these conflicts? Our previous analysis in which the individual in face-to-face primary groups was the focus of consideration of person-physical setting relationships confronts us with two important implications: first, that research on population change and conflict must also be longitudinal in character, that is, its usefulness will depend on the extent to which the problem is addressed over time or in successive stages of the life-cycle; and second, that the different individuals and groups in conflict may involve intergenerational differences or antagonisms within a given society or even subculture — and not social, religious, or ethnic differences between groups in that society or culture. Said differently, the various "stages" of the life cycle may reflect conflicts between intergenerational groups because of changing population factors. Yet here, too, cross-cultural comparisons are a must. Conflicts between children and parents, young adults and established adults, or the young(er) and aged populations may either not exist or express themselves differently in different societies or cultures.

Research in different cultures and across cultures that reverses the problem, namely, how intergroup and interindividual conflicts themselves may generate not only crowding and stress but other consequences that lead to demographic, compositional, and aggregate number changes in population, is critical in its own right. Conflict itself may indeed foster population change.

82   PROSHANSKY

Still another issue that demands attention is establishing both empirically and theoretically the links among various person-physical setting relationships such as place-identity, personal space, privacy, and territoriality. Yet as we take note of these and other research issues a final one asumes a very special importance by its methodological focus.

In brief, concerns with population change and its consequences for social conflict immediately suggest the need for a "new" methodology. Research in or out of the laboratory which is developed in the limited one- or two-variable causal paradigm will do little to answer or clarify the research issues we have discussed. It is only in the context of the real-life, on-going setting that research efforts can provide meaningful answers. A commitment to this approach implies methods concerned less with precision and quantification and more with preserving both the integrity of day-to-day phenomena that are involved in population change and human conflict and the people who are active in these settings. Inconstancy in research findings on the problem reflects the *variations* possible in translating real world phenomena into manageable cause-effect variables. Certainly such "translations" become even more hazardous as we move into other cultures and subcultures. The issue of methodology in the theoretical analysis and empirical study of population change as a source of human conflict is of fundamental importance.

Policy Implications

What policy implications follow from the analysis of the problem of population changes in relation to interindividual and intergroup conflict? To begin with, it cannot be emphasized too strongly that the space and place practitioners of any society or subculture (architects, designers, landscape architects, and planners) must view their task not simply in terms of individual tastes and needs but no less so in terms of an ever-changing physical world. It is not just the person-physical setting relationships of individuals in an ongoing normative context, but the impact on these relationships in a constantly changing physical world. Population changes that engender crowding and psychological stress represent the kind of impact whose consequences may indeed result in human conflict.

This broad policy implication in turn suggests two corollary implications. First, spaces and places in a given culture in which population changes are typical should be designed as flexible physical systems that can be modified quickly in response to changes in the demographic, compositional, and aggregate number characteristics of the members of that culture. Human conflicts resulting from population changes often occur because of the delay involved in changing physical settings so as to offset or nullify the potentials for crowding and psychological stress. The second corollary policy implication confronts us with a self-evident truth. How people use and experience space is not only a matter of who they are, what the properties of the space are, or what changes are occurring in the larger environment, but equally of how space is administered and managed. This means, of course, that space and place planning and evaluation must be a continuing function or activity in a given culture or subculture if conflict and stress are to be minimized.

However inchoate the research on cross-cultural uses of physical settings, existing research clearly points to the significance of normative value and attitudinal considerations in defining the problem of population changes as a source of conflict. For design practitioners as well as government officials in a given society or subculture the policy is clear enough: both differences between and among social groups, ethnic groups, and intergenerational groups make it necessary to design places and spaces with sufficient variations to take account of the diversity of needs and purposes of these different groups. Not only do complex Western societies often ignore these differences, but designers and architects create physical settings on the basis of implicit as well as explicit assumptions about what the "average" citizen needs and wants.

It is important to carry the implications of a policy of subcultural variation a step further. The conception and design of physical settings that characterize the day-to-day existence of individuals in a complex urban society tend to address biological needs and a minimal number of social needs of the person. Building codes and government regulations for residential, recreational, educational, medical, and employment settings provide potent evidence of this point. Fundamental environmental needs and person-physical setting relationships play a secondary role and at times no role at all, particularly when the economics of space and place development are of special importance. So many of the fundamental person-physical setting issues raised in our analysis play almost no role in the development of physical settings for purposes of living, working, relaxing, learning, or caring for one's health.

The final policy implication of our analysis is predicated on the assumption that an increasing number of different cultural and societal groups will live and experience urban life. In time most, if not all, underdeveloped nations or cultures will take their place in a world of complex industrialized urban societies. The physical socialization of the child is a critical consideration to human conflict. Environmental skills for living in a complex, technological setting must necessarily be involved in the education of the child, who must learn to understand and behave competently in physical settings just as the conventions for functioning in social settings are learned. How well a person can move through, use, and indeed modify the physical setting will depend on such skills. Such environmental skills and in turn their consequences

—environmental understanding, competence, security, and control—will determine how well needs for personal space, privacy, place-identity, and territoriality are satisfied. Surely they will determine just how much crowding and stress a particular person experiences as a result of changes in a physical setting and its inhabitants because of population changes.

REFERENCES

Adams, B., and J. Conway. "The Social Effects of Living off the Ground." In *IAEBSE Tall Buildings and People*. St. Catherine's College, Oxford: September, 1974, pp. 150–57.

Aiello, J. R., Y. M. Epstein, and R. A. Karlin. "Effects of Crowding on Electrodermal Activity." *Sociological Symposium* 14 (1975): 43–57.

Aiello, J. R., D. E. Thompson. "Personal Space, Crowding, and Spatial Behavior in a Cultural Context." In *Human Behavior and Environment*, edited by I. Altman, A. Rapoport, and J. Wohlwill, vol. 4 (1980): 107–78.

Altman, I. *The Environment and Social Behavior: Privacy, Territoriality, Personal Space, and Crowding*. Monterey, Ca.: Brooks/Cole, 1975.

Anderson, E. N., Jr. "Some Chinese Methods of Dealing with Crowding." *Urban Anthropology* 1 (1972): 141–50.

Averill, J. "Personal Control over Aversive Stimuli and its Relation to Stress." *Psychological Bulletin* 80 (1973): 226–303.

Baldassare, M. "Residential Density, Household Crowding, and Social Networks." In *Networks and Places,* edited by C. Fischer. New York: Free Press, 1977, pp. 101–15.

Baum, A., R. E. Harpin, and S. Valins. "The Role of Group Phenomena in the Experience of Crowding." *Environment and Behavior* 7 (1975): 185–98.

Baum, A., and S. Valins. *Architecture and Social Behavior.* Hillsdale, N.J.: Lawrence Erlbaum Associates, 1977.

Becker, F. D., and L. P. Friedburg. *Design for Living: The Residents' View of Multifamily Housing.* Ithaca, N.Y.: Center for Urban Development Research, 1974.

Berkeley, E. P. "More Than What You Want to Know about Boston City Hall." *Architecture Plus* (February 1973): 72–77.

Bickman, L., A. Teger, T. Gabriele, C. McLaughlin, M. Berger, and E. Sunaday. "Dormitory Density and Helping Behavior." *Environment and Behavior* 5 (1973): 465–90.

Blake, R. R., C. C. Rhead, B. Wedge, and J. S. Mouton. "Housing and Social Interaction." *Sociometry* 19 (1956): 133–39.

Boggs, D. H. and J. R. Simon. "Differential Effects of Noise on Tasks of Varying Complexity." *Journal of Applied Psychology* 52 (1968): 148–53.

Booth, A., and D. Johnson. "The Effect of Crowding on Child Health and Development." *American Behavioral Scientist* 18 (1975): 736–49.

Brookes, M. J., and A. Kaplan. "The Office Environment: Space Planning and Affective Behavior." *Human Factors* 14 (1972): 373–91.

Brunetti, F. "Noise, Distraction, and Privacy in Conventional and Open School Environments." In *Environmental Design: Research and Practice.* Proceedings of the Environmental Design Research Association, edited by W. J. Mitchell. Los Angeles: University of California Press, 1972.

Canter, D., and S. Canter. "Close Together in Tokyo." *Design and Environment* 2 (Summer 1971): 60–63.

Capellini, A., and M. Moroni. "Clinical Survey on Hypertension and Coronary Disease and their Possible Relations with the Environment in Workers of a Chemical Plant." *Medicina del Labora* 65 (1974): 297–305.

Clausen, J., and S. Clausen. "The Effects of Family Size on Parents and Children." In *Psychological Perspectives on Population,* edited by J. Fawcett. New York: Basic Books, 1973.

Cohen, S. "Environmental Load and the Allocation of Attention." In *Advances in Environmental Psychology,* vol. 1, edited by A. Baum, J. E. Singer, and S. Valins. Hillsdale, N.J.: Lawrence Erlbaum Associates, 1978, pp. 1–29.

———, D. C. Glass, and S. Phillips. "Environment and Health." In *Handbook of Medical Sociology,* edited by H. E. Freeman, S. Levine, and L. G. Reeder. Englewood Cliffs, N.J.: Prentice-Hall, 1979.

———, and N. Weinstein. "Nonauditory Effects of Noise on Behavior and Health." *Journal of Social Issues* 37 (1981): 36–70.

Cooper-Marcus, C., and L. Hogue. "Design Guidelines for High-Rise Housing." *Journal of Architectural Research* 5 (1976): 34–39.

Cooperman, D. "Social Research on Tall Habitats: A Critique and Proposal for Network Analysis." In *Human Response to Tall Buildings,* edited by D. J. Conway. Stroudsburg, Pa.: Dowden, Hutchinson & Ross, 1977, pp. 29–38.

Cozby, P. C. "Effects of Density, Activity, and Personality on Environmental Preferences." *Journal of Research in Personality* 7 (1973): 45–60.

Crowhurst, S. H. "A House Is a Metaphor." *Journal of Architectural Education* 27 (1974): 35–41.

D'Atri, D. A. "Psychophysiological Responses to Crowding." *Environment and Behavior* 7 (1975): 237–50.

Dean, L. M., W. M. Pugh, and E. K. E. Gunderson. "Spatial and Perceptual Components of Crowding: Effects on Health and Satisfaction." *Environment and Behavior* 7 (1975): 225–36.

Desor, J. A. "Toward a Psychological Theory of Crowding." *Journal of Personality and Social Psychology* 21 (1972): 79–83.

Donnerstein, E., and D. W. Wilson. "Effects of Noise and Perceived Control on On-going and Subsequent Aggressive Behavior." *Journal of Personality and Social Psychology* 34 (1976): 774–81.

Dooley, B. B. "Crowding Stress: The Effects of Social Density on Men with 'Close' or 'Far' Personal Space." Doctoral dissertation. University of California, 1974.

Draper, P. "Crowding among Hunter-Gatherers: The !Kung Bushmen." *Science* 182 (1973): 301–303.

Durlak, J. T., B. E. Beardsley, and J. S. Murray. "Observation of User Activity Patterns in Open and Traditional Plan School Environments." In *Environmental Design: Research and Practice.* Proceedings of the EDRA 3/AR and Conference, edited by W. J. Mitchell. Los Angeles: University of California Press, 1972.

Epstein, Y. M. "Crowding, Stress, and Human Behavior." *Journal of Social Issues* 37 (1981): 126–44.

Freedman, J. L. *Crowding and Behavior.* San Francisco: Freeman, 1975.

Gasparini, A. "Influence of the Dwelling on Family." *Ekistics* 216 (1973): 344–48.

Gattoni, F., and A. Tarnopolsky. "Aircraft Noise and Psychiatric Morbidity." *Psychological Medicine* 3 (1973): 628–34.

Glass, D. C., and J. E. Singer. *Urban Stress.* New York: Academic Press, 1972.

Hall, E. T. "Space and its Organization as a Factor in Mental Health." *Landscape* (1962): 26–29.

Hanke, B. R. "Urban Densities in the U.S. and Japan." *HUD International* 7 (1972): 1–24.

Harris, L., and Associates, Inc. *The Steelcase National Study of Office Environments: Do They Work?* Grand Rapids, Mi.: Steelcase, 1978.

Holahan, C. J., and S. Saegert. "Behavioral and Attitudinal Effects of Large-Scale Variations in the Physical Environment of Psychiatric Wards." *Journal of Abnormal Psychology* 82 (1973): 459–62.

Homenuck, P. *A Study of High-Rise: Effect, Preferences, and Perceptions.* Toronto: Institute of Environmental Research, Inc., 1973.

Ittelson, W. H., H. M. Proshansky, and L. G. Rivlin. "Bedroom Size and Social Interaction on the Psychiatric Ward." *Environment and Behavior* 2 (1970): 225–70.

Iwata, O. "Empirical Examination of the Perception of Density and Crowding." *Japanese Psychological Research* 16 (1974): 117–25.

——. "Factors in the Perception of Crowding and the Relationship of Crowding to Personal Space." *Psychologia* 20 (1977): 33–37.

Izumi, K. "Psychosocial Phenomena and Building Design." In *Environmental Psychology: Man and his Physical Environment,* edited by H. M. Proshansky, W. H. Ittelson, and L. G. Rivlin. New York: Holt, Rinehart and Winston, 1970, pp. 569–73.

Justa, F. C., and M. B. Golan. "Office Design: Is Privacy Still a Problem?" *Journal of Architectural Research* (1977): 5–12.

Kantor, D., and W. Lehr. *Inside the Family.* San Francisco: Jossey-Bass, 1975.

Khomulo, L. P., L. P. Rodinova, and A. P. Rusinova. "Changes in the Blood Lipid Metabolism of Man Owing to the Prolonged Effects of Industrial Noise on the Central Nervous System." *Kardologia* 7 (1967): 35–38.

Kilday, P. "Travellers Go Crazy in Big Dallas-Fort Worth Airport." *Associated Press News Service,* July 8, 1979.

Knight, R. C., W. H. Weitzer, and C. M. Zimring. *Opportunity for Control in the Built Environment: The ELEMR Project.* Amherst: University of Massachusetts, Environmental Institute, 1973.

Kokokusha, D. *Report on Investigation of Living Environment around Osaka International Airport.* Japan: Association for the Prevention of Aircraft Nuisance, 1973.

Kryter, K. D. *The Effects of Noise on Man.* London: Academic Press, 1970.

Kuper, L. *Living in Towns.* London: Cressett Press, 1953.

Kyzar, B. L. *Comparison of Instructional Practices in Classrooms of Different Design.* Final Report. School Planning Laboratory, Northwestern State College, 1971.

Lazarus, R. S. *Psychological Stress and the Coping Process.* New York: McGraw-Hill, 1966.

LeVine, R. A. "Witchcraft and Co-Wife Proximity in Southwestern Kenya." *Ethnology* 1 (1962): 39–45.

Marsella, A. J., M. Escudero, P. Gordon. "The Effects of Dwelling Density on Mental Disorders in Filipino Men." *Journal of Health and Social Behavior* 11 (1971): 288–94.

Mathews, K. E., Jr., and L. K. Cannon. "Environmental Noise Level as Determinant of Helping Behavior." *Journal of Personality and Social Psychology* 32 (1975): 571–77.

McCarthy, D., and S. Saegert. "Residential Density, Social Overload, and Social Withdrawal." *Human Ecology* 6 (1978): 253–71.

Mehrabian, A., and J. A. Russell. "A Measure of Arousal Seeking Tendency." Environment and Behavior 5 (1973): 315–34.

Michelson, W. *Man and his Urban Environment: A Sociological Approach.* Reading, Ma.: Addison-Wesley, 1970.

_____. *Environmental Change.* University of Toronto, Center for Urban and Community Studies, Research Paper no. 60, 1973.

Milgram, S. "The Experience of Living in Cities." *Science* 167 (1970): 1461–68.

Mitchell, R. "Some Social Implications of High Density Housing." *American Socio-logical Review* 36 (1971): 18–29.

Morville, J. *Children's Play on Flatted Estates.* English summary. Copenhagen: Statens Byggesorsknings Institut, Report no. 10, 1969.

Munroe, R. L., and R. H. Munroe. "Population Density and Affective Relationships in Three East African Societies." *Journal of Social Psychology* 88 (1972): 15–20.

Newman, O. *Defensible Space.* New York: Macmillan, 1972.

Parvizpoor, D. "Noise Exposure and Prevalence of High Blood Pressure among Weav-ers in Iran." *Journal of Occupational Medicine* 18 (1976): 730–31.

Paulus, P., V. Cox, G. McCain, and J. Chandler. "Some Effects of Crowding in a Prison Environment." *Journal of Applied Social Psychology* 5 (1975): 86–91.

Paulus, P. B., G. McCain, and V. C. Cox. "Death Rates, Psychiatric Commitments, Blood Pressure and Perceived Crowding as a Function of Institutional Crowding." *Environmental Psychology and Nonverbal Behavior* 3 (1978): 107–16.

Piaget, J. *Play, Dreams, and Imitation in Childhood.* New York: Norton, 1951.

Pollowy, A. *The Urban Nest.* Stroudsburg, Pa.: Dowden, Hutchinson & Ross, 1977.

Proshansky, H. M., W. H. Ittelson, and L. G. Rivlin. "Freedom of Choice and Be-havior in a Physical Setting." In *Environmental Psychology: Man and His Physical Setting,* edited by H. M. Proshansky, W. H. Ittelson, and L. G. Riv-lin. New York: Holt, Rinehart & Winston, 1970, pp. 173–83.

Proshansky, H. M., A. K. Fabian, and R. D. Kaminoff. "Place-Identity: Physical World Socialization of the Self." *Journal of Environmental Psychology* 3 (1983): 57–83.

Rapoport, A. *House Form and Culture.* Englewood Cliffs, N.J.: Prentice-Hall, 1969.

——. "Toward a Redefinition of Density." *Environment and Behavior* 7 (1975): 133–58.

Rivlin, L. G., and M. Rothenberg. "The Use of Space in Open Classrooms." In *En-vironmental Psychology: People and their Physical Settings,* 2nd ed., edited by H. M. Proshansky, W. H. Ittelson, and L. G. Rivlin. New York: Holt, Rinehart & Winston, 1976, pp. 479–89.

Rodin, J. "Density, Perceived Choice and Responses to Controllable and Uncontrol-lable Outcomes." *Journal of Experimental Social Psychology* 12 (1976): 564–78.

Saegert, S. "Crowding: Cognitive Overload and Behavioral Constraint." In *Environ-mental Design Research,* vol. 2, edited by W. Preiser. Stroudsburg, Pa.: Dow-den, Hutchinson & Ross, 1973.

———. "High-Density Environments: Their Personal and Social Consequences." In *Human Response to Crowding,* edited by A. Baum and Y. M. Epstein. Hillsdale, N.J.: Lawrence Erlbaum Associates, 1978, pp. 257–81.

———, and R. D. Kaminoff. "Background Density, Personality, and Current Susceptibility to Crowding Phenomena." Manuscript in preparation. New York: Center for Human Environments, 1981.

Sawin, D. B., R. D. Parke, and S. Dimiceli. "Privacy in the Home: A Developmental and Situational Analysis." Paper presented at the Biennial Meetings of the Society for Research in Child Development, April, 1975.

Schmitt, R. C. "Density, Delinquency, and Crime in Honolulu." *Sociology and Social Research* 41 (1957): 274–76.

———. "Implications of Density in Hong Kong." *Journal of the American Institute of Planners* 24 (1963): 210–17.

———. "Density, Health, and Social Organization." *Journal of the American Institute of Planners* 32 (1966): 38–40.

Schopler, J., and M. Walton. "The Effects of Structure, Expected Enjoyment, and Participants' Internality-Externality Upon Feelings of Being Crowded." Unpublished manuscript, University of North Carolina, 1974.

Sherrod, D. R., and R. Downs. "Environmental Determinants of Altruism: The Effects of Stimulus Overload and Perceived Control on Helping." *Journal of Experimental Social Psychology* 10 (1974): 468–79.

Simmel, G. *The Sociology of Georg Simmel,* translated and edited by K. H. Wolff. Glencoe, Ill.: Free Press, 1950, Chapter IV.

Singer, J. E., U. Lundberg, and M. Frankenhaeuser. "Stress on the Train: A Study of Urban Commuting." In *Advances in Environmental Psychology,* vol. 1, edited by A. Baum, S. Valins, and J. Singer. Hillsdale, N. J.: Lawrence Erlbaum Associates, 1978, pp. 41–56.

Smith, S., and W. W. Haythorn. "Effects of Compatibility, Crowding, Group Size, and Leadership Seniority on Stress, Anxiety, Hostility, and Annoyance in Isolated Groups." *Journal of Personality and Social Psychology* 22 (1972): 67–79.

Sommer, R. *Personal Space: The Behavioral Basis of Design.* Englewood Cliffs, N.J.: Prentice-Hall, 1969.

Spivak, M. "Sensory Distortions in Tunnels and Corridors." *Hospital and Community Psychiatry* 18 (1967): 24–30.

Steele, F. *Physical Settings and Organization Development.* Reading, Ma.: Addison-Wesley, 1973.

Stevens, S. S. "Stability of Human Performance under Intense Noise." *Journal of Sound and Vibration* 21 (1972): 35–36.

Stokols, D. "On the Distinction between Density and Crowding: Some Implications for Future Research." *Psychological Review* 79 (1972): 275–77.

_____. "The Experience of Crowding in Primary and Secondary Environments." *Environment and Behavior* 8 (1976): 49–86.

_____. "A Typology of Crowding Experiences." In *Human Response to Crowding*, edited by A. Baum and Y. M. Epstein. Hillsdale, N.J.: Lawrence Erlbaum Associates, 1978, pp. 219–55.

Sundstrom, E. "Crowding as a Sequential Process: Review of Research on the Effects of Population Density on Humans." In *Human Response to Crowding,* edited by A. Baum and Y. M. Epstein. Hillsdale, N, J.: Lawrence Erlbaum Associates, 1978, pp. 31–116.

Ullman, L. *Institution and Outcome: A Comparative Study of Psychiatric Hospitals.* New York: Pergamon, 1967.

Valins, S., and A. Baum. "Residential Group Size, Social Interaction, and Crowding." *Environment and Behavior* 5 (1973): 421–39.

Westin, A. *Privacy and Freedom.* New York: Atheneum, 1967.

Wirth, L. *Community Life and Social Policy,* edited by E. W. Marwick and A. M. Reiss. Chicago: University of Chicago Press, 1939, pp. 368–91.

Wohlwill, J., and I. Kohn. "The Environment as Experienced by the Migrant: An Adaptation-Level View." *Representative Research in Social Psychology* 4 (1973): 135–64.

Wolfe, M. "Childhood and Privacy." In *Human Behavior and the Environment: Children and the Environment,* vol. 3, edited by I. Altman and J. Wohlwill. New York: Plenum, 1978.

Wolfensberger, W. "The Normalization Principle and Some Major Implications to Architectural-Environmental Design." In *Barrier-Free Environments,* edited by M. J. Bednar. Stroudsburg, Pa.: Dowden, Hutchinson & Ross, 1977.

Zuckerman, M. "Dimensions of Sensation Seeking." *Journal of Consulting and Clinical Psychology* 36 (1971): 45–52.

4

Sociological Perspectives and Evidence on the Links Between Population and Conflict

WILLIAM R. KELLY AND OMER R. GALLE

THE DIMENSIONALITY OF CONFLICT

ALTHOUGH CONFLICT AND VIOLENCE can take various forms — from protest demonstrations, riots, coups, and strikes to revolutions — most research delineates two major dimensions of collective action: *frequency* and *severity,* or *intensity.* Measurement of the frequency of conflict or violence involves a simple count or location of all events that meet some predefined operational definition. An obvious assumption underlying the use of frequency as an indicator of conflict and violence is either that all events are relatively homogeneous or that the heterogeneity of events is unimportant. Often such assumptions are quite limiting (Snyder and Kelly 1979).

Determining the severity, or intensity, of conflict and violence is a more complex strategy that takes into account the heterogeneity of events by correlating various aspects of collective actions including factors such as size, duration, and personal and property damage. For example, one index of riot severity consists of the number of participants, duration, deaths, and injuries (Kelly and Snyder 1980). A somewhat different strategy includes the nature of violence (rock and bottle throwing, fighting, looting, or arson) (Spilerman 1976), as well as size, number of arrests, and number of injuries (see Snyder and Kelly 1979 for a discussion of issues related to the measurement of violence severity). Strategies for measuring the severity of nonviolent conflicts follow along similar lines, for example, the use of a combination of size, duration, and the number of sites of conflicts to measure protest intensity (Eisinger 1973).

Frequency and severity are often considered conceptually distinct dimensions of conflict and violence (for example, Wanderer 1968; Spilerman 1976; and Kelly and Snyder 1980). However, it is not always necessary, or desirable, to treat the frequency and severity of conflict as empirically distinct

91

if one is interested in characterizing and quantifying an *overall level* of conflict in a society, or perhaps industry. An appropriate strategy might combine indicators of frequency and intensity (Britt and Galle 1974). In the case of industrial conflict *volume* is a multiplicative function of the frequency of strikes, the duration of strike activity, and the breadth of conflict (number of workers involved per work stoppage). Generalizing beyond incidents of labor conflict, one could conceivably distinguish between the volume of conflict occurring in a society (or city or other ecological unit) and the component parts of that volume of conflict distinguished by, for example, the frequency, breadth, and duration.

In short, various strategies for measuring conflict and violence exist. The dimensionality of conflict indicates that no single measure is always appropriate. Later, we inquire whether the relation between population and conflict differs depending upon which measure is used.

On the Nature of the Determinants of Conflict and Violence

Three distinct types of independent variables influence conflicts or violence: precipitants, facilitators, and determinants. These distinctions are necessary and useful because they allow the determination of the various roles, and thus the relative import, of factors influencing violence.

Precipitants are events or situations that spark or trigger the outbreak of violence. Often the actual event that triggers violence is a routine or common occurrence that may or may not bear directly on the underlying causes of the violence. Precipitant factors are theoretically important only to the extent that they allow us to understand the dynamics or volatility of violence, not its fundamental causes. *Facilitators* are factors that are not the basic, underlying causes of violence, but rather help the process by making violence an easier, more accessible strategy. Thus we assume that the motivation to participate is present. Facilitators are structural factors that bridge the gap between motivation and participation. Facilitators of conflict or violence are often the same factors referred to as *resources for contention* — people, money, the media, and organization (Tilly 1978). The actual underlying *determinants* of conflicts or violence are the reasons or motivations for actions.

Population at Risk and Level of Analysis

A final issue concerns the varying levels of analysis characteristic of sociological theory and research on conflicts within macroecological units such as cities and universities, micro units such as households, and finally groups of varying size like labor unions. It is important to establish a conceptual link across these different levels or units of analysis. That link, for the purposes of this study, is the concept of the population at risk. A primary function of population factors in the sociological study of conflict is in determining who is available to engage in contentious activity. The concept of a population at risk transcends differing levels of analysis.

THEORETICAL EXPLANATIONS OF CONFLICT AND VIOLENCE

Most major social scientific and sociological explanations of the incidence and intensity of violence and conflict are primarily aimed at addressing conflict and violence at the national (revolutions, coups) and subnational (labor unrest, race riots) levels of analysis. However, a more recent formulation, the density/crowding hypothesis, attempts to explain household and domestic conflict and violence. With the addition of the crowding hypothesis, the major sociological approaches to conflict address various dimensions of conflict and violence on several levels of analysis.

The more directly demographic crowding/density explanation, the disorganization/rapid social change and relative deprivation arguments, share a common but fundamental social psychological concept of tension, frustration, or discontent but, nevertheless, rely to a fair extent on various dimensions of population as primary determinants of violence. The mobilization/resource management framework provides a quite different explanation, focusing on the organizational aspects of conflict and contention. Several other explanations directed mainly at the incidence of urban racial violence in the post-1964 United States are for the most part demographic approaches. These include diffusion and contagion of violence, the assembling process, and concepts of a critical mass and a population at risk to participate in conflicts and violence.

Overcrowding, Conflict, and Violence

Although concern with potentially deleterious effects of high population density has a long and rich sociological heritage (Spenser 1879–82; Durkheim 1933; Wirth 1938; and Hawley 1972), most of the recent interest in this area has been stimulated at least in part by the results from studies of a variety of animal species (Alexander and Roth 1971; Archer 1970; Calhoun 1962; Christian 1961; Deevey 1960; Keeley 1962; Perrins 1965; and Thiessen and Rodgers 1961). For many species, high population density appears to lead to higher levels of aggression than observed in less dense aggregations. The difficulties of imputing, through analogous reasoning, a similar relationship between high population density and aggressive or conflictual behavior in human populations is manifold. In the following discussion, five separate but related issues are addressed: How is the major explanatory variable — density or overcrowding — conceptualized? Under what conditions (or in what settings) is overcrowding important? How does overcrowding, in these settings, lead to particular behavioral outcomes? How is crowding dealt with in distinct cultures? What kinds of behavioral outcomes might be expected from overcrowding?

Man normally lives in a more complex environmental setting than other animals. In animal studies the usual measure of density is the number of the species divided by some areal unit measure of the domain of the species under observation. Gross density — population per unit area — for humans in an urban setting, on the other hand, is actually a composite of several different measures of land use. Urban population density is primarily a consequence of the number of dwelling units per structure, structures per net residential area, and net residential area per total area. Persons per room and rooms per dwelling unit (the other two factors involved in determining gross density) are of substantially less importance in determining overall levels of population density (Duncan and Guest 1970, 1972). It has been argued that since they are not that closely related empirically, the conceptual confusion between gross *density* and residential *overcrowding* has contributed to the ambiguity of the findings in some of the early studies of the behavioral consequences of crowding or high population density in human populations. In the present theoretical discussion we focus on *overcrowding* in primary environments and its potential behavioral outcomes rather than on the consequences of high population (gross) density (Stokols 1978). The *logic* of the argument for a "high density-pathology" linkage is implicitly similar to that proposed in the overcrowding literature, but the linkages are much more clear and explicit when referring to overcrowding than high density.

In discussing the possible relationship between crowding and behavior, care must be taken to distinguish under what conditions (or in what settings) high levels of crowding become significant. One recent typology of crowding experiences addresses this issue by differentiating between *primary* and *secondary* environments: "*Primary environments* are those in which an individual spends much time, relates to others on a personal basis, and engages in a wide range of personally important activities. Examples of primary settings are residential, classroom, and work environments. *Secondary environments* are those in which one's encounters with others are relatively transitory, anonymous, and inconsequential. Examples of these settings are transportation, recreation, and commercial areas" (Stokols 1978, p. 235). Social interferences, it is argued, will be more disruptive and frustrating in primary environments, especially if they are of long term or persistent duration. The focus of our discussion here, then, will be on the effects of overcrowding in primary environments, especially in residential settings.

In addressing the question of how, in primary environments, overcrowding leads to deleterious behavioral outcomes, the theoretical literature focuses on two analytically distinct but interrelated concepts: an excess of stimulation, or *stimulus overload,* and a *lack of privacy.* Lack of control over one's interpersonal space (lack of privacy) and receiving excess stimulation from social sources (stimulus overload) can be brought about, it has been argued, in residential settings with unusually high ratios of persons per room. The logic for this argument is fourfold:

> First, crowding results from a situation characterized by the inevitability of contact between persons, and an inability for persons to control the presence of others. Second, close proximity of persons increases the likelihood of attempted interaction. Third, a high ratio of persons to rooms will increase the degree one is obligated to be responsive to others. Fourth, in a crowded household, since everyone's daily activities may be easily observed by others, the most intimate aspects of one's "self" are exposed and one lacks the back regions which . . . are important for both the maintenance of "self" and for the effective performance of one's activities. (Gove, Hughes, and Galle 1979, p. 61)

It seems reasonable to expect that people react to incessant demands (stimulus overload) and lack of privacy resulting from overcrowding in the home with irritability, weariness, and withdrawal. Furthermore, people under these conditions are likely to be so completely involved in reacting to their immediate environment that it becomes extremely difficult for them to step back, look at their situation, and plan ahead. These increased levels of irritability could potentially lead to higher levels of conflict within the household, which in turn leads to higher levels of violence in crowded households than in uncrowded ones.

But what about cross-cultural variations in levels of overcrowding? Certainly the levels of crowding in the United States are not as high as have been observed in Hong Kong, for example. Does this mean that we should expect higher levels of maladaptive behavior among Hong Kong natives than among persons in the United States? According to the extant literature, apparently not. A key factor in understanding the effects of crowding cross-culturally is the recognition that culture determines what demands and responses are appropriate in any behavioral setting. In all cultures there are ways in which one can socially construct a situation and setting to withdraw from interaction and experience privacy, and there are sharp cultural variations in how social interaction and privacy are regulated (Hall 1966; Anderson 1972; Gregor 1977; Morgan 1981; Mitchell 1975; Altman 1975). Given these factors, the argument is advanced that the norms within a given culture would regulate social interaction so that persons in typical situations ("average" levels of crowding for that culture) would experience an optimal level of social interaction (Levi and Anderson 1975; Altman 1975). If this is the case, it follows that persons in atypical situations (persons experiencing above-average levels of crowding for their culture in their primary environments) would experience an excess of social demands and a lack of privacy. It seems likely that crowding would be experienced in most cultures by those persons who experience the highest levels of crowding—for that culture—in their primary environments (this argument is abstracted in large part from Gove et al. 1979).

With regard to the kinds of behavioral outcomes expected from excessive levels of overcrowding, relatively little differentiation has been made distinguishing frequency from severity of conflict. In fact there has been a veritable plethora of projected outcomes suggested from overcrowding, including increased morbidity and/or mortality levels, increased levels of mental illness, ineffectual care of children, along with generally increased levels of aggressiveness. These have, at one time or another, been referred to as "pathological" behavioral outcomes of overcrowding (Calhoun 1962). For the most part studies examining overcrowding as a factor leading to aggressive behavior look at the frequency of such forms of behavior, though there are some exceptions (McCarthy, Galle, and Zimmern 1975).

Much of the writing from which these analytic ideas spring and a good deal of the early evidence supporting them suffers from a lack of good fit between the theory and the data used to support the theory. Although the reasoning may be sound, most of the early studies are based on the analysis of macro-level data, the results of which were "explained" in terms of individual-level psychological states. These problems related to the classic "ecological fallacy" argument have been partially rectified in several recent studies which will be discussed later, in the section on empirical evidence.[1]

Rapid Change, Disorganization, and Relative Deprivation

The rapid social change/social disorganization argument views rapid social or demographic changes as sources of societal strain and disorganization (for example, Durkheim 1951; Kerr, Dunlop, Harrison, and Meyers 1960; Smelser 1963; Johnson 1966; and Eisenstadt 1966). Such changes, it is argued, facilitate or produce the breakdown of primary and secondary social groups and generate anomie, which in turn leads to various forms of uninstitutionalized action including collective behavior (Smelser 1963), mass movements (Kornhauser 1959), labor conflict (Kerr et al. 1960), revolution, and collective violence (Johnson 1966; Eisenstadt 1966). One formulation of the argument goes as follows:

> Social and economic change — urbanization, increases in literacy and education, industrialization, mass media expansion — extend political consciousness, multiply political demands, broaden political participation. These changes undermine traditional sources of political authority and traditional political institutions; they enormously complicate the problems of creating new bases of political association and new political institutions combining legitimacy and effectiveness. The rates of social mobilization and the expansion of political participation are high; the rates of political organization and institutionalization are low. The result is political instability and disorder. (Huntington 1968, p. 5)

Massive and/or rapid changes that physically place individuals or groups in new environments and expose them to unfamiliar ideas, norms, and cultures (or subcultures) may create collective disorganization or bewilderment. This disorganization or bewilderment may lead to collective discontent which in turn may lead to collective violence or conflict (Feierabend, Feierabend, and Nesvold 1969). The types of social changes which the rapid change/disorganization theorists posit are principally demographic, including urbanization, migration, industrialization, and structural modernization. Undoubtedly there are socioeconomic factors as well, but demographic changes appear to be the primary determinants of disorganization, anomie, discontent, and thus collective violence.

   The relative deprivation or achievement discrepancy explanation of conflict and violence (for example, Davies 1962; Feierabend and Feierabend 1966; Gurr 1968, 1970), also referred to as systemic frustration, rising expectations and the J-curve, relies primarily on the hypothesized link between frustration and aggression (see Dollard, Doob, Miller, Mowrer, and Sears 1939, or Berkowitz 1962). Briefly, achievement discrepancy theorists reason that the gap between individuals' expected and achieved welfare (generally economic but not restricted to that) is the most important determinant of collective violence. One focus on revolution is explicitly extended to include other forms of contention and violence such as student protests and riots. "Revolution is most likely to take place when a prolonged period of rising expectations and rising gratifications is followed by a short period of sharp reversal, during which the gap between expectations and gratifications quickly widens and becomes intolerable. The frustration that develops, when it is intense and widespread in the society, seeks outlets in violent action" (Davies 1969, p. 547).

Although the major expectations and achievements are economic in the relative deprivation formulations, demographic factors are not irrelevant. For example, shifts in the age structure or the size of particular cohorts of individuals, due mainly to fluctuations in fertility, have been linked to structural strains, limited resources, and thus (presumably) frustration, discontent, and conflict (Ryder 1974). Other formulations of the achievement discrepancy explanation rely at least implicitly on demographic factors, and a similar logic applies. Realization of expectations depends in part on the availability of resources. When populations grow or change composition, resources may become scarce, interfering with or inhibiting achievement.

There are several major problems with the frustration and strain explanations of conflict and violence, and all are serious. One is the probability that these explanations can be tautological. One may observe some form of conflict or violence at a particular time, and in searching backward in time, likely find at some point evidence of a disruptive demographic shift (rapid migration or a sizable increase in urbanization) or the conditions producing an expectations or achievement gap. The obvious problem is that there may be no relation between those antecedent conditions and the incidence of violence.

Another related problem is the attribution of particular psychological states of frustration, anomie, strain, and discontent to individuals from macro-level structural changes. We question the assumption of a link between structural changes and individual psychological states especially as far as that involves the further assumption that individuals are influenced to roughly the same extent, producing roughly the same (necessary) level of strain or frustration. Compare Miller, Bolce, and Halligan (1977) and more recent research on overcrowding, for example, Gove et al. (1979), for similar views and attempts to overcome these problems.

A final problem with these two approaches is the tendency to characterize the participants in conflicts as marginal, unassimilated individuals. Whether due to deprivation and frustration, or dislocation and anomie, violent action tends to lack legitimacy in the view of the established social order and is viewed as meaningless and irrational. The disorganization and deprivation theories exclude "purely instrumental accounts of rebellion, in which violence is simply the most efficient means available in accomplishing some collective end" (Tilly 1975, p. 20).

Resource Mobilization

The mobilization/resource management approach treats violence as a by-product of "political organization and the day-to-day struggle for power"

(Tilly 1970, p. 2; see also Tilly 1969, 1975; Snyder and Tilly 1972; Snyder and Kelly 1979; Gamson 1968, 1975; and Oberschall 1973). Collective conflict and violence is a function of a group's control over relevant resources, their contention for power, and finally the resistance of that contention by authorities and other contenders (Snyder and Kelly 1976a). Of primary importance is the role of demographic processes or population movements within the context of the mobilization perspective. One scholar points out the departure of mobilization theory from the relative deprivation and rapid change perspectives:

> Large structural changes in a society like urbanization and industrialization do not in themselves generate collective violence or other acute forms of conflict, but they strongly affect the number, identity, and organization of the contenders which in turn determine the predominant forms and loci of conflicts. In the short run, the magnitude of conflict depends on an interaction of the tactics of contenders and the coercive practices of the government. In the longer run, the magnitude of conflict depends on the established means by which contenders can enter and leave the polity and the frequency with which entries and exits actually occur. (Tilly 1970, p. 4)

Thus rather than invoking notions of strain, frustration, anomie, and disorganization (although an unspecified but necessary level of anger or discontent is assumed), the resource mobilization perspective views population shifts such as migration, urbanization, and cohort size as important as far as determining who is where when. The essential importance of demographic factors lies in how population shifts affect the *costs* of mobilizing individuals into contending groups. The cost of mobilization, among other factors, is a primary determinant of whether groups form, and thus enter into, contentions, conflicts, and violence.

However, the mobilization of participants for collective action and violence is not solely dependent on massive population shifts or other major demographic changes. Organizational issues are important as well. For example, labor conflict demonstrates how contenders can be mobilized at a relatively low cost without the major structural/demographic changes often linked to larger macro-level conflicts. Labor unions provide the *organizational structure* that links relatively large numbers of workers together in a definable and limited space. All else equal, labor unions are capable of low-cost mobilization of workers for collective action by means of existing organizational structure and communication networks.[2]

The availability of large numbers plays a central role in various formulations of the more general mobilization perspective. A cost-benefit model of nonconventional challenges (contentions for power, conflicts, violence, and so on) has been formulated (Oberschall 1979). Net benefit from conflict is a function of, among other factors, the probability of obtaining the collective goods under contention and the cost of collective action. As far as costs are concerned, the argument postulates safety in numbers. The size of the contending group bears directly on the costs of collective action as well as the probability of success. Large contenders are hard to ignore, repress, and co-opt. But what influences group size and thus the likelihood of contention and conflict? The ease of mobilization — available numbers in a limited space. An example cited is the U.S. riots of the 1960s:

> Rioting occurred precisely where and when the conditions for strategic interaction were present and would lead to massive participation and low collective action costs: large size of black population; ease of informal communication in black neighborhoods in the warm months, when people hang out in the streets; and weekends, when opportunity costs are low. The growth of a riot ideology, that is, of a collective action repertoire of rioting, helps explain the increase in frequency and severity over the years. (Oberschall 1979, p. 65)

In general the resource mobilization/resource management frameworks views collective action as a function of groups' shared interests, intensity of organization, mobilization of the resources under the group's collective control, and repression or social control strategies of authorities or other groups. Assuming shared interests and a particular level of discontent, a group's capacity to engage in collective action or contend for power is dependent upon its ability to mobilize resources such as money, communication, weapons, but most important, manpower. It is the importance placed on people as resources that makes demographic considerations fundamental in this approach.

While the resource mobilization framework appears to overcome some of the conceptual problems characteristic of the relative deprivation and rapid change models, it too suffers from limitations. One such shortcoming is an overemphasis on organization, resources, authorities, third parties, tactics of contention — and too little attention paid to *collective interests* and how they develop. For our purposes, however, mobilization theory adds considerable insight into the link between major demographic processes and various dimensions of conflict and violence.

Population as a Factor

There is a fairly extensive literature on the role of *size* as it relates to militancy of labor conflict, both in terms of the frequency of work stoppages and the severity or violence of strikes (Snyder and Kelly 1976). The theoretical rationale underlying these relationships involves the idea that there is strength in numbers: before labor contends with management, it should demonstrate the ability to act collectively—that there is solidarity among workers concerning potential conflicts, and that labor can impose distinct disadvantages on management by engaging in some form of collective action. Another example of the importance of population size, distribution, and proximity in accounting for conflict is the pre-1964 era of U.S. urban racial violence, the so-called communal riots (Janowitz 1969). Urban riots are typical of the contested terrain disturbances. They were primarily the outgrowth of the logic of metropolitan growth which placed large groups of recent migrants in segregated but proximate areas. The violence has been described as "ecological warfare" because it involved the proximity of conflict groups.

Several others have noted the positive relationship between the number of nonwhites in cities and the location of urban racial violence in the United States during the 1960s (McPhail 1971; Spilerman 1970, 1971). The role of available numbers for the riot process has been detailed:

> First, a necessary condition for the initiation of civil disorder is a large number of persons with a period of unscheduled or uncommitted time at their disposal. . . . Some persons are more likely than others to be riot participants, but not because they are "riot-prone" or because we can infer other motivational tendencies from their attributes; rather, their attributes crudely describe the presence or absence of their contacts and relationships with others which decrease or increase their availability for riot participation by virtue of the behaviors others can address to them. (McPhail 1971, p. 1070)

An explanation of the role of nonwhite population size as it relates to racial violence cites federal inaction regarding blacks, racial solidarity, and the national media as major factors transforming racial conflicts and riots into national phenomena. Thus, if the underlying causes of the riots were national in scope (rather than local or city specific), then the location of riots should reflect the size of the black population in different cities rather than local differences in indicators of absolute or relative well-being. But a non-linear relationship is specified for the black population size-violence link. There must be a threshold effect or *critical mass* below which one would not expect violence to occur (Spilerman 1971).

Thus the larger the riot (all else equal), the larger the *population at risk of rioting* must be. The implicit assumption is that the relevant population at risk is the black population in a city, thus the connection between minimum population at risk size (the critical mass) and incidence of disorder.

A slightly different interpretation of the effect of size and the logic of a minimum population criterion comes to a similar conclusion (Granovetter 1978). The researcher argues that the probability of a riot (or other form of collective actions or innovations) is a function of the distribution of proclivities or thresholds for participation among the population at risk and the size of that population:

> Suppose that before an incident is reported as a "riot" the equilibrium number of rioters must reach some level, and that a city has, each time a crowd gathers, the same probability of reaching this particular equilibrium. (Such a probability is determined by the underlying distribution of riot thresholds from which each crowd is drawn.) If this probability is, say, 0.10 . . . , then we may think of each incident as a Bernoulli trial with probability of success (a large riot) of 0.10. It is then clear that the expected number of large riots is a function of the number of incidents, since the mean of the binomial is the number of trials multiplied by the probability of success. In a community sufficiently small that only one "trial" occurred over a specified time period the chances are 90 percent that no large riot would occur. But in a larger city where 10 incidents occurred the chance of no riot falls to $(0.90) = 0.35$, even though the distribution of thresholds is the same. (Granovetter 1978, p. 1432)

This type of logic concerning the link between size and violence is evident in the literature on diffusion of collective violence (for example, Pitcher, Hamblin, and Miller 1978). The diffusion argument reasons that collective violence is in part a function of vicarious learning, or learning via observation. However, diffusion theorists are quick to point out that learning should not be equated with behavior. Thus one may expect aggression when a threat exists *and* when potential participants have observed others successfully using aggression against those responsible for the threatening conditions. Or put differently, people will engage in collective violence when they are motivated (by threat, discontent) and when they think violence may work (observational learning). Population size influences the likelihood of observational learning as well as the potential number of individuals who may observe such behavior. Differential equations modeling the imitation and diffusion processes have been developed. In most instances the models are quite successful in predicting the distribution of various forms of collective violence, including lynching, civil disorders, machine breaking, and revolution (Pitcher et al. 1978).

The theoretical importance of population or group size is evident and appears to hold at differing levels of analysis including the interactional dynamics of the riot process (McPhail 1971), the escalation of labor conflict to labor violence (Snyder and Kelly 1976b), and the aggregate distribution of violence across time and space (Granovetter 1978; Pitcher et al. 1978; Spilerman

1970, 1971). However, it is important to note that the size or critical mass argument is limited to particular forms of collective violence, specifically those that are sufficiently collective, requiring large numbers of participants.

Summary of Theoretical Explanations of Conflict

Studies of population-violence linkages are extremely diffuse, in terms of both subject matter and measures used. The independent, or predictor variable — density or overcrowding — is fairly constant, but *what* it predicts is extremely variable, from mortality and morbidity through fertility, mental health, and sometimes including measures of interpersonal conflict or violence, such as juvenile delinquency rates, homicide, or interpersonal arguments leading to physical conflict in the home.

POPULATION AND VIOLENCE: EMPIRICAL EVIDENCE

In their review of the consequences of rapid population growth, the National Academy of Sciences (1971) cites evidence that crowding increases the incidence of infectious disease through the greater opportunity for spread of infection and that animal experiments and experience with humans confirm that social stresses due to crowding may produce physiological disturbances in the organism (National Academy of Sciences 1971). Five measures of population density have been correlated with nine indicators of pathology, including suicide rates, admissions to mental hospitals, juvenile delinquency, and adult crime. Persons per acre correlated much more strongly with the pathology measures than did any of the other component measures of density. In an analysis of data for Chicago community areas, it was found that although persons per acre was not significantly related to these rates, persons per room was.

Several studies using cities as units of analysis have attempted to examine the effects of overcrowding on murder rates. A positive relationship between a set of density variables and homicide rates was found for 171 U.S. cities in both 1950 and 1970, although the relationships were greatly reduced after social class and racial composition controls were introduced (McCarthy, Galle, and Zimmern 1975). Using a larger sample of U.S. cities (N equals 389), the researchers found overcrowding and city size to be positively correlated with homicide (Gove, Galle, McCarthy, and Hughes 1976). The relationship for overcrowding (but not city size) was reduced to insignificance after controls were introduced. Others, using an even larger set of U.S. cities, found a small relationship between density and a variety of personal and property crimes (Booth, Welch, and Johnson 1976). This study, however, used census data from 1960 and crime data from 1967, a time lag which is probably great enough to distort the relationship they found (McPherson 1973).

The effect of population density and crowding on health and social behavior was assessed among 145 economic-geographic regions in the Netherlands (Levy and Herzog 1974). After economic status and population heterogeneity were controlled for, density was positively associated with only age-adjusted death rates, and weak or inverse relations were found between crowding (persons per room) and the other measures including admissions to mental hospitals, delinquency, and divorce.

In other non-U.S. studies, eighteen urban areas in New Zealand were found to have a fairly strong positive relationship between density and psychological disorder, and weak and inconsistent relationships between crowding and several pathological behavioral outcomes (Collette and Mebb 1974). Unfortunately, no socioeconomic controls were used in this study. In a study of census tracts in Edmonton, Alberta, Canada, using controls for income and national origin, it was found that building type (the relative predominance of multiple dwelling units) had a positive association only with juvenile delinquency and public assistance rates, but the relationships of those dependent variables with density and overcrowding were not significant (Gillis 1974).

A study of Peoria, Illinois, using city blocks rather than census tracts, controlled for a large set of other variables, examined the relationship among measures of density and crime and mortality (Choldin and Roncek 1976). Compared to the effect of some of their control variables, that of density was relatively weak; however, it was significantly related to child and infant mortality and the general crime rate and more strongly related to the violent crime rate.

In sum, ecological studies of overcrowding, high population density, and various rates of pathological behavior show very mixed results. Part of the difficulty of generalizing from these studies arises from confusion among the several aspects of high population density, particularly overcrowding versus structural density (persons per acre). Our summary assessment is a cautious affirmation of a positive relationship between crowding and some rates of pathological behavior. Although social structural factors are highly intercorrelated with high levels of structural density and interpersonal crowding, there does appear to be a small but significant amount of explained variance in certain rates of behavior that can be attributed to density and/or overcrowding independently of other social structural factors.

Because individual inferences from aggregate data have inherent limits, to establish accurately relations for individuals it is necessary to utilize data obtained from individuals. Unfortunately, there are relatively few of these, but we shall briefly review from here. In these studies the outcome and control variables are typically measured for individuals, while the density measure may refer to an aggregate index (persons/area) or specifically to the individual living circumstances (persons/room).

A 1970 study found that high levels of density were associated with poor mental health (Marsella, Escudero, and Gordon 1970). Further research found that high levels of crowding were related strongly to complaints about lack of space and lack of privacy, as well as to levels of general unhappiness and amount of worrying, primarily among the poor (Mitchell 1971). A survey in Toronto looked at the effects of overcrowding (Booth 1976). Among the factors examined in relation to crowding were adult health, reproductive behavior, child health and development, family relations, community life, and political activity. It was found that the net of control variables, neighborhood crowding, generally was unrelated to their dependent variables. Subjective perception of crowding was related slightly to poor family relations. Objective and to a lesser extent subjective household crowding was related weakly to poor physical health. The conclusion was that "crowded conditions seldom have any consequence, and even when they do their effects are very modest" (Booth 1976, p. 1). This rather negative assessment has been challenged, however, on the basis of both the sample and the methods of analysis (Gove and Hughes 1980).

The other major survey study of overcrowding as it relates to various behavioral outcomes was done in the city of Chicago. In this study a sample of around two thousand households was selected in a way to minimize the collinearity between socioeconomic status, race, and crowding (Gove et al. 1979). A randomly selected adult in each household was interviewed, and information was obtained regarding their subjective experience of crowding, their objective levels of crowding, and a variety of behavioral outcomes. It was concluded that crowding does appear to have significant effects on a number of behavioral outcomes which are of relevance to the current discussion. First of all, persons per room is a good objective measure of crowding, and the effects of crowding (as measured by persons per room) tend to be largely explained or interpreted by the subjective experience of crowding, which largely involves the respondent feeling excessive social demands and a lack of privacy. The experience of crowding is (1) strongly related to poor mental health, (2) strongly related to poor social conditions in the home, (3) strongly associated with poor child care (but only moderately associated with poor interaction between parent and child), (4) significantly associated with poor social relationships outside the home where the effects of crowding are modest (Gove et al. 1979, p. 79). In this analysis, race, sex, education, income,

age, and marital status are used as control variables, and investigators conclude that crowding does have substantial effects on a number of behavioral outcomes.

A number of cautious conclusions may be drawn. First, the range
of behavioral outcomes which crowding and/or high density has been used
to account for is substantial. Second, although the findings do seem to be
somewhat ambiguous due to both some confusion in the measurement of
crowding and/or density and mixed success in controlling for other relevant
variables, high levels of density and crowding do seem to have a reasonably
consistent and significant effect on a number of behavioral outcomes. Persons who live under conditions of high density and overcrowding may be expected to have higher proneness toward aggressive behavior. Because of the
higher levels of stress or irritability experienced by those in overcrowded conditions, they may be expected to be more likely to respond in an aggressive
or violent manner to perceived threats or aggravations. This tendency toward
aggressive behavior, while apparently consistent over a number of studies, does
not seem in any case to be very large.

Rapid Change, Disorganization, and Relative Deprivation

The link between revolution and rapid growth of urban population
has been suggested:

> On the surface, the most promising source of urban revolt is clearly the slums
> and the shanty towns produced by the influx of the rural poor. In many Latin
> American cities during the 1960s from 15 to 30 percent of the population
> lived in the appalling conditions which prevailed among the favelas, ranchos,
> and barriadas. Similar slum towns were emerging in Lagos, Nairobi, and other
> African cities. The rise in urban population in most countries clearly exceeded
> the rise in urban employment. Unemployment rates in the cities frequently
> amounted to 15 or 20 percent of the labor force. Clearly, these social condi-
> tions would seem to be ripe to generate not only opposition but revolution,
> and in the 1960s American policy-makers became increasingly concerned
> about the probability of violence and insurrections sweeping the cities of many
> countries to whose economic and political development the United States was
> committed. (Huntington 1968, p. 278)

For the most part, however, the anticipated violence did not occur. Four factors have been suggested to account for the apparent conservatism and ac-
quiescence of recent urban migrants: (1) an increased standard of living due
to migration to the city; (2) rural values, attitudes of deference, and political

passivity; (3) immediate concerns of food, housing, and employment which occupy much time and generally necessitate working through existing institutions; and (4) the nature of social organization in urban slums which may, because of general feelings of distrust, preclude mobilization. However, other evidence appears to discount the link between rapid change (migration) and violence (National Advisory Commission 1968). The available evidence suggests that typical rioters are unmarried males between fifteen and twenty-four years old. Their employment status is no different from others, and they are *not* migrants (see also McPhail 1971 for a review of evidence supporting these conclusions). Evidence from the French Revolution further questions the salience of the rapid change-violence relation (for example, Rude 1959, 1964; Pickney 1964).

Finally, direct empirical tests of the rapid-change thesis cast further doubt on its usefulness as an explanation of collective violence. Although French collective violence did in fact fluctuate in the century following 1830, that fluctuation did not correspond to the pace of urban growth (Lodhi and Tilly 1973). Cross-sectional comparisons of collective violence and urban growth showed weak to nonexistent relationships. Other analyses also indicate either weak, mixed, or no support for the rapid change model (Gurr 1968; Hibbs 1973; Sofranko and Bealer 1971). One researcher concludes that "on balance (given that arguments may be rendered more or less plausible but not fully rejected), there appears to be little empirical justification for holding to rapid change *per se* as an important determinant of collective violence (Snyder 1977, p. 13). It is likely that there is something unique about the urban setting, not the actual process of urbanization, which facilitates particular forms of collective action and violence (Lodhi and Tilly 1973).

As noted earlier, population variables generally play a secondary or facilitative role in most formulations of the achievement discrepancy or relative deprivation explanations. However, it has been suggested that much of the discontent, conflicts, and violence during the 1960s was largely a product of the increase in the size of the youth population, specifically the cohort of persons aged fourteen to twenty-four. It is argued that "we would do well to consider the extent to which current discontent with the process by which children are turned into adults is attributable less to systemic flaws than to engulfment by numbers" (Ryder 1974, p. 46). The fourteen-to-twenty-four-year-old cohort increased by 52 percent from 1960 to 1970, leading to the conclusion that the decade of the 1960s was statistically unique. However, others have contested this "invasion of barbarians" argument:

> The rise [in the youth cohort] started in 1953, and though it picked up somewhat by 1960, it was still very steady through 1972. There was no sudden influx of youth in 1958 when the student movement started, or in 1965

> when any other movements began to take off. . . . Finally, the students, the
> youth, and the generation gap did not go away about 1972, but remained as
> high as ever. Yet most movements did go away. (Perrow 1979, pp. 197–98)

In short, this purely demographic explanation for the rise of social movements, conflicts, and collective violence during the 1960s appears inadequate
when the timing of these events is considered.

Available evidence also suggests that other formulations of the
achievement discrepancy perspective, which may *implicitly* include population-
related explanations, have little empirical support. A cross-national analysis
of the gap in educational attainment and in economic development (the types
of deprivation specified in earlier analyses) indicates these factors are unrelated to the frequency of violence (Hibbs 1973). The study using French time
series data finds no link between annual fluctuations in the prices of food
and manufactured goods and an index of industrial production (all assumed
to be indicators of deprivation) and the number of participants in collective
violence (Snyder and Tilly 1972). Similar null effects were found regarding
the gap between expectations and achievements and violence (Snyder and Kelly
1976b). A study using Italian time series data found no relation between the
probability of labor dispute becoming violent and indicators of sudden drops
in welfare as well as rising expectations. Other attempts to correlate indicators of absolute and relative deprivation and collective violence have been
generally unsuccessful as well. Analyses of the urban racial violence of the
1960s indicate the inadequacy of deprivation arguments for explaining intercity variation in frequency and intensity of the riots (for example, Spilerman
1970, 1971, 1976; Jiobu 1971, 1974; Ford and Moore 1970; Downes 1968, 1970;
however, see Morgan and Clark 1973 for an exception to this body of evidence).
Although earlier studies indicated some relation between deprivation and violence, more recent analyses indicate otherwise (for example, Davies 1962;
Feierabend and Feierabend 1966; Gurr 1968; and Bwy 1968). On balance, then,
it appears that conclusions about the limits of conflict and violence to the
discrepancy between expectations and achievements are difficult to make.

Resource Mobilization

Recent research aimed at evaluating the empirical importance of the
resource mobilization theories, or the relative importance of deprivation, rapid
change, and mobilization arguments, has provided a fair amount of support
for the mobilization approach. Much of the evidence supporting this approach
is indirect, often taking the form of mobilization theory's ability to account
for relationships that are inconsistent with the other approaches (Snyder 1977).

For example, since mobilization theories stress the problematic nature of the organization or mobilization of discontent, they can help explain why particular structural changes which probably would produce strain or frustration, such as during the 1930s Depression, did not then lead to widespread collective violence. Along this line of reasoning is evidence concerning the timing and location of collective violence with regard to urbanization. The relation between the number of participants in collectively violent events and urbanization (rate of change in the proportion residing in urban areas of 10,000 or more population), migration, urbanity (the proportion residing in urban areas of 10,000 or more population at a given point in time), and other factors for French departments at various time periods during the nineteenth century (1841, 1846, and 1851) has been analyzed (Lodhi and Tilly 1973). Plots of the gross long-term trends in their indicator of collective violence and urbanization indicate an overall negative relation—the greater the urban growth, the lower the level of violence. Analyses of cross-sectional variation by department at several time points indicate that, while violence and urbanization are unrelated, urbanity and violence have a strong positive relation: "Frequencies (of collective violence) are strongly shaped by the structures of the social setting in which men find themselves—rather than the rates at which those structures are changing" (Lodhi and Tilly 1973, p. 313). An analysis of the French revolution of 1830 lends further support to the importance of urbanity and the unimportance of the process of urbanization. Participation in the violence associated with the 1830 revolution was concentrated in the urban departments (Rule and Tilly 1972). However, multiple regression analysis which evaluated the relative importance of urbanization, urbanity, net migration, and other social characteristics of the departments indicated low positive effects of urbanization, low negative effects of net migration, but large positive effects of urbanity. In short, "the presence of cities, in other words, makes collective violence more likely; the disruption caused by rapid urban growth—or at least by rapid in-migration—does not" (Rule and Tilly 1972, p. 70).

Further support for the mobilization arguments is provided by related research (Snyder and Tilly 1972; Snyder 1975; Snyder and Kelly 1976b; Shorter and Tilly 1974; Britt and Galle 1972, 1974). Comparisons of the relative explanatory power of deprivation and mobilization models using French time series data indicates that the mobilization argument is clearly superior to the expectations/achievements model for explaining variation in annual fluctuation in the number of participants in collective violence (Snyder and Tilly 1972). Further research contrasting mobilization and expectations/achievements arguments with time series data on industrial conflict for France, Italy, and the United States finds clear support for the mobilization model and inconsistent support for the deprivation argument. "In all three countries prior to World War II the organizational/political model explains fluctuations in industrial conflict well. In each case union membership as a measure of labor's organizational capacity for collective action is a significant predictor of the frequency and size of industrial conflict" (Snyder 1975, p. 274). Similar results indicating the importance of size and reflecting the organizational capacity for collective action have been reported (Shorter and Tilly 1974). Regression analyses of French time series data, covering the period 1890 to 1938, show that union membership has the largest net effect on both the size and frequency of industrial conflict.

An analysis of the relation between unionization and industrial conflict notes a strong positive relation between degree of unionization and the intensity of conflict (Britt and Galle 1972, 1974). Redefining the dependent measures of industrial conflict, this study found unionization effects on various dimensions of conflict (Britt and Galle 1974). Degree of unionization has a strong positive impact on the frequency of strike activity. Degree of unionization is also related to the breadth of industrial conflict (breadth is defined as the number of workers involved in strikes relative to the number of strikes). Finally, unionization tends to shorten the length of strikes, evidenced by the negative relation between duration and degree of unionization. In general, this research indicates that, as the size of the population at risk of striking increases, strikes tend to be more frequent, broader, and shorter.

Several cross-sectional analyses of the relation between labor militancy and size of the work establishment indicate consistently strong positive correlations (for example, Cass 1957; Cleland 1955; Revans 1956; Prost 1964). A recent study investigated the effects of number of strike participants (a dimension of size conceptually distinct from size of work place or size of union but empirically related) on the probability of a strike becoming violent. The results from the analysis of Italian time series data show a steady increase in the probability of violence as a function of the number of strikers (Snyder and Kelly 1976b).

Other Aspects of Population

A considerable amount of additional research not directly linked to mobilization theory further underscores the empirical importance of size for understanding the frequency and severity of conflicts and collective violence. The critical mass or size of population at risk arguments are fundamental for explaining intercity variation in the frequency and severity of violence (Spilerman 1970, 1971, 1976; Downes 1968).

The population size argument appears to be important for understanding other forms of conflict as well. Intercity variation in the frequency (but not the intensity) of all *nonviolent* protest in a city was found to be in part a function of city size (Eisinger 1973).

Finally, a fair amount of research focusing on student protest has attempted to isolate the structural conditions leading to student uprising. One study found that the most important predictor of the frequency of student demonstrations was the size of the college or university (Scott and El-Assal 1969). Another notes: "It is not surprising that demonstrations occur more often in large universities and colleges than in small ones. Active protest requires a minimum number of committed students who are willing to take the time and risk not only to participate but also to provide leadership and to solicit the support of others" (Blau and Slaughter 1971, p. 176). Since university size is correlated with other factors which may respond to student needs, these other factors should be controlled for when correlating size and protest (Blau and Slaughter 1971; Astin and Bayer 1971). This is the strategy often used when evaluating the relation between violence and protest and city size. Most of these studies indicate that controlling for other plausible factors does not substantially alter the relation between size of institution and the frequency and seriousness of student protest (McPhail and Miller 1973).

The assembling process, also referred to as "situational mobilization," appears at least intuitively to explain the mobilization of individuals for collective actions which are primarily spontaneous (Snyder 1977). Such situational mobilization depends on available individuals at a given time and place and communication of verbal and nonverbal cues. To our knowledge the only direct empirical test of the assembling process is an analysis of a student rally following a basketball game. The evidence from that study indicates the importance of verbal and nonverbal instructions which suggest or specify the movement to a common time-space location and thus facilitate the convergence of individuals at that location. Descriptions of the racial disorders of the 1960s, as well as earlier forms of urban racial violence, provide indirect support for the assembling process (National Advisory Commission 1968; Grimshaw 1960). That is, patterns of riot participation are consistent with the major aspects of situational mobilization.

The empirical models of the diffusion of collective violence do not directly evaluate the role of population size (Pitcher et al. 1978). We noted earlier that population size plays a fundamental but, in present formulations, implicit role in the models of diffusion. Thus empirical tests of these models only reflect the plausibility of the assumptions concerning population size. Overall the differential equation models of diffusion do quite well in explaining the variance in several forms of violence (riots, coups, revolutions, guerrilla warfare) in a wide range of places and times (nineteenth and twentieth centuries). A conclusion has been formulated: "The relative successes here in terms of explained variance, replication, and generality suggest these other questions might be profitably investigated in the context of this diffusion model. The constitutive imitations processes as well as the interactive nature of conflict appear to be too powerful to ignore" (Pitcher et al. 1978, p. 34).

Although many studies have noted the empirical importance of ethnicity for accounting for variation of conflict and violence, much less attention has been directed toward sorting out the theoretical and conceptual impacts of race and ethnicity.

Sociological research invokes two interrelated impacts of race or ethnicity. First is the concept of available numbers or the population at risk. This is the most commonly invoked usage or assumption of the impact of race or ethnicity. It is also the least satisfying. The implicit meaning is that race and/or ethnicity represent (or are correlated with) many other explicit and often unmeasured factors. It is not just sheer size of a population that accounts for intergroup conflicts but rather attributes associated with race or ethnicity that also provide the motivation to become violent. The more hardships a particular group experiences, the more significant racial or ethnic characteristics become for delineating conflict groups.

SUMMARY AND CONCLUSIONS

In sorting through the several theories of conflict and violence, two have sufficient viability to warrant further examination, testing, and refinement: the *overcrowding/density model* at the individual or household level and the *resource mobilization perspective* at the more aggregate or collective level. A general assessment of these models is now presented by posing three questions: Are there consistent effects of population variables on conflict and violence in each of them? Are those effects stable across different *forms* of conflict and violence, as well as the major *dimensions* of conflict and violence (such as frequency and severity)? Are there unexplored potential linkages between the individual household level model of overcrowding and pathological behavior and the more aggregate level resource mobilization model of conflict?

Density/Overcrowding

The density/overcrowding literature is diffuse with regard to the type of behavior the model attempts to explain, and somewhat ambiguous with regard to the strength of the effects of the predictor variable (density or overcrowding). Despite these caveats there is a consistent effect of high levels of crowding in primary environments, an effect resulting from stimulus overload and lack of privacy, which in turn leads to a general proneness towards more aggressive and potentially violent behavior. Although the evidence for this assertion appears in a sufficiently large number of different studies, such that one can have confidence in its consistency, it is at the same time a fairly modest effect. The amount of variance explained by density or crowding factors, while statistically significant in quite a few studies, is in virtually none of these studies of a very large magnitude. Therefore the relationship between overcrowding and potentially aggressive behavior should be framed in terms of *proneness, motivation,* or a *general tendency* toward such behavior. While the forms of conflict or violence are somewhat variable in these studies, ranging from interpersonal fights in the household to homicides, the effect appears to be reasonably consistent across them — stress, tenseness, and irritability leading to a higher probability of reacting to a given situation (or stressor) with more aggressive behavior. Generally, sociological studies do not distinguish specifically the dimensionality of conflict. They tend to focus primarily on the frequency of conflict, though types of conflict or violence are by definition more severe than others (homicides as opposed to arguments with spouse).

Resource Mobilization

The available evidence is sufficiently broad in scope and the empirical relations are sufficiently strong to conclude that there is a consistent and important influence of population variables on conflict and violence. Not only does the resource mobilization related research indicate statistically significant and substantively important effects of population or group size, but these effects do not appear to be dependent upon particular forms of conflict or violence. Size affects violent (riots) as well as nonviolent (urban protest) collective actions. It is an important factor for various forms of violent and nonviolent conflicts. Size of the population at risk explains much of the variation in industrial violence, race riots, revolutionary violence, other forms of urban violence, and prison disorders (Wilsnack 1976). Size is also an important factor in understanding different forms of nonviolent collective action like student protest and urban protest.

Recent research indicates that the impact of population size is not dependent on particular dimensions of conflict and violence for the most part. Union size affects the frequency of labor conflict as well as the size of the conflict and its duration or intensity (Britt and Galle 1974; Shorter and Tilly 1971; Snyder 1975). All else equal, the larger the population at risk participating in industrial conflict (measured by unionization), the more frequent, more intense, larger in size, and shorter the conflict will be. The larger the strike itself, the more likely it will be violent (Snyder and Kelly 1976b). City size influenced both the frequency and severity of U.S. racial violence during the 1960s and the frequency and intensity of urban protest (Spilerman 1971, 1976; Downes 1968; Eisinger 1973; note, however, that this effect differs by race of the protest group). Further cross-sectional analysis of French departments in the years 1841, 1846, and 1851 present mixed evidence on the impact of urbanity (percent in urban areas) on several indicators of collective violence, including number of participants, number killed, number wounded, and number arrested (Lodhi and Tilly 1973). Urbanity is consistently related to number arrested, and in a later period (1851) city size has large net effects on all four indicators. The larger the city, the wider was the participation, and the greater the number wounded, killed, and arrested. However, these relationships do change, particularly in 1841 and 1846.

Finally, studies of student protest indicate that university size is the most important factor in explaining variation in the frequency and seriousness of protest, the latter measured according to whether demonstrations were concerned with only internal university issues or external issues as well (for example, Blau and Slaughter 1971).

Multilevel Linkages

The effects of population variables appear to be quite robust across different forms and dimensions of conflict and violence. Equally important, population-related effects transcend different levels of analysis from large ecological areas (cities or even nations as a whole) to smaller groups such as labor unions and universities, down to smaller ecological units like households. It is important to remember, however, that although population variables appear to influence conflict and violence in both the overcrowding and mobilization perspectives, they do so in quite different ways.

The major difference is whether the population-related factor is viewed as an underlying determinant or a facilitative factor in affecting the frequency or severity of the conflict. Density or overcrowding is conceptualized primarily as an *underlying determinant* that affects the proneness or propensity to engage in conflict and violence. On the other hand, the mobilization perspective views population size (or population at risk) as a factor that permits the mobilization of participants and thus *facilitates* conflict and violence.

Another difference between these two perspectives is in the level of conflict each addresses. The mobilization approach is oriented toward *group* conflicts on a macro level. Unions strike against management; blacks riot against police and political authority. Conversely, the overcrowding research focuses primarily on individual level propensities to engage in aggressive action and thus provides a qualitatively different perspective on the dynamics of conflict.

A comprehensive theory of conflict and violence should contain both elements of motivation (variously referred to as discontent or proneness to act aggressively) and opportunity (factors that facilitate the mobilization of resources to act collectively). Individuals probably must experience discontent as a precondition to engaging in conflict and violence, but the structural opportunities for collective action must be present as well. The two models discussed in these pages were developed independently of one another, and, as far as we know, no attempt has ever been made to conceptually link the two approaches into one general demographic perspective on conflict. It appears to us that such a linkage may be useful. Consider that the macro-level research we have reviewed (resource mobilization) discounts individual-level motivation to act. It assumes that some level of discontent is present in the population, but, relative to the organizational and demographic factors that facilitate conflict, that level of discontent is fairly invariant — or at least the distribution of discontent is sufficiently stable within populations. This relative invariance of discontent (most often indicated using *economic variables*) is in part why factors impinging on the potential to mobilize account for major spatial and temporal differences in conflict and violence.

The overcrowding research, focusing precisely on individual motivation or proneness toward aggressive action, suggests that variations in levels of overcrowding may indeed result in variations in the propensity toward aggression. This suggests a fairly unique source of discontent compared to traditional economic explanations of deprivation. Despite the relative lack of empirical success of economic models, linking the motivation to participate in conflict and violence to density and overcrowding might prove fruitful. In short, our evaluation of the current state of sociological research on population and conflict points toward the benefits future research may realize from the linkage of macro- and micro-level explanatory models.

Our discussion of the empirical and theoretical literature does not produce a clear statement regarding the policy implications for third world stability and development, but we speculate a little. The trend in the growth of cities in developing nations continues at a rapid pace. This urban growth provides the size component central to the mobilization perspective. Further urban growth in the third world results in increasing overcrowding, a pattern not found in contemporary developed societies (Carnahan, Gove, and Galle 1974). Given these conditions, we should see massive conflicts and collective violence now and in the future in many cities in the developing world. In spite of rapid growth, third world cities have been surprisingly calm. Regardless, population growth and its consequences cannot be ignored. Demographers are well aware of the socioeconomic, health, and demographic consequences of rapid population growth. It is becoming increasingly clear that population factors are also destabilizing forces. We do not paint a pessimistic picture, but we think that the available evidence suggests that population policies should be developed in the awareness of all the consequences of growth, one of which is civil unrest.

NOTES

1. By "ecological fallacy" we refer to the potential errors that may come about by inferring individual relationships on the basis of aggregate level correlations, which was first pointed out by Robinson (1950). One of the examples used by Robinson was the negative correlation (minus 0.526) across states between percent foreign born in the state and the percent of the population illiterate, while at the individual level the relationship between nativity and literacy was in the opposite (positive) direction.

2. This is not, of course, to deny that the initial costs of organizing the workers into unions may have been quite high (see, for example, Brooks 1971). Once, however, the workers have been organized into unions, the costs of mobilizing these workers are substantially reduced.

REFERENCES

Alexander, B. F., and E. M. Roth. "The Effects of Acute Crowding on Aggressive Behavior of Japanese Monkeys." *Behavior* 39 (1971): 73–90.

Altman, I. *The Environment and Social Behavior.* Monterey, Ca.: Brooks/Cole, 1975.

Anderson, E. N. "Some Chinese Methods for Dealing with Crowding." *Urban Anthropology* 1 (1972): 141–50.

Archer, J. "Effects of Population Density on Behavior in Rodents." In *Social Behavior in Birds and Mammals,* edited by J. H. Crook. New York: Academic, 1970.

Astin, A. W., and A. E. Bayer. "Antecedents and Consequences of Disruptive Campus Protests." *Measurement and Evaluation in Guidance* 4 (1971): 18–30.

Berkowitz, L. *Aggression: A Social-Psychological Analysis.* New York: McGraw-Hill, 1962.

Blau, P., and E. Slaughter. "Institutional Conditions and Student Demonstrations." *Social Problems* 18 (1971): 475–87.

Booth, A. *Urban Crowding and Its Consequences.* New York: Praeger, 1976.

———, S. Welch, and D. R. Johnson. "Crowding and Urban Crime Rates." *Urban Affairs Quarterly* 2 (1976): 291–307.

Britt, D., and O. Galle. "Structural Antecedents of the Shape of Strikes." *American Sociological Review* 39 (1974): 642–51.

_____. "Industrial Conflict and Unionization." *American Sociological Review* 37 (1972): 46–57.

Brooks, T. R. *Toil and Trouble: A History of American Labor.* New York: Dell, 1971.

Bwy, D. "Political Instability in Latin America: The Cross-Cultural Test of a Causal Model." *Latin American Research Review* 3 (1968): 17–66.

Calhoun, J. B. "Population Density and Social Pathology." *Scientific American* 206 (1962): 139–48.

Carnahan, D. L., W. Gove, and O. Galle. "Urbanization, Population Density, and Overcrowding." *Social Forces* 53 (1974): 62–72.

Cass, M. "The Relationship of Size of Firm and Strike Activity." *Monthly Labor Review* 80 (1957): 1330–34.

Choldin, H., and D. Roncek. "Density, Population Potential, and Pathology: A Block Level Analysis." *Public Data Use* 4 (1976): 19–30.

Christian, J. J. "Phenomena Associated with Population Density." *Proceedings of the National Academy of Science* 47 (1961): 428.

Cleland, S. *The Influence of Plant Size on Industrial Relations.* Princeton, N.J.: Princeton University Press, 1955.

Collette, J., and S. Webb. "Urban Density, Crowding, and Stress Reactions." Paper presented at the meeting of the Pacific Sociological Association, San Jose, Ca., 1974.

Davies, J. C. "The J-Curve of Rising and Declining Satisfactions as a Cause of Some Great Revolutions and a Contained Rebellion." In *Violence in America: Historical and Comparative Perspectives,* edited by H. D. Graham and T. R. Gurr. New York: Signet, 1969, pp. 671–709.

_____. "Toward a Theory of Revolution." *American Sociological Review* 27 (1962): 5–19.

Davis, K. "The Urbanization of the Human Population." *Scientific American* 213 (1965): 41–53.

Deevey, E. S. "The Hare and the Haruspex: A Cautionary Tale." *The Yale Review* 49 (1960): 161–79.

Desor, J. A. "Toward a Psychological Theory of Crowding." *Journal of Personality and Social Psychology* 21 (1972): 79–83.

Dollard, J., L. Doob, N. E. Miller, O. H. Mowrer, and R. R. Sears. *Frustration and Aggression.* New Haven, Ct.: Yale University Press, 1939.

Downes, B. T. "A Critical Re-examination of the Social and Political Characteristics of Riot Cities." *Social Science Quarterly* 51 (1970): 349–60.

_____. "Social and Political Characteristics of Riot Cities, a Comparative Study." *Social Science Quarterly* 49 (1968): 504–20.

118

Duncan, O. D. "Path Analysis: Sociological Examples." *American Journal of Sociology* 72 (1966): 1–16.

Durkheim, E. *Suicide.* New York: Free Press, 1951.

Eisenstadt, S. N. *Modernization: Protest and Change.* Engelwood Cliffs, N.J.: Prentice-Hall, 1966.

Eisinger, P. K. "The Conditions of Protest Behavior in American Cities." *American Political Science Review* 67 (1973): 11–28.

Feagin, J. R., and H. Hahn. *Ghetto Revolts: The Politics of Violence in American Cities.* New York: Macmillan, 1973.

Feierabend, I. K., and R. L. Feierabend. "Aggressive Behavior Within Policies, 1948–1962: A Cross-National Study." *Journal of Conflict Resolution* 10 (1966): 249–71.

Feierabend, I. K., R. L. Feierabend, and B. A. Nesvold. "Social Change and Political Violence: Cross-National Patterns." In *Violence in America: Historical and Comparative Perspectives,* edited by H. D. Graham and T. R. Gurr. New York: Signet, 1969, pp. 606–67.

Fireman, B. and W. A. Gamson. "Utilitarian Logic in the Resource Mobilization Perspective." In *The Dynamics of Social Movements,* edited by M. Zald and J. McCarthy. Cambridge, Ma.: Winthrop, 1979, pp. 8–44.

Ford, W. F., and J. H. Moore. "Additional Evidence of the Social Characteristics of Riot Cities." *Social Science Quarterly* 51 (1970): 339–48.

Galle, O., and W. Gove. "Overcrowding, Isolation, and Human Behavior: Exploring the Extremes in Population Distribution." In *Social Demography,* edited by Karl Tauber and James Sweet. New York: Academic, 1978, pp. 95–132.

Galle, W., W. Gove, and J. McPherson. "Population Density and Pathology: What are the Relationships for Man?" *Science* 176 (1972): 23–30.

Gamson, W. A. *The Strategy of Social Protest.* Homewood, Ill.: Dorsey, 1975.

———. *Power and Discontent.* Homewood, Ill.: Dorsey, 1968.

Gillis, A. R. "Population Density and Social Pathology: The Case of Building Type, Social Allowance, and Juvenile Delinquency." *Social Forces* 53 (1974): 306–14.

Gove, W., and M. Hughes. "The Effects of Crowding Found in the Toronto Study: Some Methodological and Empirical Questions." *American Sociological Review* 45 (1980): 864–70.

Gove, W., M. Hughes, and O. R. Galle. "Overcrowding in the Home: An Empirical Investigation of its Possible Consequences." *American Sociological Review* 44 (1979): 59–80.

Gove, W., O. Galle, J. McCarthy, and M. Hughes. "Living Circumstances and Social Pathology: The Effect of Population Density, Overcrowding, and Isolation on Suicide, Homicide, and Alcoholism." Unpublished paper.

Granovetter, M. "Threshold Models of Collective Behavior." *American Journal of Sociology* 83 (1978): 1420–43.

Grimshaw, A. D. "Urban Racial Violence in the United States: Changing Ecological Considerations." *American Journal of Sociology* 66 (1960): 109-19.

Guest, A. M." Families and Housing in Cities." Doctoral dissertation, University of Wisconsin, Madison, 1970.

_____. "Patterns of Family Location." *Demography* 9 (1972): 159-71.

Gurr, T. R. *Why Men Rebel.* Princeton: Princeton University Press, 1970.

_____. "A Comparative Study of Civil Strife." In *Violence In America: Historical and Comparative Perspectives,* edited by H. D. Graham and T. R. Gurr. New York: Signet, 1969, pp. 544-605.

_____. "A Causal Model of Civil Strife: A Comparative Analysis Using New Indices." *American Political Science Review* 62 (1968): 1104-24.

Hannan, M. *Aggregation and Disaggregation in Sociology.* Lexington, Ma.: Lexington Books, 1971.

Hauser, P. M., and O. D. Duncan. *The Study of Population.* Chicago: University of Chicago Press, 1959.

Hibbs, D. A., Jr. *Mass Political Violence: A Cross-National Causal Analysis.* New York: Wiley, 1973.

Huntington, S. P. *Political Order in Changing Societies.* New Haven, Ct.: Yale University Press, 1968.

Janowitz, M. "Patterns of Collective Racial Violence." In *Violence in America: Historical and Comparative Perspectives,* edited by Hugh Graham and Ted Robert Gurr. New York: Signet, 1969, pp. 412-44.

Jenkins, J. C., and C. Perrow. "Insurgency of the Powerless: Farm Workers, Movements (1964-1972)." *American Sociological Review* 42 (1977): 249-68.

Jiobu, R. M. "City Characteristics and Racial Violence." *Social Science Quarterly* 55 (1974): 52-64.

_____. "City Characteristics, Differential Stratification, and the Occurrence of Interracial Violence." *Social Science Quarterly* 52 (1971): 508-20.

Johnson, C. *Revolutionary Change.* Boston: Little, Brown, 1966.

Keeley, K. "Prenatal Influence on Behavior of Offspring of Crowded Mice." *Science* 135 (1962): 44.

Kelly, W., and D. Snyder. "Racial Violence and Socioeconomic Changes among Blacks in the United States." *Social Forces* 58 (1980): 739-60.

Kerr, C., J. T. Dunlop, F. H. Harbison, and C. A. Myers. *Industrialism and Industrial Man.* Cambridge, Ma.: Harvard University Press, 1960.

Kirkham, J. F., S. Levy, and W. Crotty. *Assassination and Political Violence.* Washington, D. C.: USGPO, 1970.

Kornhauser, W. *The Politics of Mass Society.* Glencoe, Ill.: Free Press, 1959.

Levy, L., and A. Herzog. "Effects of Population Density and Crowding on Health and Social Adaptation in the Netherlands." *Journal of Health and Social Behavior* 15 (1974): 228-40.

Lodhi, A. Q., and C. Tilly. "Urbanization, Crime, and Collective Violence in 19th-Century France." *American Journal of Sociology* 79 (1973): 296–318.

McCarthy, J., O. Galle, and W. Zimmern. "Population Density, Social Structure, and Interpersonal Violence: An Intermetropolitan Test of Competing Models." *American Behavioral Scientist* (1975): 771–91.

McPhail, C. "Civil Disorder Participation: A Critical Examination of Recent Research." *American Sociological Review* 36 (1971): 1058–73.

_____, and D. L. Miller. "The Assembling Process: A Theoretical and Empirical Examination." *American Sociological Review* 38 (1973): 721–35.

McPherson, J. M. "A Question of Causality: A Study in the Application of Regression Techniques to Sociological Analysis." Doctoral dissertation, Vanderbilt University, 1973.

Marsella, A., M. Escudero, and P. Gordon. "The Effects of Dwelling Density on Mental Disorders in Filipino Men." *Journal of Health and Social Behavior* 11 (1970): 288–94.

Milgram, S. "The Experience of Living in Cities." *Science* 167 (1970): 1461–68.

Miller, A. H., L. H. Bolce, and M. Halligan. "The J-Curve Theory and the Black Urban Riots: An Empirical Test of Progressive Relative Deprivation Theory Using Both Objective and Perceptual Indicators." *American Political Science Review* 71 (1977): 964–82.

Mitchell, R. "Some Social Implications of High Density." *American Sociological Review* 36 (1971): 18–29.

Morgan, W. R., and T. N. Clark. "The Causes of Racial Disorders: a Grievance-Level Explanation." *American Sociological Review* 38 (1973): 611–24.

National Academy of Sciences. *Rapid Population Growth.* Baltimore: Johns Hopkins University Press, 1971.

National Advisory Commission on Civil Disorders. *Report.* New York: Bantam, 1968.

Oberschall, A. "Protracted Conflict." In *The Dynamics of Social Movements,* edited by M. N. Zald and J. D. McCarthy. Cambridge, Ma.: Winthrop, 1979.

_____. *Social Conflict and Social Movements.* Englewood Cliffs, N.J.: Prentice-Hall, 1973.

Perrins, C. M. "Population Fluctuations and Clutch Size in the Great Tit." *Journal of Animal Ecology* 34 (1965): 601–47.

Perrow, C. "The Sixties Observed." In *The Dynamics of Social Movements,* edited by M. N. Zald and J. D. McCarthy. Cambridge, Ma.: Winthrop, 1979.

Pinkney, D. "The Crowd in the French Revolution of 1830." *American Historical Review* 70 (1964): 1–17.

Pitcher, B. C., R. L. Hamblin, and J. L. L. Miller. "The Diffusion of Collective Violence." *American Sociological Review* 43 (1978): 23–35.

Prost, A. "La C. G. T. a l'Epoque du Front Populaire: Essai de Description Numerique, 1934–1939." Paris: Colin, 1964.

Rapoport, A. "Some Perspectives on Human Use and Organization of Space." Paper presented at Australian Association of Social Anthropologists, Melbourne, 1972.

Revans, R. W. "Industrial Morale and Size of Unit." *Political Quarterly* 27 (1956): 303–11.

Robinson, W. S. "Ecological Correlations and the Behavior of Individuals." *American Sociological Review* 15 (1950): 351–57.

Rude, G. F. *The Crowd in History.* New York: Wiley, 1964.

_____. *The Crowd in the French Revolution.* New York: Wiley, 1959.

Rule, J., and C. Tilly. "1830 and the Unnatural History of Revolution." *Journal of Social Issues* 28 (1972): 49–76.

Ryder, N. In *Youth: Transition to Adulthood,* edited by J. Coleman et al. Chicago: University of Chicago Press, 1974.

Schmidt, D. E. "Crowding and the Urban Environments: An Integration of Theory and Research." In *Residential Crowding and Design,* edited by J. Aiello and A. Baum. New York: Plenum, 1979.

Schmitt, R. "Density, Health, and Social Disorganization." *Journal of the American Institute of Planners,* 32 (1966): 37–40.

Scott, J. W., and M. El-Assal. "Multiuniversity, University Size, University Quality, and Student Protest: An Empirical Study." *American Sociological Review* 34 (1969): 709.

Shorter, E. L., and C. Tilly. *Strikes in France, 1830 to 1968.* Cambridge: Cambridge University Press, 1974.

Smelser, N. J. *Theory of Collective Behavior.* New York: Free Press, 1963.

Snyder, D. "Collective Violence: A Research Agenda and Some Strategic Considerations." *Journal of Conflict Resolution* 22 (1978): 499–534.

_____. "Collective Violence: A Research Agenda and Some Strategic Considerations." Unpublished manuscript. Department of Sociology, Indiana University, Bloomington, 1977.

_____. "Institutional Setting and Industrial Conflict: Comparative Analyses of France, Italy, and the United States." *American Sociological Review* 40 (1975): 259–78.

Snyder, D., and W. R. Kelly. "Strategies for Investigating Violence and Social Change: Illustrations from Analyses of Racial Disorders and Implications for Mobilization Research." In *The Dynamics of Social Movements,* edited by M. N. Zald and J. D. McCarthy. Cambridge, Ma.: Winthrop, 1979, pp. 212–37.

_____. "Racial Violence and Social Change: U.S. Cities, 1960–75." National Institutes of Mental Health Grant no. MH29817-01, 1976a.

_____. "Industrial Violence in Italy, 1878–1903." *American Journal of Sociology* 82 (1976b): 131–62.

Snyder, D., and C. Tilly. "Hardship and Collective Violence in France, 1830 to 1960." *American Sociological Review* 37 (1972): 520–32.

Sofranko, A. J., and R. C. Bealer. "Modernization Balance, Imbalance, and Domestic Instability." *Economic Development and Cultural Change* 20 (1971): 52–72.

Spilerman, S. "Structural Characteristics of Cities and the Severity of Racial Disorders." *American Sociological Review* 41 (1976): 771–92.

_____. "The Causes of Racial Disturbances: Tests of an Explanation." *American Sociological Review* 36 (1971): 427–42.

_____. "The Causes of Racial Disturbances: A Comparison of Alternative Explanations." *American Sociological Review* 35 (1970): 627–49.

Stokols, D. "A Typology of Crowding Experiences." In *Human Response to Crowding,* edited by Baum and Y. Epstein. Hillsdale, N.J.: Erlbaum, 1978.

_____. "The Experience of Crowding in Primary and Secondary Environments." *Environment and Behavior* 8 (1976): 49–86.

Thiessen, D. D., and D. A. Rodgers. "Population Density and Endocrine Function." *Psychological Bulletin* 58 (1961): 441–51.

Tilly, C. *From Mobilization to Revolution.* Reading, Ma.: Addison-Wesley, 1978.

_____. "Revolutions and Collective Violence." In *Handbook of Political Science,* vol. 3, edited by F. I. Greenstein and N. W. Polsby. Reading, Ma.: Addison-Wesley, 1975.

_____. "From Mobilization to Political Conflict." Unpublished paper. Department of Sociology, University of Michigan, Ann Arbor, 1970.

_____. "Collective Violence in European Perspective." In *Violence in America: Historical and Comparative Perspectives,* edited by H. D. Graham and T. R. Gurr. New York: Signet, 1969, pp. 4–42.

Wanderer, J. J. "1967 Riots: A Test of the Congruity of Events." *Social Problems* 16 (1968): 193–98.

Wilsnack, R. W. "Explaining Collective Violence in Prisons: Problems and Possibilities." In *Prison Violence,* edited by A. Cohen, G. Cole, and R. Bailey. Lexington, Ma.: Lexington Books, 1976.

Wohlwill, J. F. "Human Adaptation to Levels of Environmental Stimulation." *Human Ecology* 2 (1974): 127–47.

5

Economic Dimensions of Conflict

JOHN R. HARRIS AND VIJAYA SAMARAWEERA

CONFLICT AND COMPETITION OVER SCARCE RESOURCES

THE CRUDEST COMMON MODEL of population and conflict posits that, as population increases, resources (especially but not exclusively land) become relatively scarce giving rise to competition among individuals and groups. With increasing population, competition intensifies and eventually leads to conflict and violence. Such conflict arises within local groups in the social context of families, clans, or other levels of primary social organization. Within national states such conflict takes place in the political context and in extreme cases leads to regionally based civil wars. At the international level domestic scarcity leads to foreign adventurism in search of *lebensraum*, resulting in war. Thus civil wars, regional disturbances, or international conflicts are attributed at least in part to population pressures.

In this chapter we will argue that such a model is misleadingly simple. While there are conditions in which population growth leads to violence, there are other possible outcomes. Each of the steps intervening between population pressure and conflict needs to be examined in some detail: the relationship between population growth and scarcity, the forms of competition that arise from scarcity, conditions under which competition can be considered conflict, and conditions under which conflict erupts into violence. Our argument is that competition and conflict may arise at local levels, at regional levels within nation states, and at international levels between sovereign states. A range of institutions exists at each level which has in part the purpose of mediating conflict to avert violence. Therefore, to understand the link between population change and violence we must examine the mediating institutions at each of these levels.

Resource Issues: Range and Scope

In examining the relationships between population, resources, scarcity, and conflict, the intuitive attraction of simple lineal explanations must be avoided, for these relations are played out in specific and often complex situations. Population variables constitute but one category — albeit a crucial category — of the host of factors that bear upon stability or change in resource availability and use. When population does influence resources in society, the relationship is often multifaceted: demographic factors may appear as causes, correlates, consequences, or even as symptoms of the dynamics of resource use.

In this chapter we recognize the critical importance of population variables for understanding resource use. Furthermore we recognize the legitimacy of positing causal linkages between these demographic factors and competition and conflict over resources. However, we do argue against the general applicability of any overall model that relates these variables without considering the varied institutional frameworks through which these economic relationships are channelled.

The population variables to focus on in the population/resources/ conflict calculus are amply clear, and their definitions are now firmly established by convention in the literature: the size, composition, and distribution of population and changes in each of these. However, since other demographic terminology — for instance, the term "optimum population" — is not equally clear, definitions will be offered in context as the discussion proceeds.[1]

What is meant by resources is a more complex question. Much of the economic writings devoted to population and its economic dimensions draws attention to only three referent variables in defining the resources structure of societies: land, labor, and capital. Scarcity is defined in terms of relative endowments of these factors so that, as population increases relative to land, land becomes scarce relative to labor or labor becomes plentiful relative to land. This simplification of resource endowments has allowed the formulation of rigorous and tractable models of economic growth. However, such a taxonomy is clearly inadequate to accommodate the complexity of economic development and the interaction between population and resource use (see, for example, Kuznets 1966).

There is a strong bias in the literature in favor of referents that are meaningful in strict economic terms. These include variables such as natural resources, "human capital," and technology. The principal criteria for defining and including a resource variable is the degree to which it can be conceived as entering a production function — to the extent that it can be considered an input into a process for the production of goods or services.

To be sure, the nonmaterial variables have not been entirely ignored in discussions on population and resource use: perhaps the most notable examples are those writings that highlight "social and psychic space" rather than physical resources as the determinants of strains and stresses in the demographic context (see, for example, Day and Day 1964 and Hall 1966). However, these writings are flawed by an artificial dichotomy between physical and nonphysical resources which usually differentiates and ranks nonphysical resources as the most potent constraint on population.[2] This chapter takes the view that whatever is perceived as a resource by the society concerned should be brought within the ambit of discussion.

Scarcity in economic terms merely indicates that more of a particular resource is desired than exists. Scarcity is determined by both the numbers of people relative to the asset and the technology that enables individuals to employ such assets. Technological changes that increase agricultural yield are commonly referred to as land augmenting because of their ability to decrease relative land scarcity.

Competition arises from situations of scarcity since several individuals or groups simultaneously establish claims on the limited resources available. Inconsistent competing claims on resources give rise to conflict, which in the absence of other mediating institutions results in the establishment and maintenance of claims through superior force.

In fact in most human societies institutions have been developed for mediating conflicting claims and enforcing the resultant allocations of resources according to rules that are generally accepted to be fair or legitimate. The nature of the institutions, the rules that are accepted, and the means of enforcement vary widely among societies, but the function of mediating competing claims to avert violent conflict in face of scarcity is virtually universal. Therefore the emergence of violence is a sign of institutional failure.[3]

Underlying and animating the discussion which is to follow on the competition and conflict that arise out of the interaction of population with resources lies the view that resources, renewable and nonrenewable or deteriorating and nondeteriorating, are finite. The argument that resources are finite is not meant to foreclose developments in technology and human ingenuity that some commentators firmly believe will enable mankind to rise above the physical limitations imposed upon numbers.[4] We do not adopt the simplistic Malthusian proposition that population increase necessarily outruns the means of subsistence available. However, conflict over resources can be as intense in static or dwindling as in growing populations.

Historically, conditions arise when resources in a society are defined as finite, and therefore scarcity exists. If resources were considered to be infinite, there would be no scarcity and hence no competition — casual observation of extant societies suggests that such a state of affairs is not prevalent. We argue that the critical elements in the determination of scarcity are the impressions and assessments of the population concerned. The perceived condition may not necessarily portray the empirical situation. Of course, empirical realities play a critical role in shaping perceptions along with other variables such as ideological and political forces.[5] In viewing competition and conflict over resources explicitly within the realm of social relations, the subjective definition of the situation as well as the underlying realities must be identified.

The voluminous literature on the economic implications of population dynamics will reveal that the relationship between scarcity and conflict is usually presented as a given, as an inevitable and logical outcome of the operative dynamics. This chapter explores the dimensions in which population dynamics (taken to mean changes in the three variables of size, composition, and distribution of population) create and change conditions of scarcity in particular contexts and, in turn, how specific institutions mediate the responses on the part of populations to these changes. The nature and form of conflicts that arise out of these settings will be explored as well.

The Role of Institutionalized Settings
as Mediators between Population and Conflict

Virtually every institution in society, whether social, cultural, economic, or political, has the potential of functioning as a mediator of conflict. As such, one must look not only at institutions explicitly designed to resolve overt conflict but also at those that limit the emergence of conflict by molding perceptions and legitimating certain claims. Cultural institutions including religion are powerful in establishing who is entitled to make what kind of claims on scarce resources and what kind of claim-making behavior is acceptable.

Competition and conflict are usually generated within the "rules of the game" — but how the rules are set and enforced are the most important determinants of the games that are played out. An analogy can be drawn from the anthropological literature on dispute resolution in society: the insistence of some early anthropologists working in non-Western settings that only formally constituted adjudicative bodies should be defined as pertinent in dispute resolution eventually proved inadequate. Dispute resolution is very much a part of social control in society, something that cannot be conveniently packaged and legitimized in the form of particular explicit institutions only (see Abel 1973).

It is as important to give attention to implicit nonformal mechanisms in conflict mediation as to those institutions formally constituted as mediators. The ultimate workings of nonformal institutions are as crucial in explaining the relationship between population and conflict as changes in, say, immigration policies of states responding to internal population dynamics.

Institutions require a broad interpretation if their full potential as conflict mediators is to be realized. Such institutional variety undercuts the different conviction displayed by the early literature on population — that institutions in society respond to changes in population in an inevitable and unilinear fashion. This was no doubt a Malthusian legacy, for the laws he propounded on the relationship between "the power of population" and "the power in the earth to produce subsistence" were distinguished by strict immutability and mathematical regularity. The issues that dominated the history of demography as a discipline — the controversy as to whether mortality or fertility was the key determinant in preindustrial Europe's population changes (see Ohlin 1970) — reflect a propensity to seek predictable responses from institutions to population dynamics or, to put it differently, to establish universal unilinear relationships. Demographic responses to changes in resource structures vary remarkably, as do the responses of resource dynamics to changes in population variables. To exemplify, it is now commonplace to echo and re-echo Schumpeter's (1947) seminal suggestion that the economy would respond to population growth in fashions varying from stagnation to innovation.

The general framework we will adopt in this chapter is applicable to industrialized as well as developing countries. While our examples are often drawn from the developing countries, parallel cases could be found in industrialized nations. Of course, patterns of scarcity, forms of conflict, and institutionalized response vary depending on the degree and kind of development.

We shall also stress the role of social institutions as conflict mediators at the local level. However, it is arguable that at least in Western countries traditional social networks, extended families, and organized religion play a less significant role. Finally, the discussion of international conflict implicitly juxtaposes the interests of the developing and the more developed countries — a subject which has provoked an inconclusive debate over a "new international economic order."

Differentiation among Local, National, and International Levels

The scale and forms through which population dynamics change scarcity, the degree to which competition over resources gives rise to conflict, and the institutions that mediate conflict differ significantly at different levels and in different sectors of societies. Macro-level investigations to the exclusion of micro-level studies reveal only an incomplete picture of the interrelations between population and resources.

Analyses of population dynamics are most often conducted at the national level, and many of the United Nation's projections are at a multinational regional level. In cases such as Africa, the projections are given for the continent as a whole. Apart from obvious problems of data reliability at these levels of aggregation,[6] crude densities do not reflect the actual experience of populations with density. These figures combine the inhabited (and habitable) areas with uninhabitable regions in their calculations. When the data are adjusted to compensate for the distortions, a different and certainly more valid picture emerges, and the differential experience of the countries and regions that fall within the statistical unit becomes clear.[7] Population estimates can also be divided between rural and urban areas. In particular, differential fertility behavior is found in many countries between two sectors. This disaggregated information is then useful in projecting population dynamics and in understanding the determinants of such differential behavior.

While at one stage natural resources were given great weight, especially in delineating population distribution by means of simple correlations between population and climatic/vegetation regions, it is now recognized that physical resources alone cannot account for distributional patterns.[8] While in purely agricultural or extractive economies resources are the principal determinants of real incomes, in modernizing economies much of the true scarcity is in relation to jobs and prized services (such as education and housing) in the modern sector. Population changes interact with resource availabilities (broadly defined) in specific ways in particular subregions. Population increases make land, resources, modern sector jobs, and housing more scarce and thereby intensify competition and potential conflict, but the impact of such competition will vary substantially among subregions of a country and in different economic and social sectors.

The drama of competition and conflict is played out in specific locations, markets, and polities, with different players, rules, and scripts giving rise to different outcomes. We must now delineate the specific functions of conflict mediation at local, national, and international levels. At this point we examine those institutions that function instead of or along with markets at each of the levels.

Rules governing competition and mechanisms for conflict resolution at the local level are provided by basic social institutions such as families, clans, or ethnic ties. The basis of allocations at this level has been described as reciprocity with the rules for economic transactions reflecting the social order in which such transactions are embedded (see particularly Polyani 1957, Chapter 13).

At the national level the apparatus of the modern nation state has responsibility for setting the basic rules under which access to resources is allowed, the judicial systems for enforcing those rules, and an intrusive political and administrative structure that directly and indirectly mediates conflict over scarcity. In most states the principal institutions are political, with the legitimate authority having some monopoly on the exercise of force. The basis of most of the transactions in these systems has been referred to as redistributive — taxes and tribute are contributed to the sovereign state, and services and privileges are in turn distributed to individuals on the basis of political criteria.

Institutions for conflict mediation at the international level are extremely weak. While there is considerable voluntary adherence to treaties and generally understood rules of behavior, claims to resources continue to be made on the basis of force or threat of force. Despite the growth of multinational bodies including the United Nations and various regional organization such as the OAS, OEDC, OAU, and ASEAN, problems of legitimacy abound. Therefore it is no accident that the most dangerous arena in which conflict erupts into violence is the international one. While violence at communal levels and civil wars are hardly rare, the mechanism of the nation state makes these forms more readily contained.

A SIMPLE ECONOMIC MODEL OF SCARCITY AND COMPETITION

The model of economics that permeates the literature from the time of Adam Smith through classical writers such as Ricardo, Malthus, Marx, and J. S. Mill and continues as the basic paradigm through the present shows the relationships between resources and the production of goods and services. Specifically, land, labor, and capital can be combined in production; the total amount of production will be determined by the amount and quality of resources employed and the efficiency with which they are combined. It is also posited that diminishing returns will apply as any one factor is increased relative to all others. The simple arithmetic of this hypothesis yields the further implication that, although in the former case total output will continue to rise as labor is added, the average output per *person* will decline.

Therefore within given technology, if population increases and land remains fixed, output per person will decline. This fundamental dynamic presented by Smith and Ricardo is wholly adopted also by Malthus and Marx. Within this framework it is possible that additional factors of production can be supplied that will further increase output. Capital inputs are the most obvious addition — capital may be provided for augmenting land supplies by clearing forests, draining swamps, terracing, and so forth, or may also take the form of machinery and implements that increase the power of labor to till the soil. But still, if land in fact is supplied in a finite amount, the addition of capital will also suffer from diminishing returns as land becomes more scarce, although the point will be reached with higher output than would have been the case in absence of the capital inputs. Similarly, if additional capital is put in place with labor not increasing, more output will be produced, the

Responses to Changing Scarcities

While the market can be a powerful adjusting force in avoiding confrontations and conflict, its success is contingent upon all actors passively responding to impersonal forces and accepting outcomes as inevitable. The basic mechanism of changing scarcities being reflected in factor earnings and giving rise to equilibrating changes in factor supplies does not always work. When it does, the results may not be acceptable to many.

Most modern societies have set as goals improved living standards for the majority of their population. If population adjusts according to Malthusian principles, any attempt to raise living standards will be undone by population growth. In the process wages will be lowered back to bare subsistence levels. If population does not respond in this way and instead stabilizes or at least grows more slowly than capital formation, and if technology improves so that labor becomes relatively more scarce, improved living standards will be achievable. But if earnings are declining, responses other than passive acceptance with eventual biological adjustment are possible.

Most economies have not allowed capital formation to be determined only by the response of capitalists to incentives. Various communal and public institutions play crucial roles in determining levels of savings, their allocation to investments in specific sectors, and the returns from investment that flow to private owners. All types of economies approach the question of savings, investment, and returns to savings very differently, and there are huge degrees of variation among countries within each of these categories. The market model does not really ask how claims are established to assets, particularly land and natural resources. Rather it is assumed that some distribution of endowments has been made and accepted; thus transactors passively accept and respond to market signals, *given* the patterns of asset ownership that have been bequeathed from the past.

Competition never becomes conflict in such an idealized world. Changing patterns of scarcity cause some to gain and others to lose, but all accept this outcome as the workings of a fair game and have incentives to do better next time—to work harder, to acquire scarce resources by saving and investing in physical assets and skills. It is the claim of free marketers that left to itself the market will take care of scarcity as well as is possible and that all other outcomes arising from market interference would be worse. Without accepting the full dogma, it is still useful to recognize market forces as being impersonal, relatively automatic, and thereby reducing overt conflict.

Markets allocate only within a limited framework in which claims to ownership or use of scarce resources are given. The contribution of Marx was to point out specific mechanisms by which acceptance of preexisting property rights would change. Marx believed that workers would eventually seize all property and labor would be rewarded with its average rather than its marginal product. Exploitation of workers through payments to owners of other factors would thereby cease. This approach highlights the fact that claims on scarce resources are socially determined and not a law of nature.

Trade and Resource Mobility

While the previous discussion has not defined the geographic unit within which factor supplies and scarcity are to be measured, the appropriate units are those that have resources mobile within and immobile between them. Then, and only then, is it legitimate to aggregate the units of labor, capital, and land as inputs into production processes and to describe the total amounts available. If resources are mobile between units, then the endowment within any unit is poorly defined; while if they are immobile within the unit, their productive potential depends crucially on their distribution within that unit.

Take the simplest idealized economy in which family units have preexisting allocations of land and in which there is no market for either land or labor. Then, each family will use its own labor and capital resources along with its land to produce output. In such circumstances families will be richer or poorer depending on their endowments of labor and capital relative to their land. For example, if markets were allowed to develop in labor, large families would offer some of their labor to the larger landowners who would find it profitable to hire this labor. Factor flows would continue in this way until each unit of labor was combined with the same amount of land in all holdings — that is, the factor combinations for production would be the same in all farm sizes. The returns to *labor* would be the same on all farms, and the returns per acre of land owned would also be the same. However, members of some families would be richer than others because of their larger land holdings.

The point of this example is that market forces, if allowed to function, will lead to movements of factors from situations of scarcity to situations of plenty until the levels of scarcity are equalized. This can also be shown to lead to the greatest possible output and to benefit all transactors. The families with small amounts of land increase their living standards by being able to sell some of their labor; the large landowners are better off by being able to buy labor to work on their land. But note that the definitions of "better off" are all relative to the initial distribution of land which was posited to be unequal. With a different distribution of land, the outcome would be different (see Eberstadt 1979).

Likewise at the national level there will be incentives for abundant factors to move to regions where the same factor is relatively more scarce. Population will flow from the land-scarce regions to the land-plentiful ones, from the capital-scarce to the capital-rich regions. Similarly, there may be capital flows from the capital-rich to the capital-scarce regions in search of higher returns. Such movements will tend to equalize earnings of similar factors, but note that in each case the inflow of factors, by reducing their scarcity, will reduce the earnings owners of those factors had been enjoying. Thus poor immigrants will drive down the wages of workers in the richer regions, and capital inflows will drive down the returns capitalists were enjoying in the poor regions.

Thus the stage is set for factor mobility to lead to conflict. When the migrant workers or capitalists are "foreign," the rules of market allocations are likely to come under pressure, and social and political organizations will arise to protect the owners of scarce resources. Thus workers in the rich areas will use political and social pressures to exclude the migrants, while capitalists in the poor areas will organize to prevent free capital inflow. The arena for conflict becomes social and political, and the outcomes will not be solely those dictated by impersonal market forces. The specific outcomes, and acceptance of them, will depend crucially on the particular social and political institutions. In general we expect social institutions to be most important at the local levels, with national political institutions being crucial in preserving or curtailing population and capital mobility within countries. Political institutions likewise affect international factor movements.

In some instances the market, working through factor movements, may accentuate rather than mediate conflicts arising over scarce resources. However, the market also provides a more subtle and pervasive substitute for factor movement through the specialization in production with trade in commodities. A large corpus of theory and empirical work in economics is devoted to the effects of specialization and trade. The basic proposition that is widely, but not universally accepted is that trade in goods substitutes for movement of factors and has similar effects in equalizing factor returns, *given* the preexisting distribution of assets.

Trade in commodities not only substitutes for movement of factors but also substitutes impersonal for personal points of contact between competitors. These different forms of competition, the ways in which competition becomes personalized, and conditions under which such personalized competition erupts into open conflict and even violence are mediated crucially by various institutions.

THE LOCAL LEVEL

By way of exemplification we examine in this section three different types of responses of societies to scarcity at the local level, taking increases in density as the contextual framework of scarcity. Clifford Geertz's discussion of "agricultural involution" in colonial Java offers a striking example of how society sought to cope with increase in density and the consequent pressure on land as a resource. In Geertz's usage "involution" means the inward elaboration of detail of an established form or pattern in "an effort to provide everyone with some niche, however small, in the overall system" (Geertz 1963, p. 82). The critical problem the Javanese faced was the absorption of a growing population. The constraints that operated within the framework of the Javanese peasant economy precluded a fundamental breakthrough: the Javanese had no way of transforming already intensive farming in the direction of extensive farming since colonial laws and rules effectively barred them from expanding into uncultivated areas. For our purposes the significance of Geertz's presentation lies in the capacity the Javanese displayed, hamstrung as they were by structural and cultural constraints, of meeting the challenge of increasing numbers by transforming the character of the scarce resource, land. Geertz thereby implies that Javanese society avoided, or at least delayed, conflict through the mediating device of involution.

That increases in density tend to force technical changes and bring about improved agricultural practices has often been argued (see Boserup 1966), and the Javanese experience — by no means an isolated example — points to the importance of changes in tenurial arrangements, tenancy relationships, and employment of labor in the realization of the overriding goal of enhancing the carrying capacity of land (see Geertz 1963). What is observable here in essence is a process of intensification of agriculture, the substitution of labor and/or capital for the scarce factor, land (van de Walle 1975, p. 142).

The processes of adaptation to the new demographic realities, whether through innovation, transformation, or elaboration of existing land usage, underscores the dynamic nature of man's relationship to land as a resource, the immense potential of human ingenuity, and the exploitative powers of land. The experience of numerous societies belies the validity of abstract "optimum" population-land ratios posited so often in the literature. This is not to deny that societies could face what has been termed "critical density" (Allan 1965) — the level beyond which deterioration of land becomes inevitable — nor to preclude the possibility of identifying "danger signals" that are suggestive of pressure of numbers on land (see the "danger signals" enumerated in Hance 1968). It is equally evident that the direction in which a society would move to accommodate demographic changes and the point at which a departure would be made for accommodation cannot be projected in advance. Further the processes of change do not necessarily meet with success in either the short or the long run. Geertz saw "agricultural involution" in Java as an ultimately self-defeating process in that there was a point beyond which the "Gothic over-elaboration" could not be carried out.[10]

In fact the increasing premium placed on land for its productive capacities and the process of change that is initiated to permit land to carry a greater burden could bring about new forms of competition and conflict. Litigation over land has made this competition and conflict visible in many societies. For example, in rural Hausaland population growth resulted in the end of the rotation of agricultural land and the emergence of individual land tenure. The resultant trend away from customary rights inevitably brought in its wake a new and heightened competition over land (see Goddard, Mortimore, and Norman 1975). If changes in tenurial arrangements due to demographic factors have strained the internal cohesion of societies at the local level, then changes wrought in tenancy relationships because of the need to absorb new labor on land—the appearance of sharecropping, for example—have given rise to considerable social tension, if not to outright conflict.

Historically, the expansion of frontiers is the more common response of societies to higher densities. The expansion itself could take a highly formalized character—to the extent of imposing political and legal control over the new areas—or it could be carried out by individuals or groups without formal backing, as is the case with "squatting." In either case the presence or absence of other groups with actual or potential rights over the land in targeted areas is crucial to the success of frontier expansion.

Thus, where population distribution reveals nodes of high density separated by corridors of low density or unoccupied land, as in the case of several countries in West Africa (see Hance 1975), expansion of the cultivation frontiers can be carried out without major confrontations. Again, where the expansion meant the reclamation of waste lands, in nineteenth-century Ireland, for example (see Connell 1965), or the exploitation of land abandoned due to depopulation, as in West Central Mexico in the nineteenth century (see Cook 1970), open competition and conflict rarely emerged.

In general the newly opened-up lands have been subjected to extensive rather than intensive cultivation, and the intricate land usage developments seen in Java are largely absent here. This leads to a question that was of central importance to the classical political economists concerning the productivity of lands newly brought into cultivation. The Ricardian assumption that new land is likely to be marginal or less productive was validated by the European experience, but it by no means has universal validity. Certainly the experience of nations placed before vast frontiers—the United States and Australia, to name two conspicuous examples—was precisely the opposite. The key factors to note, though, are quite different: the availability of "breathing space" and sources of food supply for the new members of society.

Migration, the movement of individuals or groups from one habitat to another, could be identified as the classical response of societies to perceived situations of scarcity. Indeed it could even be asserted that the extent to which migration occurs is "a meaningful measure of relatively deficient resources at home" (see Caldwell 1975). In discussing migration as a mediating mechanism for scarcity,[11] two central questions have to be raised: In what ways does migration change the situation of scarcity, whether potential or actual, that initially prompts the movement of people? What consequences does such migration have for those areas receiving the migrants?

As a societal response migration can take either an institutionalized or a spontaneous character. In its institutional form migration functions explicitly to maintain an equilibrium between resources and population, and to that extent it is social control in action. The precise optimum number for a society in relation to its resources is a matter that may be debated at length — witness the search for the ideal for the *polis*. But it is arguable that societies that value migration for its mediating function carry within themselves an understanding as to the point at which the migration of its members becomes desirable. The migration itself may touch particular individuals, thus some pastoral tribes in East Africa call for the migration of individuals associated with disputes to prevent further discord (see Gulliver 1966), or it may involve identifiable segments within society — those who were required to migrate to form colonies in classical Greece provide the best example (see Boardman 1973). Of course the socioeconomic backgrounds of the migrants may vary considerably within society as well as between societies. Those who moved out are eventually likely to reap the benefits of their action, but the intended beneficiary of outmigration is the natal society. Its equilibrium between resources and numbers will be assured, and ideally the society concerned will never pass the threshold of overt conflict.

Spontaneous migration, the movement of people on the basis of specific impulses rather than under conventions established by the society at large, is likely to be quite erratic as compared to migration under institutional promptings. The best examples of this type of migration are to be found in the movement of peoples under famine conditions (see, for example, Bhatia 1967). Spontaneity, however, does not mean that formal trappings are absent altogether. Thus, for example, the modern-day outmigration of the Frafra people of Northern Ghana who sought to escape the region's stringent survival system has taken the character of a "social network of chain migration" involving both specific families and clan members (Nabila 1975). There is no doubt that this type of migration benefits the societies that produced the migrants, but the underlying motivating factor is the betterment of the migrants themselves. With spontaneous migration there is no assurance that the threshold of competition and conflict over resources would not be reached since the decision to migrate is taken on an individual basis rather than under societal guidelines.

The mediating function of migration for natal societies is unquestionable. Labeling migration an "escape view" is certainly appropriate, given the numerous studies showing how outmigration eases initial conditions of scarcity. Thus, to return to the Frafa of Northern Ghana, their movement led to the reduction of population density and therefore a more favorable relationship between numbers and resources (Nabila 1975, p. 75).

Migrations have other implications for the natal communities and it is worth briefly focusing on them. In some contexts migration functions as a channel of mobility and thus plays a crucial role in diffusing potential sources of social disruption. The decision by low-ranking Indian castes, who had become economically powerful but received no commensurate social recognition in terms of the caste system, to move out of their respective villages to establish new settlements rather than attempt the drastic revision of the existing order of social stratification could be taken as an example here (this process has been documented for several historical periods; see, for example, Sanyal 1975).

Migration results in the dispersion of what was originally a single community, and the relationship that develops subsequent to the outmigration is important for all involved. For the purposes of this discussion three different situations can be identified: where an unambiguous separation occurs, where the relationship is articulated, and where the migrants remain dependent on the mother community. In instances where the migrants achieve a new and distinctive identity—as in the case of the colonist in classical Greece—the resource use patterns of the two groups will not necessarily conflict.

In the second situation the noteworthy factor is the temporal dimension of the migration.[12] Such migration is usually seasonal, even if for an extended period of time, and it is best expressed in the vivid description used for Nigerian agricultural laborers who seasonally migrate from the north to the south: "people who ate away the dry season elsewhere" (Mabogunje 1975). The ambiguity of the relationship to the natal group that results can be a source of strength as well as weakness. The income flow, entrepreneurial and technological skills, knowledge, and experience the migrants bring on their return home lead to more efficient resource use, as a considerable number of studies testify (see, for example, the data on Ghana in Caldwell 1969 and in Hart 1970). The very same factors, however, could function in an adverse fashion. Thus the remittances of Indians now working in the Persian Gulf countries have resulted in intense competition over land in their respective natal areas to the detriment of those who have no access to such outside funds (Weiner 1981).

The conflict that could arise in situations where the new settlements become dependencies of the old are multifarious. The key issue is for whose benefit the resources of the new settlements are to be exploited: Is it for the benefit of the mother country or for the benefit of the settler population? This issue was a dominant theme in the evolution of European settlements overseas during the imperial era (Saul 1960).

Migration could of course have an entirely negative impact for the societies concerned. Reference to two characteristic features of rural communities that have faced the migration of their members to urban areas is illuminating: the unfavorable sex ratio against women and the high dependency rate of the population. The first affects reproductive capacities and the second places extra burdens on the mother community's resources. Together both factors deeply affect the capacity of the community concerned to exploit the available resources. The unfavorable consequences of the migratory process within the larger context of the national level become more prominent: even a cursory glance at the considerable literature on urban growth in developing countries reveals the manifold problems faced by urban centers that have been forced to absorb, alongside their own natural increase, burgeoning migrations from the rural areas (see, for example, Hance 1970).

Whether a particular region will become the locus of new settlement will depend on a host of so-called "pull" factors—in contrast to the "push" factors (see Lee 1966) that propelled individuals and groups out of their natal lands. What history has amply shown is that migrants have been attracted as much to heavily populated regions as to uninhabited or thinly populated areas. If the settlement becomes established without potential or actual rival claimants, no serious problems will arise, unless of course the settlers themselves compete and conflict over their new resources. However, if the migrants encounter an established population, conflicts may become pronounced.

The relationship that would eventually emerge between the new arrivals and the original habitants would be determined by a variety of factors. Most notable, the respective resources of the two groups will shape the struggle that ensues—the history of European expansion overseas provides ample examples. Also crucial is the type of settlement the newcomers choose to carry out in terms of nature and strategy of relations with the host communities.

THE NATIONAL LEVEL

Most modern analyses of economic growth and change have been conducted at the national level. As a result most of the vast extant development and population literature deals with dimensions of the problems of population change within sovereign states, and most of the policies discussed are also intended to be exercised at that same level (see Birdsall, Fei, Kuznets, Ranis, and Schultz 1979).

The most obvious problem of population growth is that, given the limited ability of developing countries to save and invest resources productively, population growth requires much of the new output to be devoted to meeting the needs of the additional members of the society rather than increasing per capita availabilities. Thus massive efforts of mobilizing resources for development are required just to maintain present living standards.

Pressure on arable land is a second evident phenomenon. In the absence of new frontiers to be settled (and such settlement still requires substantial capital), the arable land per person will decline, and land will become increasingly scarce as the classical economists predicted. While new technologies (the green revolution) and intensified cultivation methods, particularly irrigation, effectively augment land, producing sufficient food for expanded populations is extremely problematical in many countries (see *Proceedings; The World Food Conference of 1976* 1977; Brown 1970; and *The Twenty-Ninth Day* 1978). Not only does population press on existing land, but there are also cases where population growth may actually reduce cultivable land through irreversible processes of erosion and desertification (a few of the many studies which have treated this theme for the Sahel region include Kates, Johnson, and Haring 1977; Houerou 1977; and Swift 1977).

In addition to land other resources come under pressure. While much attention has been paid in recent years to the problem of depletion of non-renewable resources, excessive rates of extraction may also cause renewable resources such as forests, fisheries, clean water, and air to be diminished alarmingly.[13] One of the most alarming situations is widespread deforestation in many countries arising from fuel wood harvesting exceeding natural growth of the forests. The results are a fuel crisis in rural areas, increased erosion, changing rainfall patterns, and reduced retention of water during dry seasons.

The fact that population growth leads to rapid labor force growth means that high rates of capital formation are required to provide sufficient productive jobs to absorb these new workers. In the absence of such high rates of job creation, population growth becomes manifest as a crisis of unemployment and underemployment. Finally, an expanded population requires corresponding increases in investment in schools, hospitals, housing, water supply, and so forth, in order to maintain constant levels of services.

Not only are these changing patterns of scarcity affected by growth of population, but they are influenced crucially by the second dimension of population dynamics — changes in population composition. As is well known, a rapidly growing population will have larger proportions in younger age groups, thereby initially increasing dependency ratios (the proportion of non-working persons to economically active), and thereafter increasing sharply the rate of growth of the labor force through entrance of new, large cohorts. Furthermore improvements in health also increase the dependent population in older age groups. There is some limited evidence that increased dependency ratios reduce savings ratios while simultaneously increasing the share of investment required to provide education and health services (see Birdsall, Fei, Kuznets, Ranis, and Schultz 1979).

One intriguing hypothesis suggests that, following demographic change, periods in which the cohort of young adults is particularly large are periods of revolutionary change (Moller 1968). Certainly the problem of employment for new entrants to the labor force, particularly given increasing levels of formal education, raises the problem of youth unemployment which has been persistent through recent history in industrializing countries and has reached crisis proportions recently in the United States, Western Europe, and many developing countries such as Sri Lanka (see Osterman 1980 for a particularly interesting analysis of the special workings of youth labor markets).

Other dimensions of composition include ethnic divisions where differential population growth rates for different groups present specific problems in multiethnic societies. The rural-urban dimension of composition is also one that causes great problems in developing countries in terms of changing political demands, the explosive potential of discontented urban groups, and the massive requirements of resources to maintain urban service levels.

The third dimension of population dynamics, distribution, also has import for the ways in which patterns of scarcity change within nation states. Since neither resources nor population growth are uniform within national spaces, differential scarcities cause potential for movements of population from poor and densely populated regions to richer and less densely populated ones and from rural to urban areas. We have already mentioned the potential for conflict provided by such population movements.

Points of Political Tension

Population growth and resulting changing patterns of scarcities will give rise to systematic adjustments if markets are allowed to function freely. To summarize briefly: land rents as well as the share of income going to landlords will rise; returns to capital will rise; real wages will fall and/or employment become hard to find at prevailing wage rates; population will migrate within the country from areas of land shortage to areas of relatively plentiful land, thereby depressing real wages most in the previously best-off areas; internal capital flows may be redirected toward the labor-surplus areas of the country, although this depends very much on infrastructure and complementary inputs; there will be a relative shift of the growing population out of agricultural areas toward areas in which demand for labor is greater (mostly cities); and relative prices of food will rise, thereby further depressing real wages.

Although the scenario envisioned will have increasing shares of income going to landowners and capital owners, it is by no means certain that such increased incomes will be plowed into productive investment. Furthermore the rates of private savings may well decline if the dependency ratio rises, thereby increasing public sector capital requirements for providing social infrastructure. Therefore it is not a foregone conclusion that adjustments to population growth will cause an increase in capital formation sufficient to maintain or increase per capita stocks of capital.

But even if the market were to work in this idealized manner, it is not divinely ordained that this is the only adjustment process that should be accepted as fair by all participants. Indeed the nation state's political institutions function to protect individuals and groups from untrammeled market outcomes. At the very least these institutions should afford people a means for articulating their grievances and assuring that they have some power to affect terms under which they gain access to resources.

At least three main issues are likely to become politicized as market adjustments to population growth take place: land, employment, and regional disparities. Different polities respond differently to each of these issues, and their particular responses will depend on individual political processes, the individual regime's legitimacy and its willingness and ability to employ coercion. In idealized models of political pluralism the system arranges compromises such that all parties accept outcomes as reasonable and comply with the agreements. A leadership successful in mobilization obtains agreement or at least compliance from the masses to pursue particular policies. Political legitimacy here implies at least tacit acceptance of the system's appropriateness including its allocational rules.

When legitimacy breaks down, regimes attempt to enforce compliance through coercion. Most modern nation states have a legal monopoly on the use of coercive force to gain compliance: the police, courts, jails, and so forth are the institutions of coercion. The knotty question is what levels of coercion are necessary and proper for the maintenance of a regime that is regarded as legitimate — and at what level does coercion exceed legitimate bounds and the regime be properly considered repressive and totalitarian. We raise this issue in order to compare the institutionalized mediation of conflict designed to avoid violence with the overt or potential coercive violence exercised by the political institutions themselves. Our contention that successful institutional mediation averts violent conflict and is therefore desirable assumes a more or less pluralistic, consensual, and legitimate political system — which is not always prevalent internationally.[14]

The political ideology may also have a distinct preference for certain types of outcomes and work directly to obtain them. Discontent can be reduced through compromises and improved political performance or repression, but in some cases discontent will erupt into violence.

The first area in which conflict is likely to become politicized is that of land (see Lipton's article in Lehman 1979). In any specific case the political modifications associated with conflict over land can be understood only in terms of specific political institutions. Clearly, population growth intensifies competition for and conflict over land. Political institutions can mediate that conflict and have done so. It is significant that frequently political mediation arises from the fear that the alternative is violence. While peasant uprisings, or the threat thereof, have been a potent source of support for change, the threat and use of violence to maintain privileged access to land is the major support of counterrevolutionary actions.

The second principal issue that becomes politicized is employment. Those who cannot find employment — or at least cannot find employment that they consider appropriate to their training and at wages they consider adequate — feel aggrieved and are generally unwilling to accept passively their condition. Although much has been written (and feared) about the violent potential of unemployed youth in sprawling cities, the eruption of the unemployed into violence has been surprisingly infrequent in recent years. However, not only open unemployment but also wage erosion of the employed can cause deep discontent. Demonstrations, general strikes, and riots have been common manifestations of this discontent in the urban life of developing countries.[15]

The employment problem is in fact much more complex: the issue is not merely distribution of a given set of jobs but rather the creation of different levels of employment at particular conditions of work, pay, and security. To increase the levels of employment, capital formation must be accelerated in sectors in which labor absorption will be high. In addition appropriate policies for trade, regulation of employment, the burden of taxes on employment, and so on, have to be pursued (ILO 1972, 1976). While means of improving employment prospects are indirect and relatively undramatic, the political articulation of demands for more jobs at better pay is dramatic, visible, and immediate. In fact the principal demands in terms of employment are for relatively well-paying jobs for the relatively well educated in most developing countries. The political response most frequently has been to increase wages in public employment, to legislate increases in minimum wages in private sectors, and sometimes also to increase employment in the public sector (ILO 1972). When such employment is not accompanied by increased productivity (which has been frequent), the result has been to use more public revenue for wages, thereby reducing rates of new capital formation.

Technology then becomes biased against labor intensity in response to higher relative wage costs in the "modern" sectors. It can be argued with considerable empirical support that, although expanded employment can cause labor scarcity and pull real wages up sharply (as in Japan and Korea), attempts first to raise real wages work against expanding employment (see Harris and Todaro 1970; Lipton 1978). Pluralistic political institutions will have difficulty in mediating demands for expanding employment since the measures that meet immediate demands of the most articulate are likely to be counterproductive in the long run. The issue is likely to intensify and become more intractable in face of continuing rapid population increases.

The third area of conflict that comes to the political system for adjudication is that of regional disparities. Since scarcities are unevenly distributed within a national space, disparities in living standards, employment, levels of services, and rates of growth vary considerably. It is not surprising that the regional allocation of government-controlled resources is a subject for intense political competition within most countries. Furthermore in countries with pluralistic and democratic institutions regional affiliations become the basis for political organization. Parties in power maintain their electoral bases by rewarding their faithful with relatively large allocations (Nigeria and India provide particularly good examples). Thus opposition to governing regimes becomes regionally based with considerable potential for secessionist movements and civil war. The quest for maintaining national unity in many countries is the attempt to maintain legitimacy of the nation state in face of secessionist forces and potential civil war.[16]

The political problem facing nations is how to maintain common rights of citizenship, including the right to move and live with uniform legal protection within all parts of the national space, in face of strongly articulated demands by local groups to limit the inflow of "outsiders" (see Weiner 1978).

In addition to these interregional problems many countries have also tried, albeit with little success, to limit population movements to the major cities in order to prevent the uncontrolled growth of unserviced slums and unruly urban masses (Harris and Todaro 1969; Harris 1979). Again the political process is critical to the working out of rules governing who will and who will not be allowed privileged access to the cities.[17]

In summary, at the national level market solutions are neither completely appropriate nor are they passively accepted by all economic actors. Therefore political demands are made to ameliorate the consequences of population and regional interests. Solutions have to be provided through political institutions, and failure to mediate conflict results in repression, civil war, or communal violence.

THE INTERNATIONAL LEVEL

While the consequences of population growth for changing patterns of scarcity *among* nation states are virtually congruent with the impact on regions *within* nation states, the existence and functioning of mediating institutions are obviously very different. The principal differences flow from the fact that there is no counterpart to sovereignty for international institutions; thus international agreements are enforceable only through voluntary compliance, and imposition of will through force by stronger upon weaker countries is not uncommon.

In the three decades following World War II an "international economic order" has prevailed in which the generally accepted principles governing economic relations among nation states have included movement toward free trade in goods and relatively free international movement of capital (see Rosenstein-Rodan 1981 for a brief and lucid discussion of the emergence of the postwar international economic order). In addition there has been some agreement that some forms of resource transfer should be made from the richer countries to the relatively poor, which corresponds quite directly to transfer from labor-scarce to labor-abundant economies. Agreements on freedom of trade have been developed under the aegis of the General Agreement on Trade and Tariffs (GATT), supplemented by the institution of the United Nations Commission for Trade and Development (UNCTAD); insuring freedom of capital movements and harmonization of the world financial systems has been the function of the International Monetary Fund (IMF); and resource transfer has become partly the responsibility of the International Bank for Reconstruction and Development (The World Bank and Affiliates), various national aid programs, and regional development institutions (African Development Bank, Asian Development Bank, Inter-American Development Bank, for example).

Following our earlier discussion of market responses to differential scarcities, the desire to free world trade from excessive protection and restriction should provide opportunities for labor-abundant countries to specialize in production of labor-intensive goods which they would then trade for capital-intensive goods produced in countries with relative labor scarcity. While there are many qualifications to the theory required before one can hold with great certainty that free trade will in fact work in such ways, it is clear that a number of countries have been quite successful in exporting labor-intensive goods in the 1960s and 1970s and that these countries have also had relatively high rates of growth of employment and increasing real wages, lending at least partial support to the propositions (World Bank 1979, Chapters 4 and 7). Furthermore there has been systematic revision of preference to favor entry of exports from developing countries through GATT and specifically through the Lomé Convention agreement between the European Common Market and a large group of African, Pacific, and Caribbean countries (Alting von Geusau 1977).

At the same time, in recent years it has been evident that as soon as labor-intensive imports from labor-surplus countries significantly reduced output of the same goods (particularly textiles and shoes) in the labor-scarce countries, cries for protection ring out, and "voluntary restrictions" have been imposed on the exporters under the threat of more systematic protection. The problem of voluntary compliance and the potential for unilateral action by the stronger countries have made this avenue of development appear precarious to many countries so that the full scope for expanding the international division of labor has not been exploited. However, in recent years, under the umbrella title of "North-South Dialogue," guarantees of free access to industrialized-country markets by the labor-surplus countries have been sought.

In fact much of the recent discussion about the need for a new international economic order is predicated on the observation that the existing system is not sufficiently responsive to the needs of the poor countries which are, virtually by definition, abundant in labor and scarce in capital and complementary resources (see Hansen 1979 and Brandt 1980). Much of the thrust of this dialogue (or more frequently talking past each other) has been that new supranational institutions are required to establish rules for allocation that will work better in the interests of poor countries and serve some of the representational functions conventionally served by governmental institutions (particularly parliaments) within nation states. The problems of compliance and enforcement remain intractable, given the lack of legitimate supranational institutions with at least minimal coercive power (see Rosenstein-Rodan 1981).

In addition to efforts to make international markets work more effectively and to institute some forms of systematic resource transfers based on equity considerations, there have also been a number of proposals for integration into common markets, free trade areas, or economic communities at the multinational regional level. The most notable success has been the European Common Market; the Central American Common market was considered quite successful in the late 1960s and early 1970s; the Latin American Free Trade Area received mostly verbal support although the Andean Pact has developed some mechanisms for cooperation; the East African Economic Community was a model of success until its demise in 1979; the Association of South East Asian Nations (ASEAN) is a voluntary consultative group in which voluntary harmonization of policies is undertaken; and the Economic Community of West African States (ECOWAS) has become firmly established with a treaty and secretariat and mechanisms for harmonization of investment policies.[18]

The impetus for such regional cooperation is to achieve the gains of international trade within a limited area while being able to shape specific policies for gaining some protection for infant industries and reaping benefits of scale economies, which may be difficult or impossible for small countries competing completely in the world market. Indeed the standard model of trade governed by comparative advantage (another name for differential scarcities) is quite static, and there is reason to believe that always adhering to short-run advantage may not be consistent with long-term comparative advantage.

In addition to providing for freer trade among member countries, some of the agreements, notably the EEC and ECOWAS, also provide for free movement of population within the common market areas. As in the individual country case such factor movements will tend to equalize scarcities, but more direct forms of conflict between nationals of different countries become possible under such arrangements.

Potential Points of Conflict

While greater economic integration among countries can lead toward relative equalization of scarcities, we again can point out the differences between relatively impersonal relationships embodied in trade in goods and more personalized relationships arising from movement of workers and capital. While it can be shown that such relationships can improve the welfare of each country where all goods and services are aggregated into an index such as GNP, it is clear that different groups within each country will be affected differently. Worker groups in richer countries will resist immigration of low-wage workers from other countries, and they will join with employer groups in labor-intensive industries in calling for protection against imports of competing goods.[19] At the same time organized labor in rich countries will try to erect barriers to capital outflow by multinational companies from their countries while local entrepreneurs in poor countries will seek protection from untrammeled competition with foreign capital.

Thus political pressures will be applied to sovereign governments to accept only those parts of international integration that are of direct advantage to particularly well-organized groups within each country. The result is that countries are understandably hesitant to tie their economies too closely to the world economy when they thereby become highly vulnerable to unilateral decisions of other countries over which they have no control.[20] But such actions can easily escalate into trade wars with potential for further violent clashes.

Because of sovereignty and the lack of effective multinational institutions, neither market nor politically adjudicated adjustments are often allowed to run their course. Rather, action can be taken unilaterally by individual countries to which other countries are vulnerable. Certainly there is a plethora of international organizations and forums with much attendant verbiage and declarations of cooperation, but aborted cooperative agreements can become the cutting edge of serious conflict.[21]

Perhaps the most interesting implication is that common market agreements seeking greater integration might best be restricted to facilitating trade and capital movements. Agreements including free movement of people may just intensify points of conflict, as seems to have been the case recently between the Ivory Coast and Ghana under the ECOWAS agreement.[22]

CONCLUSION: MARKETS, INSTITUTIONS, AND CONFLICT

Differential population dynamics cause patterns of scarcity and hence competition for and conflict over scarce resources to change. Markets are a relatively impersonal way of mediating such conflict and can work so long as all parties are willing to accept the outcomes of these adjustment processes. There is no reason to believe that all will, or should, passively accept market outcomes, however; institutions have developed to mediate conflicts according to other principles. At the lowest levels of social organization we find families, clans, tribes, and other basic groups that accord access to scarce resources and validate claims to goods and services. Such allocations are made according to principles of reciprocity in which one's ability to make claims is a function of one's position within the social organization. At the level of the nation state political institutions have emerged to adjudicate claims and allocate scarce resources according to principles of redistribution. Claims are established and made effective in these systems based on one's position and status within the political system.

These institutions at both local and national levels can be effective in mediating conflict over scarcity so long as various participants respect the legitimacy of the institutions and are willing to accept the allocations that are made. In a less volatile scheme national allocations can also be effective so long as the state maintains sufficient coercive power to enforce its allocations. But at the international level the institutions for mediating conflict and competition between states are weak, and the very attempt to mediate claims may merely intensify conflict. The general point is that population growth increases scarcity of land and employment opportunities, and conflict over them is likely to become intense. However, such conflict can be mediated in many ways that avert violence.

Violence need not be an automatic consequence of population growth and changes in population distribution. But the actual outcomes depend on the particular patterns of scarcity that emerge and the institutions of markets, social organization, and political organization that serve to mediate conflict. In these terms violence represents a breakdown or failure of other mediating institutions. Certainly, reductions in rates of population growth will serve to reduce points of intense conflict that could erupt into violence. Yet the institutional capacities for mediation must also be examined. It is possible that better institutional development can lead to more humane and equitable means of dealing with intensified patterns of scarcity.

NOTES

1. Since our concern is to present working definitions, no extended discussion will be offered in defining the terms used. For a discussion of the problems of defining population variables see Choucri (1974).

2. Indeed, in the view of one commentator (Ackerman 1966), space functions as "the ultimate Malthusian control, beyond the reach of the cleverest space-adjusting techniques." Arguments such as these are based upon the biological premise that beyond a certain point crowding (and complexity) begin to take a toll on the human (and animal) constitution. It is to be noted that this premise lies behind much of the recent writings that decry large-scale systems (cities, for instance) which are seen as essentially incompatible with human nature. See, for example, Sale (1980).

3. We fully recognize, of course, that the emergence of violent conflict may in some cases be preferable to the maintenance of repressive institutions. Our chapter, however, does carry an implicit assumption of conflict avoidance as a goal.

4. The assumptions upon which such optimistic projections are based and the parameters of the projections themselves vary greatly. See, for example, the detailed analysis of technology and resource-use patterns projected to the year 2000 in Fisher and Potter (1964). For an extreme presentation of the optimistic view, one which considers the placing of arbitrary limits for future world population "man-hating," see Zhavoronkov (1965).

5. Winter (1980), for example, examines the ideological concerns and political factors that led to the fear of population decline in Western Europe during the seven decades from 1870 to 1940.

6. This is especially true in the case of the developing countries. See, for example, essays which discuss African census material in Ominde and Ejiogou (1972). However, the developed countries are by no means exempt from the same strictures. Note, for example, the problems faced in identifying the Mexican-American population in the United States discussed in Grebler, Moore, and Guzman (1970). The unique problems faced by historical demographers are

well known; and serious problems lie with developing countries. Omissions, misrepresentations, and faulty or inadequate analysis are the more common drawbacks for both civil registration systems and sample surveys. Differences in definition and in data collection procedures only compound these problems when comparative analysis is attempted. See the review of the literature on historical demography in the "Introduction" by Glass in Glass and Eversley (1965).

7. See, for example, Hance (1970), and Morgan and Pugh (1969). The importance of moving beyond crude density data can be illustrated with reference to Niger, admittedly an extreme case. In 1969 for the country as a whole the density was 8 per square mile; for those parts not desert it was 35; and for the arable areas it was 200 per square mile; see Issaka Dankoussou et al., "Niger," in Caldwell (1975).

8. There is a growing body of literature on the importance of cultural determinants in population change, both through anthropological studies and KAP surveys, but the precise significance of cultural determinants in comparison to other variables continues to be closely debated. Also, widely different terminology — "urbanization," "industrialization," "secularization," to name but a few — is used to denote the non-traditional forces and movements that have an impact on population dynamics. What each of these terms subsumes can vary remarkably. How "modern" is "modern behavior" and how "traditional" is "traditional behavior" are questions for which unambiguous answers have yet to be provided. There are serious doubts as to whether the urban-rural differential in respect to fertility rates can be conceptualized wholly in terms of the impact of modernization. However, at the empirical level data has been presented for particular contexts. See, for example, Caldwell (1968), who is careful to take into consideration socioeconomic differences to be found in the cities.

9. Probably the best-known recent prognosis is provided in Meadows et al. (1972). Several other works can be cited whose appraisals are distinguished by more sober and thoughtful language than that of the Club of Rome report. See Borgstrom (1969); and Holdren and Ehrlich (1971). For a different perspective, one colored by the writer's religious thinking about artificial birth control, see Clark (1967).

10. Geertz (1963), p. 81. Geertz also sees the initiation of "agricultural involution" as resulting in the loss of a key opportunity to "modernize" the Javanese economy.

11. For obvious reasons we exclude from the discussion annual life-cycle migrations such as those of pastoral nomads or fishermen, as well as the movements of political refugees and pilgrims. The discussion will be restricted to situations where migrations occur because of scarcity.

12. The temporal dimension is often the function of the spatial dimension of the migration concerned. See the discussion of the "inverse distance principle" developed for population movements in Mexico in Cook (1970).

13. See Ward and Dubos (1972); *Report of the United Nations Conference on the Human Environment* (1973); and *Man in the Living Environment* (1972). The July 1981 United Nations Conference on Energy in Nairobi further explored issues of depletion of energy resources.

14. Thanks (or blame) for bringing this issue to our attention is due to our editor, Steven Miller, who is a political scientist.

15. For Sri Lanka, see Obeyesekere (1974). For background on the 1979 "rice riots" and the 1980 coup in Liberia, see "Tolbert in Trouble" (1979) and "Which Side Were You On?" (1980).

16. The Nigerian Civil War (Biafra) and the successful secession of Bangladesh from Pakistan are both examples. Simmering potential conflicts are a problem for many African regimes as well as Pakistan, Thailand, the Philippines, Malaysia, Burma, etc. Lest this phenomenon

be viewed simplistically as tribalism, the cases of Canada and Belgium as well as the American Civil War should be kept in mind. The problem of national unity in the face of cultural sub-nationalism is discussed in Olorunsola (1972). For a discussion of the rebellions in Zaire, see Young (1971).

17. In general, restriction of movement to towns is pressed by middle classes who wish to preserve relatively high levels of amenities and who have concepts of appropriate standards for the "city beautiful."

18. Regional economic integration among developing countries is a subject for periodic revival of interest followed by disappointments. For euphoric statements of what could be gained, see Green and Seidman (1968) and the Monrovia Declaration of African Heads of State (1980).

19. See the positions taken by different groups testifying to the 1981 President's Commission on Immigration in the *U.S. Immigration Policy and the National Interest: The Final Report and Recommendations of the Select Commission on Immigration and Refugee Policy to the Congress and President of the United States* (1981).

20. Note the hysterical reaction of the U.S. public and Congress to the fact of U.S. dependence on Arab oil ("Can the Arabs Really Blackmail Us?" 1973) and on foreigners seeking to invest in major American corporations. The headlong rush to "Project Independence" for oil can be explained only in terms of an extreme desire to avoid international interdependence.

21. Note the widespread retaliation of Tanzania against Kenya which became part of the common market breakup. Three years later the borders are still closed, and direct air traffic is prohibited between these neighbors.

22. See "Ghana-Ivory Coast Tensions Still High" (1981) for a brief discussion of the rising tensions between the Ivory Coast and Ghana arising from the death of forty Ghanaians jailed under suspicion of being illegal immigrants even though the ECOWAS agreements provide for free movement of peoples.

REFERENCES

Abel, R. L. "A Comparative Theory of Dispute Institutions in Society." *Law and Society Review* 8 (1973).

Ackerman, E. A. "Population and Natural Resources: Statement by the Moderator." In *Proceedings of the World Population Conference, Belgrade, 30 August–10 September 1965,* vol. 1, "Summary Reports." New York: United Nations Department of Economic and Social Affairs, 1966.

African Heads of State. *The Africa We Want by the Year 2000.* Addis Ababa: Organization of African Unity, 1980.

Allan, W. *The African Husbandman.* Edinburgh: Oliver and Boyd, 1965.

Alting von Geusau, F. A. M., ed. *The Lomé Convention and a New International Economic Order.* Leyden: Sitjhoff, 1977.

Anderson, E. N. "Some Chinese Methods for Dealing with Crowding." *Urban Anthropology* 1 (1972): 141–50.

Bhatia, B. M. *Famines in India: A Study in Some Aspects of the Economic History of India, 1860–1965.* Bombay: Asia Publishing House, 1967.

Birdsall, N., J. Fei, S. Kuznets, G. Ranis, and T. P. Schultz. "Demography and Development in the 1980s." In *World Population and Development: Challenges and Prospects,* edited by P. M. Hauser. Syracuse, N.Y.: Syracuse University Press for the United Nations Fund for Population Activities, 1979.

Boardman, J. *The Greeks Overseas,* 2nd ed. Harmondsworth: Penguin, 1973.

Borgstrom, G. *Too Many.* Toronto: Collier-Macmillan, 1969.

Boserup, E. *The Conditions of Agricultural Growth.* Chicago: Aldine, 1966.

Brandt, W. *North-South: A Programme for Survival.* Cambridge, Ma.: MIT Press, 1980.

Brown, L. R. *Seeds of Change: The Green Revolution and Development in the 1970s.* New York: Praeger for the Overseas Development Council, 1970.

_____. *The Twenty-ninth Day: Accommodating Human Needs and Numbers to the Earth's Resources.* New York: Norton, 1978.

Caldwell, J. C. *African Rural-Urban Migration: The Movement to Ghana's Towns.* Canberra: Australian National University Press, 1969.

_____. *Population Growth and Family Change in Africa: The New Urban Elite in Ghana.* Canberra: Australian National University Press, 1968.

_____, ed. *Population Growth and Socioeconomic Change in West Africa.* New York: Columbia University Press for the Population Council, 1975.

"Can the Arabs Really Blackmail Us?" *New York Times Magazine.* September 23, 1973.

Choucri, N. *Population Dynamics and International Violence: Propositions, Insights, and Evidence.* Lexington, Ma.: Lexington Books, 1974.

Clark, C. *Population Growth and Land Use.* London: Macmillan, 1967.

Connell, K. H. "Land and Population in Ireland, 1780–1845." In *Population in History: Essays in Historical Demography,* edited by D. V. Glass and D. E. C. Eversley. Chicago: Aldine, 1965, pp. 423–33.

Cook, S. "Migration as a Factor in the History of Mexican Population: Sample Data from West Central Mexico, 1793–1950." In *Population and Economics: Proceedings of Section Five of the International Economic History Association, 1968,* edited by Paul Deprez. Winnipeg, Manitoba: University of Manitoba Press, 1970, pp. 279–302.

Dankoussou, I., S. Diarra, D. Laya, and I. D. Pool. "Niger." In *Population Growth and Socioeconomic Change in West Africa,* edited by J. C. Caldwell. New York: Columbia University Press for the Population Council, 1975.

Day, L. H., and A. T. Day. *Too Many Americans.* Boston: Houghton Mifflin, 1964.

Deprez, P., ed. *Population and Economics: Proceedings of Section Five of the International Economic History Association, 1968.* Winnipeg, Manitoba: University of Manitoba Press, 1970.

Dubos, R. and B. Ward. *Only One Earth: The Care and Maintenance of a Small Planet.* New York: Norton, 1972.

Durkheim, E. *The Division of Labor in Society,* translated with an introduction by G. Simpson. New York: Macmillan, 1933.

Eberstadt, N. "China: How Much Success?" *New York Review of Books* 26 (May 3, 1979): 39–44.

Fisher, J. L., and N. Potter. *World Prospects for Natural Resources: Some Projections of Demand and Indicators of Supply to the Year 2000.* Baltimore: Johns Hopkins University Press, 1964.

Geertz, C. *Agricultural Involution: The Process of Ecological Change in Indonesia.* Berkeley: University of California Press, 1963.

"Ghana-Ivory Coast Tensions Still High." *Africa News* 16 (1981).

Glass, D. V., and D. E. C. Eversley, eds. *Population in History: Essays in Historical Demography.* Chicago: Aldine, 1965.

Goddard, A. D., M. J. Mortimore, and D. W. Norman. "Some Social and Economic Implications of Population Growth in Rural Hausaland." In *Population Growth and Socioeconomic Change in West Africa,* edited by John C. Caldwell. New York: Columbia University Press for the Population Council, 1975.

Grebler, L., J. W. Moore, and R. C. Guzman. *Mexican-American People: The Nation's Second Largest Minority.* New York: Free Press, 1970.

Green, R. H., and A. Seidman. *Unity or Poverty? The Economics of Pan-Africanism.* Harmondsworth: Penguin, 1968.

Gregor, T. *Mehinaku: The Drama of Daily Life in a Brazilian Indian Village.* Chicago: University of Chicago Press, 1977.

Gulliver, P. *The Family Herd: A Study of Two Pastoral Tribes in East Africa.* London: Routledge and Kegan Paul, 1966.

Hall, E. T. *The Hidden Dimension.* Garden City, N.Y.: Doubleday, 1966.

Hance, W. A. "Population and Resources." In *Population Growth and Socioeconomic Change in West Africa,* edited by John C. Caldwell. New York: Columbia University Press for the Population Council, 1975, pp. 119–35.

_____. *Population, Migration, and Urbanization in Africa.* New York: Columbia University Press, 1970.

_____. "The Race between Population and Resources." *Africa Report* 13 (1968): 6–12.

Hansen, R. D. *Beyond the North-South Stalemate.* New York: McGraw-Hill, 1979.

Harris, J. W. "Internal Migration in Indonesia." In *The Urban Impact of Internal Migration,* edited by J. W. White. Chapel Hill, N.C.: Institute for Research in Social Science, 1979.

_____, and M. P. Todaro. "Migration, Unemployment, and Development: A Two-Sector Analysis." *The American Economic Review* 60 (1970).

_____, and M. P. Todaro. "Urban Unemployment in East Africa: An Economic Analysis of Policy Alternatives." *East African Economic Review* 4 (1969).

Hart, K. "Small-Scale Entrepreneurs in Ghana and Development Policy." *Journal of Development Studies* 6 (1970): 104–20.

Hawley, A. H. "Population Density and the City." *Demography* 9 (1972): 521–29.

Holdren, J. P., and P. R. Ehrlich. *Global Ecology: Readings Toward a Rational Strategy for Man.* New York: Harcourt, Brace, Jovanovich, 1971.

Houerou, H. N. "The Nature and Causes of Desertization." In *Desertification: Environmental Degradation in and around Arid Lands,* edited by M. Glantz. Boulder, Co.: Westview, 1977.

International Labour Office. *Employment, Growth, and Basic Needs: A One-World Problem: World Employment Conference of 1976.* Geneva: International Labour Office, 1976.

International Labour Office. *Employment, Incomes, and Equality: A Strategy for Increasing Productive Employment in Kenya.* Report of the Inter-Agency Team Financed by the United Nations Development Programme and Organized by the International Labour Office. Geneva: International Labour Office, 1972.

Kates, R. W., D. L. Johnson, and K. J. Haring. "Population, Society, and Desertification." In *Desertification: Its Causes and Consequences,* edited by the Secretariat of the United Nations Conference on Desertification, Nairobi. Oxford: Oxford University Press, 1977.

Kuznets, S. *Modern Economic Growth: Rate, Structure, and Spread.* New Haven, Ct.: Yale University Press, 1966.

Lee, S. E. "A Theory of Migration." *Demography* 3 (1966): 47–57.

Lehmann, D., ed. *Peasants, Landlords, and Governments: Agrarian Reform in the Third World.* New York: Holmes and Meier, 1974.

Levi, L., and L. Anderson. *Psycho-Social Stress: Population, Environment, and Quality of Life.* New York: Halstead, 1975.

Lipton, M. *Employment and Labour Use in Botswana, Final Report.* Gaborone: Ministry of Finance and Development Planning, Republic of Botswana, 1978.

———. "Toward a Theory of Land Reform." In *Peasants, Landlords, and Governments: Agrarian Reform in the Third World,* edited by David Lehmann. New York: Holmes and Meier, 1974.

Mabogunje, A. L. "Migration and Urbanization." In *Population Growth and Socioeconomic Change in West Africa,* edited by J. C. Caldwell. New York: Columbia University Press for the Population Council, 1975.

Meadows, D. H., D. L. Meadows, J. Randers, and W. W. Behrens III. *The Limits to Growth: A Report for the Club of Rome's Project on the Predicament of Mankind.* New York: Universe Books, 1972.

Mitchell, R. "Ethnographic and Historical Perspectives on Relationships between Physical and Socio-Spatial Environments." *Sociological Symposium* 14 (1975): 25–40.

Moller, H. "Youth as a Force in the Modern World." *Comparative Studies in Society and History* 10 (1968): 237–60.

Morgan, L. H. *Houses and House Life of the American Aborigines.* Washington, D.C.: USGPO, 1881.

Morgan, W. B., and J. C. Pugh. *West Africa.* London: Methuen, 1969.

Nabila, J. "Depopulation in Northern Ghana: Migration of the Frafa People." In *Interdisciplinary Approaches to Population Studies: Proceedings of the West African Seminar on Population Studies, University of Ghana, Legon, 30 November–4 December 1972,* edited by A. S. David, E. Laing, and N. O. Addo. Legon: Population Dynamics Programme, University of Ghana, 1975, pp. 70–83.

Obeyesekere, G. "Some Comments on the Social Background of the April 1971 Insurgency in Sri Lanka (Ceylon)." *Journal of Asian Studies* 43 (1974): 367–84.

Ohlin, G. "Historical Evidence of Malthusianism." In *Population and Economics: Proceedings of Section Five of the International Economic History Association, 1968,* edited by P. Deprez. Winnipeg, Manitoba: University of Manitoba Press, 1970.

Olorunsola, V. A., ed. *The Politics of Cultural Sub-Nationalism in Africa.* Garden City, N. Y.: Doubleday, 1972.

Ominde, S. H., and C. N. Ejiogou, eds. *Seminar on Population Growth and Economic Development in Africa.* New York: Heinemann Educational for the Population Council, 1972.

Osterman, Paul, *Getting Started.* Cambridge, Ma.: MIT Press, 1980.

Polanyi, K. "The Economy as Instituted Process." Chapter 13 of *Trade and Market in the Early Empires: Economics in History and Theory,* edited by K. Polanyi, C. M. Arensberg, and H. W. Pearson. Glencoe, Ill.: Free Press, 1957.

President's Commission on Immigration. *U.S. Immigration Policy and the National Interest: The Final Report and Recommendations of the Select Commission on Immigration and Refugee Policy to the Congress and President of the United States.* Washington, D.C.: March 1, 1981.

Rosenstein-Rodan, P. N. "The New International Economic Order." Lecture. Boston: Boston University, 1981.

Sale, K. *Human Scale.* New York: Coward, McCann, and Geoghegan, 1980.

Sanyal, H. "Social Mobility in Bengal: Its Sources and Constraints." *Indian Historical Review* 2 (1975): 68–96.

Saul, S. B. *Studies in British Overseas Trade, 1870–1914.* Liverpool: Liverpool University Press, 1960.

Schumpeter, J. A. "The Creative Response in Economic History." *The Journal of Economic History* 7 (1947): 149–59.

Spencer, H. *Principles of Sociology.* New York: Appleton, 1879–82.

156   HARRIS AND SAMARAWEERA

Swift, J. "Sahelian Pastoralists: Underdevelopment, Desertification, and Famine."
    Annual Review of Anthropology 6 (1977):457–68.

"Tolbert in Trouble." African News 12 (April 27, 1979).

United Nations. Man in the Living Environment, Report of the Workshop on Global
    Ecological Problems Prepared for the 1972 United Nations Conference on
    the Human Environment at Stockholm. Madison: University of Wisconsin
    Press for the Institute of Ecology, 1972.

————. Report of the United Nations Conference on the Human Environment, Stock-
    holm, 5–16 June 1972. New York: United Nations, 1973.

Van de Walle, E. "Population and Development." In Population Growth and Socio-
    economic Change in West Africa, edited by J. C. Caldwell. New York: Co-
    lumbia University Press for the Population Council, 1975.

"Which Side Were You On?" Africa News 14 (April 21, 1980).

Winter, J. M. "The Fear of Population Decline in Western Europe, 1870–1940." In
    Demographic Patterns in Developed Societies, edited by R. W. Harris. Lon-
    don: Taylor and Francis, 1980, pp. 171–98.

Wirth, L. "Urbanism as a Way of Life." American Journal of Sociology 44 (1938):
    1–24.

World Bank. World Development Report, 1979. Washington, D.C.: World Bank, 1979.

World Food Conference. Proceedings: The World Food Conference of 1976, June 27–
    July 1, Iowa State University, Ames, Iowa, USA. Ames: Iowa State Univer-
    sity Press, 1977.

Young, M. C. "Rebellion and the Congo." In Rebellion in Black Africa, edited by R. I.
    Rotberg. London: Oxford University Press, 1978.

Zhavoronkov, N. M. "Chemistry and the Vital Resources of Mankind: The Uses of
    Substitutes and their Industrial and Economic Significance." In Proceedings
    of the World Population Conference, Belgrade, 1965, Volume III, Selected
    Papers and Summaries: Projections, Movement of Population Trends.

6

Political Dimensions of Conflict

EDWARD E. AZAR AND NADIA E. FARAH

COMPLEXITY OF CONFLICT

THE CONCEPT "CONFLICT" usually refers to a wide range of phenomena ranging from interpersonal aggression to wars, the most extreme forms of violence. The proliferation of explanations is indicative of the concept's nonspecificity and high flexibility.

Certain explanations of conflict are located in the social psychological sphere. In this perspective conflict is variously caused by certain innate biological necessities, by the effect of the social environment on the human psyche, or through the impact of experience and learning. (Lorenz 1966; Ardry 1961; Graham and Gurr 1969; Davies 1969; Galtung 1964; Bandura 1973; Fromm 1973).

Another broad explanation tends to locate the causes of conflict within one or the other of the social structures. Traditional Marxism relegated the causes of conflict to the economic sphere (Luxembourg 1968). The functionalists stressed the ideological as a predominant factor—culture and values (Hines 1980; DeVos et al. 1975; Coser 1972). Others have emphasized the political sphere, while peace researchers have attached equal importance to all of the social structures in the generation of conflict. (Morgenthau 1973; Carr 1964; Galtung 1971).

An understanding of the nature of conflict necessitates an identification of the causes of the conflict within the totality of the social system. Social systems are in effect composed of different structures determined by the specificity of the system and the historical situation. Economic and political conflicts are not mutually exclusive. They are highly dynamic and interconnected in all their various forms and dimensions.

The authors wish to thank Rosemary Blunck and Mohamed Said of the Center for International Development for their help and significant contributions.

The transformation of a set of social antagonisms into political conflict entails a power conflict. Political conflict is defined as "a crisis in the stabilized forms of political interactions whether between states or social groups within a state." These stabilized forms of interactions are contingent upon differential political power relations between states and/or social groups. In this context political power is a *structural concept* referring to relative political power relations conditioned by the economic and ideological relations *underpinning* the political structure.

As a result of deep structural changes in the economy, the conflict might emerge first in economic terms. The economic crisis may be triggered by a failure of the market system, through some contrived scarcity of resources, or through an engineered rapid change in one or the other of the main economic sectors. On the other hand, conflict may be located in the political structure itself. Political crises may be incited by a power struggle within the power block over political hegemony or an external threat or intervention. Crisis may emerge in yet another way through ideological breakdowns within the dominant consensus. More specifically, these kinds of crises are either crises of the system or within the system.

The structural relations that condition international interactions can also transform the conflict into an open political one between states. In this context three types of relations are relevant: relations of dependence, relations of interdependence, and relations of relative independence. A crisis in economic relations may be transformed into political conflict depending on the structural relations existing between the conflictive parties.

In ideological terms two major cleavages exist in the second half of the twentieth century; the traditional East/West cleavage (or communism/capitalism) and the North/South cleavage. Most of the ideological conflicts waged today on the world level stem from these two cleavages. This does not preclude the existence of other ideological cleavages; rather they are incorporated within one or the other of these categories. Ideological and political conflicts are intertwined, as evidenced in the existing political cleavages in the world system, in the struggle for hegemony (or power politics), and in the formation of military and strategic alliances. Interstate wars are a clear form of conflict, and the intervention of foreign powers in intra- or interstate wars is usually couched in highly ideological terms expressing such sentiments as the defense of the free world or the advancement of the world revolution.

PROTRACTED SOCIAL CONFLICT

Since 1945 extensive conflict has occurred in the third world (Azar 1973). Political conflict in the poor nations has predominantly taken the form of protracted social conflicts. Protracted social conflicts mean hostile interactions that extend over long periods of time and fluctuate in frequency and intensity. They are characterized by strong equilibrating forces and the absence of a distinct end (Azar 1979; Azar and Eckhardt 1979; Azar et al. 1978). Protracted social conflicts are rooted in ethnicity and/or nationalism. They are fundamentally ideological in nature. Ideology is manifested in the goals of the conflict, expressed in demands for secession, national liberation, rights for self-determination, autonomy, or equal rights. This type of conflict arises from highly unequal socioeconomic structures, characteristic of third world nations, where channels of mediation and arbitration are either absent or blocked to the dominated groups (Azar and Farah 1981). Such conflict usually takes an intense political form. It is partly a legacy of the colonial past, the large role of the post-independence state in the social system (Van Den Berge 1971; Schermerhorn 1970; Hunter 1966), and the crisis of underdevelopment.

Although protracted social conflict is mostly characteristic of third world social systems, it is not simply confined to them. Whenever the proper conditions exist, such conflict emerges in the advanced industrial nations (Nairn 1977; Glazer and Moynihan 1975).

Protracted social conflicts are conflicts over the distribution of resources and rewards in the society between distinct ethnic groups (as opposed to social classes in general). This is not to say that class affiliations are absent from the social systems of the third world. Interethnic alliances based on class, rather than on ethnic criteria, can emerge. However, ethnicity and class are so intertwined, and ethnic affiliation is so strong, that conflict is waged on ethnic, not on class lines (Legum et al. 1979). Conflict in this situation may be essentially located in the political structure, even if the causes are economic or ideological. Ethnic conflict is concomitant with the predominance of political power relations in the distribution of economic resources and social rewards in the society. This fact is reflected in the centrality of the state in the social system. Access to power then is a necessary condition in the determination of social positions (Lenski 1966). The dominant role of the political structure (the state) in most third world countries has been created by the specific policies pursued by the colonial powers prior to independence. Most third world nations before colonialism were highly static but fairly homogeneous societies. Their political and ideological institutions corresponded to and legitimized the economic relations embedded in the organization of their productive structures. The predominantly agricultural and/or tribal economic systems were based on communal ties of social organization. The political system rested on a hierarchical patriarchal order that allowed, more or less, popular participation. The legitimacy of the political order was entrenched in a religious ideology that sustained, maintained, and reproduced the system successfully for centuries (Amin 1976).

Change did not occur from within the static social system but externally through colonial penetration. The colonizers heavily modified certain aspects of the system while maintaining others (such as ethnic affiliation) (Smith 1969). This unequal pattern of modification and change shattered the previous homogeneity of third world societies. The economy was reoriented from a basic needs strategy to a fulfillment of the growth requirements of the European metropolises. While labor intensive techniques were maintained, the communal social relations that sustained them were replaced by capitalist relations of production such as the institution of private property in agricultural land and the modification of contract and inheritance laws. The forced monetarization of the economy imposed the rules of the market system from above.

The imposition of alien social relations on the old system of production led to the marginalization of a substantial part of the labor force, an increase in poverty levels, and growing systems of inequalities between social groups. Revolts in the system were immediately curbed through the use of excessive force and coercion. For a long time the new economic and social changes were enforced by the colonial occupation forces. Even when the colonialist powers tried later to establish local governments modelled on the European parliamentary systems, these governments were at the mercy of the occupation army — the use of force was the *modus vivendi,* the supreme organizational principle in third world social systems (De Vos and Romanucci-Ross 1975).

The new national governments inherited these disjointed social systems, as well as the political and the socioeconomic institutions of colonialism. It is not accidental that the logic of the system, dominated by highly unequal power relations and the use of force, imposed itself on the newly independent states. The state, with its monopoly on the use of force, was the only viable institution capable of maintaining the cohesion of the society. However, the relative weakness of the national state, the raised expectations of freedom and equality that developed through the struggle for independence, and the development policies adopted by most of the third world nations in the last two to three decades resulted in the spread and intensification of internal (and interstate) conflicts. These conflicts were mostly protracted social conflicts. The structural roots of the protracted social conflict lie in the history of colonialism. Its perpetuation and intensification resulted from the increased political and economic inequalities promoted by the policies of the new states.

In the struggle for independence the population forgot, or suppressed, their ethnic rivalries in order to present a unified front against the colonizers. The ideology of the independence movements was highly nationalistic and stressed not only the unity of the people but their economic and political equality (Nairn 1977). Decolonization in the majority of cases happened through the transfer of power to a national group either directly or through some form of elections or universal suffrage. Usually the new ruling elite, in societies where ethnic stratification is still relevant, happened to have a strong ethnic identity.

In some cases the imposition of the power of one ethnic group over the others resulted immediately in internal turmoil and in demands for secession by ethnic groups. In the majority of the other cases, the conflict emerged later when the new elites failed to incorporate the diverse ethnic groups in the system by delivering the previously promised equal rights.

It is now well documented that inequalities increased rather than decreased through the development policies adopted in the third world (Grove 1979; Adelman and Morris 1973). The nationalist movement led to the emergence of populist regimes in the first years of independence. Populism was manifest in a multitude of laws implemented as soon as some of the new nationalist governments came to power, such as land reform, minimum wages, free education, and free health care. Populist measures were usually accompanied by the implementation of developmental policies known as import substitution. Import-substitution, highly entrenched in the western modernization perspective, was seen as the first step in a national industrialization that would spread from the relatively easy stage of consumer goods production to the development of heavy industry and self-sufficiency. These development programs disregarded the dependent nature of third world economies and, most important, the real needs of a predominantly rural and poor population.

The new policies resulted in the creation of a small, highly capital intensive industrial sector which was overpriced and inefficient. The costs mounted in terms of import prices, higher foreign debts, persistent deficit in the balance of payments, and the inability of this form of development to spread its benefits to the majority of the population. Populist policies became harder to maintain, and chronic inflation and unemployment became the permanent features of the new societies. The limited development that occurred benefited only the elites in power, without the assumed trickle-down effects to the rest of the population (Cardoso and Faletto 1979; O'Donnell 1973, 1978).

In ethnically diverse societies greater inequalities coincided with the differential access of ethnic groups to economic resources contingent on their access to power. The centrality of the state in the development process, and its extended role in the economic sector, led to the immediate transfer of the economic conflict over the distribution of resources and rewards to a clearly visible political conflict.

Most of these conflicts have resulted in the emergence of clear authoritarian regimes where the military has intervened through the use of force. Numerous military coups have suppressed the conflict for a while by the establishment of coercive and repressive regimes. In some cases the use of force and coercion has itself led to the intensification of the conflict into open civil wars or mass revolutions (O'Donnell 1973; Sunkel 1973; Nun 1969).

In cases of internal struggle within third world nations, the dominance of the state, built on highly unequal power relations, can be identified as the major source of the protracted social conflict. Access to economic resources is determined by the political elite, hence the inevitability that struggle in the economic sphere will be immediately translated into a political conflict. The structural roots of the conflict, in terms of excessive inequalities, were the major factor in the struggle over hegemony in the political structure. The very weakness of social groups prevented any single group from extending its political hegemony over the society without the help of the military.[1]

The ideological structure that reflected in the early years the ideology of the dominant modernizing elites broke down in the process. A new ideology centering around the discarded traditional values (Islamic revivalism, self-reliance, cultural authenticity) is prevalent today in the third world in an effort to reorient the society. The populist development strategy of the post-independence period is being replaced by a new development strategy that advocates self-reliance and the satisfaction of the basic needs of the majority of the population (Sunkel and Fuenzalida 1974).

The success of the new trend will depend on its ability to integrate different ethnic groups into the mainstream of the social endeavor and to reduce inequalities in both the economic and political spheres. Otherwise the world may witness new divisions that would add to the intractability of the conflict and to the general instability of third world regimes.

INTERSTATE CONFLICT

There are many theories and explanations for interstate conflicts. Several schools are reviewed whose contributions have given some scope to understanding conflict among nations.

The power politics or realist school explains conflict as a function of political power relations. According to this perspective, the absence of a central authority and of an international police force results in an anarchic international system. Independent states are compelled to use force in order to safeguard their own national interest (Osgood and Tucker 1967). Some scholars in this tradition believe the national interest to be state security. The survival of the state is a basic goal of foreign policy (Schuman 1969). Others are more inclined to define the national interest in terms of power rather than security (Morgenthau 1973). Unequal power positions in the international system incite the more powerful states to impose their will on weaker actors (the power vacuum thesis) (Schuman 1969; Schwarzenberger 1964). Military force and capabilities are the major tools in such an insecure and unstructured international system (Wallace 1973; Spiegel 1972). Even when economic capabilities are pointed out as an element of power, they are reduced to complementing military strength in interstate power play (Brown 1974; Knorr 1973; Kindleberger 1970). The use of force, or threat of using force, is the major mechanism of stability and maintenance of the balancing of power in the international system (Osgood and Tucker 1967). The quest for power in this perspective is both the cause of international conflict and the means to regulate interstate relations.

Marxist theory, on the other hand, explains interstate conflict in economic terms. International conflict is an outcome of the dynamics of the capitalist system. Interstate conflicts depend on the pattern of class relations within the capitalist states. The state as such is not the major actor in interstate relations. The dominant class served by the state is the real actor (Poulantzas 1975). The capitalist state is perceived as a simple tool of the ruling bourgeoisie that uses it as an instrument of domination within the society and to extend its economic interests in other societies.

The dynamics of capitalist accumulation require expansion outside of the capitalist countries to counteract the falling rate of profit during periods of recession (or economic crisis). The outward expansion is carried out by the capitalist state through the use of its military power in dominating weaker societies in order to secure markets and ensure sources of raw materials (colonialism) or by exporting capital (imperialism) (Lenin 1939). The search for external outlets results in an intercapitalist competition over colonies and investment opportunities. These processes initiated two world wars in the twentieth century and still threaten the existing system (Mandel 1975).

A third perspective perceives interstate conflict as an outcome of psychological motivations and attitudes. The causes of conflict are located in the ideological sphere. Images, belief systems, and misperceptions are considered to be the medium through which the field of action and conflict is appropriated (Boulding 1956; Holsti 1962; Jervis 1968). Conflict is an outcome of subjective factors that systematically distort the incoming information and images of others, including the perceptions of enemies and their actions. These subjective factors indulge the decision-makers in a self-created world and may instigate several psychological mechanisms conducive to aggression and conflict.

A fourth explanation may be designed as a structural thesis of international relations. It is conceived as a system of domination-subordination.

The different spheres of social relations (political, economic, ideological) are all considered to be equally responsible for the generation of interstate conflict (Galtung 1971).

Finally, the lateral pressure thesis argues that aggression and outward expansion are rooted in the population, economic and growth dynamics of a society. A growing population increases its demand for resources, especially in the face of changing, more complex technology. In most societies the increased demand for resources cannot be met within national boundaries, hence lateral pressures will be created to attain them through external expansion (Choucri and North 1975).

These five alternative theses offer complementary explanations for conflict among nations. In certain cases power politics is the predominant dynamic and plays a major role in the generation and the resolution of a conflict. In other cases the economic motives have the upper hand (colonial history of the third world). The dominance of one sphere in explaining a certain conflict does not negate the existence or importance of the others. The transformation of an economic or an ideological conflict into a clear political conflict will depend on the nature of the structural cleavages embedded in the international system.

The historical development of the international system resulted in three major patterns of structural relations: relations of dependence, interdependence, and relative independence.

These relations were both the cause and the outcome of contending worldwide ideologies. Western European ideology had complete hegemony until the creation of the Soviet Union in 1917 and the emergence of an opposing ideology, socialism, as a concrete force in international relations. Since the mid-sixties, however, a rising critique by the third world of both Western ideologies (capitalism and socialism) has crystallized into a third world view that challenges these systems while incorporating elements from both of them.

The antagonistic relations of dependence, interdependence, and relative independence may erupt into open political conflicts, or may be diverted to other forms of conflict (economic), depending on the position of the conflicting parties in the international stratification system.

Outward expansion led to a new worldwide division of labor that established an international system characterized by unequal relations between the center of economic growth (North) and the colonies (South). The relations led to accelerated growth in the center countries while they enforced a cycle of underdevelopment and backwardness in the periphery (Wallerstein 1979; Frank 1967). The system of *unequal relations* is maintained, even after the political independence of most third world nations, through the processes of unequal exchange in international trade and through the expansion of multinational corporations (Cardoso and Faletto 1979; Amin 1974).

Dependence is based on a harmony of interest between the center of the center nations and the center of the periphery, and on a disharmony between the peripheries of both the center and periphery. However, there is more disharmony of interests between the center and the periphery in the periphery than in the center nations (Galtung 1971). These patterns of interaction explain to a large degree why the real economic contradictions (in terms of a great inequality gap) between the North and South have sometimes resulted in crises and open violence, especially in the fifties and early sixties. However, since the 1970s these contradictions have been rarely transformed into violence.

In the fifties and sixties the nationalist movements tried to curtail their dependency relations on the West by fighting the open system of subordination (military occupation). The ensuing crisis assumed the intense political form of a liberation movement. After independence, and during the heyday of the Cold War, nonalignment was seen as a guarantee of the fragile newly independent structures. However, the perpetuation of economic dependence and the lessening of tensions between the two superpowers made the nonaligned posture harder to maintain in reality, if not in rhetoric. Since the 1970s the third world has changed course from open confrontation to the use of economic and diplomatic channels such as the demand for a new economic order and the formation of pressure groups in the United Nations, notably the Group of 77 and the Nonaligned Bloc. The ability of the peripheral countries' centers to prevent an eruption into violence of internal antagonisms depends largely on their ability to impose full hegemony on their own peripheries and on extracting some benefits from the international economic system.

POPULATION, CONFLICT, AND CONFLICT RESOLUTION

Population trends and patterns are important factors that affect the structure of social conflicts. Population growth rates, densities, age distribution, composition, and migration trends are all elements that can initiate, exacerbate, or attenuate conflictive situations. Conversely, social conflicts may also affect population trends. Inequality structures represent the field of interaction between population patterns and conflictive situations (especially in the case of protracted social conflicts).

The linkages between population growth rates and overt violence are rarely direct (Choucri 1974). Differential population growth rates contribute to the initiation or the protractedness of the conflict through their effects on the structure of economic and political inequalities.

High population growth rates themselves exacerbate inequalities (Repetto 1979; Kocher 1974; Rich 1973). These same population trends tend to deepen and reinforce the structure of economic and political inequalities. The higher the population growth rates, the higher are the dependency rates, and the lower the potential for savings and investment, and the expected growth in national product. More specifically, the poor development performance will reinforce the structure of inequalities in the absence of radical measures of income and wealth redistribution (Chenery et al. 1974).

In most underdeveloped societies households on the lower half of the income scale receive only 15 percent of total income (Repetto 1974, p. 4). High fertility rates coupled with poverty, especially if children are closely spaced, will result in less care and attention from parents, less schooling, and poorer school performance (Leibenstein 1971; Wray 1971; Mincer 1970). The necessary result of such dynamics are lower occupational status and income levels for the children of the poor, therefore more inequalities. Also differential fertility rates according to income groups will increase the concentration of wealth assets, creating greater differentials in wealth accumulation (Pryor 1973). In the long run high fertility increases the supply of labor, which may bring down wage rates, increasing income differentials (Lindert 1978).

The interaction between high fertility rates and increasing structural inequalities can lead to a vicious circle of poverty, underdevelopment, and greater population pressures, a situation that contains many elements of potentially violent conflicts.

Differential population growth rates affect the structures not only of economic inequalities but also those of political inequalities. In ethnically stratified societies, where the elites have a distinct ethnic identity, political inequalities are instituted on ethnic lines of identification. If political inequalities between ethnic groups coincide with economic inequalities, the population growth rates of the subordinated ethnic groups may outstrip those of the dominating ones. These demographic patterns, by reinforcing ethnic cleavages, will lead to conflict if political systems do not counterbalance these trends through the use of positive redistributional policies. This response is less likely where the political system is based on a scheme of segmental or ethnic representation.

Population densities were thought to have a direct impact on conflict generation. Most of the proponents of the density violence thesis base their arguments on ethnological or pathological studies, where overcrowdedness *per se* leads to deviant behavior and aggression (Galle et al. 1972; Lind 1972; Carstairs 1969). Empirical research does not, however, substantiate this proposition (Choucri 1974). What has clear empirical support is the thesis that relates densities or pressures upon available resources (in the context of inequalities) to violence (Choucri 1974; Carey 1973; Gurr and Weil 1973; Cornelius 1972, 1969; Goodman 1971).

Age distribution is another demographic variable considered to have a direct impact on the outbreak of conflicts. Some theorists assert that a youthful age distribution gives a country a certain privilege in the balance of power with other nations. Others assume that a youthful nation has a higher predisposition toward violence and aggression (Morgenthau 1973; Knorr 1970; Aron 1966). No empirical evidence has confirmed these propositions. On the other hand, a youthful population facing unemployment, especially in a context of underdevelopment and inequalities, has been found empirically to be conducive to conflict (Choucri 1974; Gurr and Weil 1973). Here again, population trends seem to operate as a stimulant to conflict through the dynamics of relative deprivation and systematic frustration created by the existing structures of inequalities.

Finally, migration trends (whether voluntary or not) alter the social composition of the society and may increase or impose new systems of inequalities. Under colonialism, for example, the colonial policies of contract labor and the encouragement of white settlements in the third world nations are a major source of some of the protracted social conflicts that we have witnessed in the last few decades. The conflict does not arise from ethnicity as such but from the competition of ethnic groups over access to resources and power, especially when migration results in more economic and political inequalities for the natives (as in the case of white settlement) (Nairn 1977; Barclay, Kumar, and Simms 1976; Schermerhorn 1970; Hunter 1966).

On the other hand, protracted social conflicts may lead to a distorted population structure directly or indirectly. This in turn will exacerbate and protract the conflictive situation.

The protracted social conflict is essentially a structural conflict rooted in deep social and economic inequality structures (Azar and Farah 1981). It may affect population trends indirectly through its impact on the development performance of a society and the structure of inequalities.

The negative impact of protracted social conflicts on development levels results from two main mechanisms. The involvement of the society in a protracted conflict diverts part of the economic resources to the military and the police forces. The channeling of resources to the military will not only decrease investments in the economic sector proper but will also deplete investment in human capital. Lower expenditures on education and health, for example, will affect labor productivities. In addition actual violence leads to the destruction of existing factories, communications systems, and other facilities, obviously impinging on development. Since, according to the demographic transition theory, the increase in economic growth is highly related to lower population growth rates, we can expect that the protracted social conflicts in this situation will reinforce the patterns of high fertility rates by reducing the negative effects of development on population trends (Coale et al. 1979; Leibenstein 1974; Kuznets 1967).

Protracted social conflicts may also reinforce and/or increase the existing patterns of economic and political inequalities. We suspect that the existence of protracted social conflicts has generated more coercion, resulting in more unequal political power relations. Protracted social conflicts also influence the distribution of economic rewards in the society, thereby increasing economic inequalities. Intermittent violence leads not only to the disruption of economic production but also to severe bottlenecks in the supply of necessities. Famines and starvation often result from such types of conflict.

Protracted social conflict may also have a direct impact on population growth rates. The strength in numbers argument is advocated by many activists engaged in ethnic conflicts either to maintain the groups' survival or to achieve their goals by backing them with votes (Renouvin and Duroselle 1967). The same argument is used in identity-related conflicts when numbers are crucial for strategic victory (Ben Gurion 1971; Brown 1969). In addition the poor economic conditions, coupled with malnutrition and famine, increase infant mortality rates (Curlin et al. 1975). The increase in infant mortality results in higher fertility rates in subsequent periods (Russell 1974). Nevertheless, the direct effect of the conflict on fertility rates in time of open violence seems to be negative, only to recover later at even higher rates before returning to preconflict levels (Curlin et al. 1975).

Short-term disruption in fertility and mortality patterns have a long-run impact on the age and sex composition of the population. These changes can have a substantial effect on the trend of differential population rates of change and therefore on the structure of inequalities and the potential for conflict.

Conflicts in their acute extensive forms may lead to a sharp reduction in the population size (especially males) (Wright 1965; Biraben 1961; Sauvy 1956). This affects the economic structure and performance of the society. These massive migrations cause dislocations and pressure on available resources and may form the basis for new internal conflicts.

The relationship between population trends and conflicts is structural, reinforcing in most cases a vicious circle of overpopulation, poverty, inequalities, and conflict.

Very briefly, we have argued that there are strong reciprocal relations between population and conflicts. We have also suggested that ideology plays a role in transforming antagonisms into violent behavior and that the persistence of inequality structures on the international and national levels will reinforce the dynamics of interaction between the existing population trends and protracted conflicts. How then, might structural inequalities be reduced or transformed so that violent conflict and adverse population trends are mitigated? Our answer is to adopt a developmental approach targeted to the alleviation of inequalities on both the international and national levels.

Within third world countries, where protracted social conflict as well as adverse population trends and patterns are prominent, development policies should be aimed not only at the satisfaction of the population's basic needs but essentially at the promotion of equal political relations and the liberalization of the political structure. Coercion is a less efficient and a more expensive means of containing conflict (Gurr and Duvall 1973). It does not solve conflict, it just suppresses it for a while, until the whole social system degenerates into extensive violence and destruction. Political development should be a prerequisite for economic development, and not vice-versa as assumed by the modernization theory. In the framework of a more open political system, policies of economic development targeted to fulfill the basic needs of the population and to achieve self-reliance on the national and international level will have a better chance to succeed. The basic secret for successful development policies is the committed participation of the people for whom development is intended.

To maintain the stability of the system, development policies should be aimed at the promotion of international policies that enable poor countries to help themselves. The demands for a new international economic order that does not stop at marginal changes but aims to establish relevant and more equitable economic relations are a step in the right direction.

NOTE

1. For example, the military takeover in Nigeria in 1966 attempted to impose the hegemony of the nascent capitalist class which was too weak to challenge directly the power of the traditional oligarchy. See also Stepan (1978); O'Donnell (1973); Nun (1969).

REFERENCES

Althusser, L. *Lenin and Philosophy and Other Essays.* London: Newleft Books, 1971.

Adelman, I., and C. Morris. *Economic Growth and Social Equity in Developing Countries.* Stanford: Stanford University Press, 1973.

Amin, S. *Unequal Development.* New York: Monthly Review Press, 1976.

_____. *Accumulation on a World Scale.* New York: Monthly Review Press, 1974.

Apter, D. "The Role of Traditionalism in the Political Modernization of Ghana and Uganda." In *Independent Black Africa,* edited by W. J. Hanna. Chicago: McNally, 1964, pp. 254–77.

Ardrey, R. *The Territorial Imperative*. New York: Atheneum, 1961.

Aron, R. *Peace and War: A Theory of International Relations*. New York: Double-day, 1966.

Azar, E. E., R. McLaurin, and P. Jureidini. "Protracted Conflict in the Middle East." *Journal of Palestine Studies* (1978): 41–69.

Azar, E. E. "Peace Amidst Development: A Conceptual Agenda for Conflict and Peace Research." *International Interactions* 6 (1979): 123–43.

Azar, E. E., and W. Eckhardt. "Protracted Conflict as a Function of Imperialism." Paper presented at the International Studies Association (Southern Section), Athens, Ga., October 2–4, 1979.

Azar, E. E., and N. Farah. "The Structure of Inequalities and Protracted Social Conflict: A Theoretical Framework." *International Interactions* 7, no. 4 (1981): 317–35.

Barbu, Z. "Nationalism as a Source of Aggression." In *Conflict in Society*, edited by A. DeReuck and I. Knight. Boston: Little, Brown, 1966, pp. 184–97.

Bandura, A. *Aggression: A Social Learning Analysis*. Englewood Cliffs, N.J.: Prentice-Hall, 1973.

Banks, A. *The Political Handbook of the World*. Albany, N.Y.: Research Foundation of SUNY, 1976.

Barclay, W., K. Kumar, and R. P. Simms. *Racial Conflict, Discrimination, and Power*. New York: AMS Press, 1976.

Barth, F. *Ethnic Groups and Boundaries*. Boston: Little, Brown, 1969.

Ben-Gurion, D. *Israel: A Personal History*. New York: Funk & Wagnalls, 1971.

Bergsten, C. F., and J. A. Mathieson. "The Future of the International Economic Order: An Agenda for Research." In *The Future of the International Economic Order*, edited by C. F. Bergsten. Lexington, Ma.: Lexington Books, 1973, pp. 1–59.

Biraben, J. N. "Pertes Allemandes au cours de la Deuxieme Guerre Mondiale." *Population* 16 (1961): 517–90.

Boulding, K. *The Image*. Ann Arbor: University of Michigan Press, 1956.

Brown, H. R. *Die Nigger Die*. New York: Dial, 1969.

Cardoso, F. H., and E. Faletto. *Dependency and Development in Latin America*. Berkeley: University of California Press, 1979.

Carey, G. W. "Density, Crowding, Stress, and the Ghetto." *American Behavioral Scientist* 15 (1972): 495–510.

Carr, E. H. *The Twenty Years' Crisis, 1919–1939*. New York: Harper and Row, 1964.

Carstairs, G. M. "Overcrowding and Human Aggression." In *Violence in America*, edited by H. D. Graham and T. R. Gurr. New York: New American Library, 1969, pp. 730–42.

Castells, M. *City, Class and Power*, translated by E. Lebas. New York: St. Martin's, 1978.

Chenery, H., M. S. Ahluwalia, C. L. G. Bell, J. H. Duloy, and R. Jolly. *Redistribution With Growth*. Oxford: Oxford University Press, 1976.

Choucri, N. *Population Dynamics and International Violence: Propositions, Insights, and Evidence*. Lexington, Ma.: Lexington Books, 1974.

_____, and R. North. *Nations in Conflict: National Growth and International Violence*. San Francisco: Freeman, 1975.

Claude, I. L. *Power and International Relations*. New York: Random House, 1962.

Coale, A. J., B. A. Anderson, and E. Harm. *Human Fertility in Russia Since the Nineteenth Century*. Princeton, N.J.: Princeton University Press, 1979.

Connor, W. "Ethnology and the Peace of South Asia." *World Politics* 20 (1969): 51–86.

Cornelius, W. A. "Urbanization as an Agent in Latin American Political Instability: The Case of Mexico." *American Political Science Review* 63 (1969): 833–57.

_____. "The Cityward Movement: Some Political Implications." *Proceedings of the Academy of Political Science* 30 (1972): 27–41.

Coser, L. "Collective Violence and Civil Conflict." Special issue of the *Journal of Social Issues* 28 (1972).

Crabb, C. V., Jr. *Nations in a Multipolar World*. New York: Harper and Row, 1968.

Curlin, G. T., L. C. Chen, and S. B. Hussain. "Demographic Crisis: The Impact of the Bangaladesh Civil War (1971) on Births and Deaths in a Rural Area of Bangaledesh." *Population Studies* 38 (1975): 87–105.

Davies, J. C. "Toward a Theory of Revolution." *American Sociological Review* 27 (1962): 5–19.

_____. "The Circumstances and the Causes of Revolution: A Review." *The Journal of Conflict Resolution* 11 (1967): 247–57.

_____. "The J Curve of Rising and Declining Satisfaction as a Cause of Some Great Revolutions and a Contained Rebellion." In *The History of Violence in America: Historical and Comparative Perspectives*, edited by H. D. Graham and T. R. Gurr. Washington, D.C.: National Commission on the Causes and Prevention of Violence, 1969, pp. 690–730.

De Vos, G., and L. Romanucci-Ross, eds. *Ethnic Identity: Cultural Continuities and Change*. California: Mayfield, 1975.

Deutsch, K. W., and J. D. Singer. "Multipolar Power Systems and International Stability." In *Analyzing International Relations*, edited by W. D. Coplin and C. W. Kegley, Jr. New York: Praeger, 1975, pp. 320–37.

Dinnerstein, H. S. *War and the Soviet Union: Nuclear Weapons and the Revolution in Soviet Military and Political Thinking*, rev. ed. New York: Praeger, 1962.

Dollard, J., L. W. Doob, N. E. Miller, O. H. Mowrer, and R. R. Sears. *Frustration and Aggression*. New Haven, Ct.: Yale University Press, 1939.

Dulles, E. L., and C. R. Dickson, eds. *Detente: Cold War Strategies in Transition*. Center for Strategic Studies, Georgetown University. New York: Praeger, 1965.

East, M. A. "Status Discrepancy and Violence in the International System: An Empirical Analysis." In *The Analysis of International Politics,* edited by J. Rosenau, V. Davis, M. East. New York: Free Press, 1972, pp. 299–319.

Fisher, S. "Long-Term Contracts, Rational Expectations, and the Optimal Money Supply Rule." *Journal of Political Economy* 85 (1977): 191–206.

Fox, R. G., C. Aull, and L. Cimino. "Ethnic Nationalism and Political Mobilization in Industrial Societies." In *Interethnic Communication,* edited by E. L. Ross. Athens: University of Georgia Press, 1978, pp. 53–77.

Frank. A. G. *Capitalism and Underdevelopment in Latin America.* New York: Monthly Review Press, 1967.

_____. *Dependent Accumulation and Underdevelopment.* New York: Monthly Review Press, 1979.

Fromm, E. *The Anatomy of Human Destructiveness.* New York: Holt, Rinehart, and Winston, 1973.

Gabel, J. *False Consciousness: An Essay on Reification,* trans. M. A. Thompson. Oxford: Basil Blackwell, 1975.

Galle, O. R., W. R. Gove, and J. M. McPherson. "Population Density and Pathology: What Are the Relations for Man?" *Science* 176 (1972): 23–30.

Galbraith, J. K. *The New Industrial State.* Boston: Houghton Mifflin, 1967.

Galtung, J. "A Structural Theory of Aggression." *Journal of Peace Research* 2 (1964): 95–119.

_____. "Violence, Peace, and Peace Research." *Journal of Peace Research* 6 (1969): 167–91.

_____. " A Structural Theory of Imperialism." *Journal of Peace Research* 8 (1971): 81–118.

_____. *The European Community: A Superpower in the Making.* Oslo and London: 1973.

Germani, G. *Authoritarianism, Fascism, and National Populism.* New Brunswick, N.J.: TransAction Books, 1978.

Glazer, N., and P. Moynihan, ed. *Ethnicity: Theory and Experience.* Cambridge, Ma.: Harvard University Press, 1975.

Goodman, A. E. "The Political Implications of Urban Development in Southeast Asia: The 'Fragment' Hypothesis." *Economic Development and Cultural Change* 20 (1971): 117–30.

Gordon, R. J., and J. Pelkmans. *Challenges to Interdependent Economies: The Industrial West in the Coming Decade.* The 1980s Project Council on Foreign Affairs. New York: McGraw-Hill, 1979.

Gouldner, A. *The Coming Crisis of Western Sociology.* New York: Basic Books, 1970.

Grove, J. D. "A Partial Test of the Ethnic Equalization Hypothesis: A Cross-National Study." In *Global Inequality: Political and Socio-Economic Perspectives,* edited by J. D. Grove. Boulder, Co.: Westview, 1979, pp. 135–62.

Gurr, T., and H. Weil. "Population Growth and Population Conflict: A Correlational Study of 84 Nations." Unpublished manuscript, Northwestern University, Evanston, Il., 1973.

Gurr, T. "A Comparative Study of Civil Strife." In *Violence in America: Historical and Comparative Perspectives,* edited by H. D. Graham and T. R. Gurr. Washington, D.C.: National Commission on the Causes and Prevention of Violence, 1969, pp. 572–632.

Haas, E. B. *Beyond the Nation-State.* Stanford, Ca.: Stanford University Press, 1964.

_____. *The Uniting of Europe,* 2nd ed. Stanford, Ca.: Stanford University Press, 1968.

Hibbs, D. A., Jr. *Mass Political Violence: A Cross-National Causal Analysis.* New York: Wiley-Interscience, 1973.

Hines, J. S. *Conflict and Conflict Management.* Athens: University of Georgia Press, 1980.

Holsti, O. R. "The Belief System and National Images." *Journal of Conflict Resolution* 6 (1962): 244–52.

Horowitz, D. "Three Dimensions of Ethnic Politics." *World Politics* 23 (1971): 232–44.

Hyde, D. *On Roots of Guerrilla Warfare.* London: Bodley Head, 1968.

Hymer, S. "The Multinational Corporation and the Law of Uneven Development." In *Economics and World Order: From the 1970s to the 1990s,* edited by J. Bhagwati. New York: 1972, pp. 113–40.

Hunter, G. *South-East Asia, Race, Culture, and Nation.* New York: Oxford University Press, 1966.

Jacobson, C. G. *Soviet Strategy-Soviet Foreign Policy.* Glasgow: R. Maclehose and Co., The University Press, 1974.

Jervis, R. "Hypotheses on Misperception." *World Politics* 20 (1968): 454–79.

Kaplan, M. A. *System and Process in International Politics.* New York: Wiley, 1957.

Keohane, R. O., and J. S. Nye, eds. *Transnational Relations and World Politics.* Cambridge, Ma.: Harvard University Press, 1972.

_____. "World Politics and the International Economic Order." In *The Future of the International Economic Order: An Agenda for Research,* edited by C. F. Bergsten. Lexington, Ma.: Lexington Books, 1973, pp. 115–79.

_____. "International Interdependence." In *International Politics,* vol. 8, edited by Greenstein and Polsby. Reading, Ma.: Addison-Wesley, 1975, pp. 363–414.

_____. *Power and Interdependence: World Politics in Transition.* Boston: Little, Brown, 1977.

Kindleberger, C. *Power and Money.* London: Macmillan, 1970.

Knorr, K. *Military Power and Potential.* Lexington, Ma.: Lexington Books, 1970.

Knorr, K. *Power and Money.* London: Macmillan, 1973.

_____, and F. N. Trager, eds. *Economic Issues and National Security.* Lawrence, Ks.: The Regents Press, 1977.

Kocher, J. E. *Rural Development, Equity, and Fertility Decline.* New York: The Population Council, 1974.

Kuznets, S. "Quantitative Aspects of the Economic Growth of Nations." *Economic Development and Cultural Change* 15 (1967): 2.

Legum, C., W. Zartman, S. Mytelka, and L. K. Mytelka. *Africa in the 1980s: A Continent in Crisis.* New York: McGraw-Hill, 1979.

Leibenstein, H. "The Impact of Population Growth on Economic Welfare: Non-Traditional Elements." In *Rapid Population Growth.* Prepared by a Study Committee of the Office of the Foreign Secretary, National Academy of Sciences, with the support of the Agency for International Development. Baltimore, Md.: Johns Hopkins University Press, 1971, pp. 175–98.

_____. "An Interpretation of the Economic Theory of Fertility: Promising Path or Blind Alley?" *Journal of Economic Literature* 12 (1974): 457–79.

Lenin. *Imperialism: The Highest Stage of Capitalism.* New York: International Publishers, 1939.

Lenski, G. *Power and Privilege.* New York: McGraw-Hill, 1966.

Lider, J. *On the Nature of War.* Swedish Studies in International Relations, vol. 8. Great Britain: Saxon House, 1977.

Lind, A. "Some Psycho-Political Effects of Population Distribution in a Postsubsistence Era." In *Political Science in Population Studies,* edited by R. L. Clinton, W. S. Flash, and R. K. Goodwin. Lexington, Ma.: Heath, 1972, pp. 55–78.

Lindert, P. *Fertility and Scarcity in America.* Princeton, N.J.: Princeton University Press, 1978.

Linz, J. "Crisis, Breakdown, and Reequilibration." In *The Breakdown of Democratic Regimes,* edited by J. Linz and A. Stepan. Baltimore, Md.: Johns Hopkins University Press, 1978, pp. 3–124.

Lodgaard, S. "Political Changes and Economic Reorientation in Europe: The Role of Industrial Cooperation." *Instant Research on Peace and Violence* 3 (1972): 145–57.

London, K. *The Soviet Impact on World Politics.* New York: Hawthorn, 1974.

Lorenz, K. *On Aggression.* New York: Harcourt, Brace, and World, 1966.

Luxemburg, R. *The Accumulation of Capital.* New York: Monthly Review Press, 1968.

Marcuse, H. *Soviet Marxism.* New York: Columbia University Press, 1958.

Mandel, E. *Late Capitalism,* rev. ed., trans. Y. O. Bris. London: Newleft Books, 1975.

Mayer, J. "Coping with Famine." *Foreign Affairs* 53 (1974): 98–120.

Midlarsky, M. I. "Power, Uncertainty, and the Onset of International Violence." *Journal of Conflict Resolution* 18 (1976): 395–431.

Miliband, R. *The State in Capitalist Society.* New York: Basic Books, 1969.

Mincer, J. "The Distribution of Labor Incomes: A Survey with Special Reference to the Human Capital Approach." *Journal of Economic Literature* 8 (1970): 1–26.

Mitrany, D. *A Working Peace System.* New York: Quadrangle, 1966.

Morgenthau, H. J. *Dilemmas of Politics.* Chicago: University of Chicago Press, 1958.

_____. *Politics in the Twentieth Century.* Chicago: University of Chicago Press, 1962.

_____. *Politics among Nations,* 5th ed. New York: Knopf, 1973.

Nairn, T. *The Break Up of Britain: Crisis and Neo-Nationalism.* London: Newleft Books, 1977.

Noel, D. L. "A Theory of the Origin of Ethnic Stratification." In *Racial Conflict, Discrimination, and Power: Historical and Contemporary Studies,* edited by W. Barclay, K. Kumar, and R. P. Simms. New York: AMS Press, 1976.

Nun, J. *Latin America: The Hegemonic Crisis and the Military Coup.* Berkeley, Ca.: Institute of International Studies, 1969.

O'Donnell, G. *Modernization and Bureaucratic-Authoritarianism: Studies in South American Politics.* Berkeley, Ca.: Institute of International Studies, 1973.

_____. "Reflections on the Patterns of Change in the Bureaucratic Authoritarian State." *Latin American Research Review* 13 (1978): 3–38.

Ogbeide, M. I. "Measles in Nigerian Children." *Journal of Pediatrics* 71 (1967): 737.

Organski, A. F. K. *World Politics,* 2nd ed. New York: Knopf, 1968.

Osgood, R. E., and R. W. Tucker. *Force, Order, and Justice.* Baltimore, Md.: Johns Hopkins University Press, 1967.

Pentland, C. *International Theory and European Integration.* London: Faber and Faber, 1973.

Poulantzas, N. *Political Power and Social Classes.* London: Newleft Books, 1973.

_____. *Fascism and Dictatorship: The Third International and the Problem of Fascism.* London: Newleft Books, 1974.

_____. *Classes in Contemporary Capitalism.* London: Newleft Books, 1975.

_____. *The Crisis of Dictatorship: Portugal, Greece, Spain.* London: Newleft Books, 1976.

Pryor, F. "Simulation of the Impact of Social and Economic Institutions on the Size Distribution of Income and Wealth." *American Economic Review* 63 (1973): 50–72.

Repetto, R. *Economic Equality and Fertility in Developing Countries.* Baltimore, Md.: Johns Hopkins University Press for Resources for the Future, 1979.

Renouvin, P., and J. B. Duroselle. *Introduction to the History of International Relations.* New York: Praeger, 1967.

Rich, W. *Smaller Families through Social and Economic Progress.* Washington, D.C.: Overseas Development Council, 1973.

Sauvy, A. "La Population de l'Union Sovietique, Situation, Croissance, et Problemes Actuels." *Population* 11 (1956): 461–80.

Schermerhorn, R. A. *Comparative Ethnic Relations: A Framework for Theory and Research.* New York: Random House, 1970.

Schuman, F. L. *International Politics,* 7th ed. New York: McGraw-Hill, 1969.

Schwarzenberger, G. *Power Politics,* 3rd ed. London: Stevens, 1964.

Senghaas, D. "Conflict Formations in Contemporary International Society." *Journal of Peace Research* 10 (1973): 163–84.

Shaw, T. M. "Kenya and South Africa: Subimperialist States." *Orbis* 2 (1977): 375–94.

Shefrin, B. M. *The Future of U. S. Politics in an Age of Economic Limits.* Boulder, Co.: Westview, 1980.

Sherman, H. J. *Stagflation: A Radical Theory of Unemployment and Inflation.* New York: Harper and Row, 1975.

Smith, M. G. "Institutional and Political Conditions of Pluralism." In *Pluralism in Africa,* edited by L. Kuper and M. G. Smith. Berkeley, Ca.: University of California Press, 1969, pp. 27–66.

Smith, T. "Social Violence and Conservative Social Psychology: The Case of Erik Erikson." *Journal of Peace Research* 13 (1976): 1–12.

Spiegel, S. L. *Dominance and Diversity: The International Hierarchy.* Boston: Little, Brown, 1972.

Steinbrunner, J. D. *The Cybernetic Theory of Decision: New Dimensions of Political Analysis.* Princeton, N.J.: Princeton University Press, 1974.

Stepan, A. *The State and Society.* Princeton, N.J.: Princeton University Press, 1978.

Sunkel, O. "Transnational Capitalism and National Disintegration in Latin America." *Social and Economic Studies* 22 (1973).

———, and E. Fuenzalida. "Transnationalization, National Disintegration in Contemporary Capitalism." *International Development Studies Internal Working Paper* 18, Brighton, England, 1974.

Sweezy, P. M. "On the New Global Disorder." *Monthly Review* 30 (1979): 1–9.

Taylor, J. G. *From Modernization to Modes of Production.* London: Macmillan, 1979.

Van den Berghe, P. "Ethnicity: The African Experience." *International Social Science Journal* 23 (1971): 507–18.

Vayrynen, R. "Economic and Military Position of the Regional Power Centers." *Journal of Peace Research* 15 (1979): 349–69.

———, and L. Herrera. "Sub-Imperialism: From Dependence to Subordination." *Instant Research on Peace and Violence* 3 (1975).

Wallace, M. D. *War and Rank among Nations.* Lexington, Ma.: Lexington Books, 1973.

Wallerstein, I. *The Capitalist World Economy.* Cambridge: Cambridge University Press, 1979.

Wray, J. D. "Population Pressures on Families: Family Size and Child Spacing." *Reports on Population/Family Planning* 9 (1971): 403–61.

Wright, Q. *A Study of War,* 2nd ed. Chicago: University of Chicago Press, 1965.

7

Population, Conflict, and Policy

DAVIS B. BOBROW

S TUDENTS OF INTERNATIONAL CONFLICT have long recognized that population matters for conflict and power (see, for example, Morgenthau 1960; Wright 1964; Organski 1968; Choucri and North 1975; Singer, Bremer, and Stuckey 1972; Cline 1975; and Knorr 1956, 1970). This chapter calls attention to the ways in which population-conflict relationships do and should matter for public policy. To that end it discusses population-conflict implications for public policy as they pose threats to a regime and obstacles to or opportunities for the objectives of partisan groups and national governments. A realistic analysis of policy implications cannot be limited to the "facts" of population and its relationships with conflict. Vivid images of the past and compelling expectations about the future, particularly demographically linked fears and prejudices, determine how political leaders judge what is feasible and important.

Available systematic evidence denies any clear, general significance for conflict of raw population numbers *per se*. Instead it makes clear the importance of population in a context of social organization, economic development, technology, political arrangements, and salient historical experience. We must avoid the trap of simplistic preoccupation with aggregate population size and growth rates. Instead we must grasp the population-conflict nexus in terms of "if . . . then" statements in which population features are some of the "ifs" and the sorts of context characteristics just noted are others. With respect to conflict, population is an intervening, independent, and dependent variable.

The images of populations held by policy-makers also may contain elements of size, composition, and distribution. These subjective profiles determine the responses of public institutions and political leaders to population matters and conflict. Images may shape the behavior of the policy system, but realities shape the consequences. Accordingly, two sorts of comparative

179

and longitudinal profiles of population are essential. The first is objective; the second deals with perceptions. Political elites are the captive of the second. Yet they are one of the sources of both.

The definition of conflict depends on the culture, social structure, economy, and political institutions of the society under analysis. This essay focuses on extreme forms of conflict — violent organized collective action for political purposes, especially war. These are the forms of conflict most irreversibly destructive in human terms, and most severely and immediately crucial for the survival of political leaders and states. We focus on types of conflict at the heart of public policy and governmental responsibilities — external and internal threats to the state, challenges to the control of state organs, and clashes over shares of benefits from and contributions to the political order.

To relate population to organized political violence, we need to distinguish several aspects of such conflicts:

- duration, for example, some conflicts go on for years, others are intermittently active and quiescent, still others are short-lived, one-time spasms;
- intensity, for example, some exact heavy casualties and economic damage on the participants and others only a minor toll;
- spatial extent, for example, some are localized in one region, others are waged throughout a nation, still others cross national lines and, at an extreme, even continents;
- precipitants, for example, events and conditions triggering conflicts may be domestic or external, economic or religious;
- participation, for example, some conflicts may involve total populations and others small fractions;
- objectives, for example, conflicts may or may not have as a major purpose changes in population distribution or the status, wealth, and power of particular population subgroups.

MILITARY CAPABILITY, WAR POWER, AND SUFFERING

This section focuses on major international conflicts and argues that the relationships between population, military capability, and war power can be understood only in relation to a nation's security objectives, technology, economy, political institutions, and social organization. Accordingly, the population-related factors that merit the most attention are those that link to these contextual features — education/skill levels, segmental divisions, and deeply felt fears and grievances related to particular population groups and subgroups.

Conventional Wisdom — Numerical Adversity and Advantage

Much conventional thinking in industrialized nations holds that population size and youth, especially of males, provide the major links between demography, military capability, and war power. Nations with larger and younger numbers of males are held to have the advantage in deterring, waging, and winning wars. Some northern elites even contend that the United States and indeed the North as a whole are threatened by "numerical adversity" due to slower rates of population growth and an increase in the age of their populations.

The premises that underlie such thinking do not stand up to what we know about the nature of military capability and war power. Instead we need to work through the relationships between population aggregates and the military labor force, the military labor force and military capability, and military capability and war power.

From Population Aggregates to Military Labor Force

Male population size and average age do not necessarily have implications for military population other than setting some maximum limit for the number of male members of the armed forces of a certain age. The relationship between population size and military population should be viewed in terms of two ratios. The first is that of military participation, or the fraction of the population under arms. The second is that of military training, the fraction of the population that while not currently under arms has received and retained training to bear arms. Both ratios are a function of national policy choices about military manning systems and the universality of their application. They need not, and historically have not, correlated with population size (see Foot 1961; Janowitz and Moscos 1979). The pertinent national policy choices are in part shaped by population-related factors and in part by other sources.

Prominent determinants of military participation and training ratios are political fears and antagonisms related to segmental divisions and labor supply-demand relationships in the economy. Segmental divisions often have implications about willingness to serve in the military and political judgments about the probable loyalty of different population subgroups should they participate in military institutions (for example, Enloe 1980; Grundy 1976; Wheeler 1976; Adekson 1976; Dominguez 1976; Guyot 1976; Mazrui 1975). Civilian labor force considerations affect the opportunity cost political leaders associate with military labor force alternatives. Military participation and training affect the availability and price of labor in the economy. The expenditures associated with military participation and training compete with other expenditures for military and civilian purposes (see, for example, McNown, Udis, and Ash 1980). While the magnitude of these opportunity costs obviously varies, their existence is universal.

Further, national policy decisions about military participation and training are shaped by security images, in particular about the nature of military threats and the ingredients of effective defense. High participation ratios follow from elite views that threats are continuous, will involve large-scale military operations, and may well arise rather quickly, over a period of days, weeks, or months rather than years. High training ratios rest on an expected time interval between warning and combat that is lengthier but insufficient for enlarging the military population from scratch.

In sum, for policy elites to assess the import of relative population size for military population size, they should take into account segmental divisions, opportunity costs for the civilian and military sectors, and threat magnitudes and warning times.

As for the age and sex characteristics of a population, their implications are more a function of policy and technology than of biology. The military usefulness of women and the middle-aged follows from the nature of military campaigns, the technology or war, and political and cultural views on sex-linked roles (see "Women as New 'Manpower'" 1978). These key variables are obviously not conveyed by standard measurements such as the size of the younger part of the male labor force.

From Military Labor Force to Military Capability

Even the most accurate comparative estimates of the current and potential size of active-duty and trained reserve military populations do not suffice for conclusions about relative military capability. The military capability stock of a nation or a political movement is a complex function involving people, organization, and goods (weapons, supplies, and logistical assets to move them) in interaction. Each can operate to enhance or detract from the others. The quantity and quality of military people, organization, and goods indicate military capability only as they are appropriate for each other. The crucial nature of appropriate matching seems clear in the current era of high technology weapons, supporting equipment (such as computers), and sophisticated means of transportation for projecting force. As a corollary of these developments, the military establishments of the major powers have experienced a decline in their needs for "combat operatives" and an increase in those for mechanics, technicians, and administrators. These trends parallel those in the labor force needs industrialized societies experience as they move away from the leading sectors of the industrial revolution to those now in vogue (notably electronics). In the age of the "military specialist," the usefulness of a military population depends on its educational/skill level (discussion in Wool 1968; Erickson 1974). High technology weapons and equipment only translate into military capability as they can be used and maintained up to their performance limits. Components of military capability function in concert. The useful military population potential will be bounded to a significant extent by the general skill level of a national population and the occupational distribution of a total labor force. Also, a more differentiated and functionally specialized military population places greater demands on military organization than in simpler periods. As in modern industry, with specialization come greater needs for horizontal and vertical coordination and information sharing.

In sum, military capability does not increase in some linear fashion with the skill and educational level of the military population. Even well-matched levels of skills and technology, when both are at a very sophisticated level, do not necessarily provide a military capability edge relative to an adversary with equally well-matched forces at a less sophisticated level. The military purpose to be served matters crucially. The combinations well-suited to a massive conventional war are strikingly different from those valuable for prolonged campaigns of disruption and harassment as in guerrilla war.

From Military Capability to War Power

The previous discussion dealt with the linkages of population-related factors to stocks of military capability in general rather than in situational terms. Yet war outcomes are not general but situational. The military success of enemies at war and the judgments of political elites about the costs and benefits of pursuing warlike policies depend not just on stocks but also on flows, that is, on replenishment and relative degradation of military capabilities. War power depends on the capacity of political systems to muster military capabilities relative to their opponents, allowing for losses. War power for a particular conflict includes the willingness of the political elite to apply that mustered capacity to waging a specific war. Population-related factors matter as they affect any of the following determinants of war power:

- stocks of military personnel and their replenishment,
- stocks of military goods and their replenishment,
- military organizational capacity and augmenting or sustaining it,
- capacity of political institutions to muster the previous assets and extract more of them,
- will of political elites to use military capability and the buttressing and eroding of that will.

This list is not limited to our previous emphasis on the ingredients of military capability. It places them in a context of political capacity and political commitment. The last determinant plays a qualitatively different role in the war power equation than the others. The relationships among the first four allow for a substantial degree of substitution. Since there is no substitute for political will, it operates on the others as a positive or negative multiplier. The literature contains two particularly relevant systematic studies. Organski and Kugler (1980) formulate an index of national capabilities that sums an internal and external component. The implication for us is that population in relation to the economy will not have a decisive implication in itself for war power.

Rosen (1972) examined forty wars between nations in the period 1815 to 1945. While his specific formulations and cases are different, there are notable general similarities between his conclusions and those of Organski and Kugler. Rosen deals with the wealth available to political leaders (based on extractions from the national economy, technology, productivity, and foreign transfers), military manpower, and casualties. The best pointer to the victor was relative wealth available to the state. As measured by central government revenue, it indicated the winner about 80 percent of the time. In the four relevant cases the side with greater revenues and a smaller population won every time. Population in terms of military manpower was not the powerful predictor. Nor was victory a function of incurring absolutely fewer casualties. What about conservation of human resources in terms of fractional loss of population? Here the two studies are not clearly reinforcing. For Rosen, the victors tended to lose a smaller fraction of their population. For the Organski and Kugler cases, the results are mixed.

In sum, population in a simple sense should not be relied on to predict war power any more than to predict conflict. Population-related factors do matter as they affect the mobilizational capacity of political institutions and, more indirectly, as they affect the resources that are available to be mustered. Population has as much to do with war power as it has to do with economic development, political development, and political commitment to particular resource uses. What conclusions can we draw from the preceding discussion?

First, population factors that create harsh trade-offs between mustering military personnel, especially skilled personnel, and economic growth limit war power. Harshness is a function of labor scarcity in militarily-relevant skills.

Second, population factors that limit government revenue limit war power. Population composition and distribution can do so, especially as they affect tax extraction.

Third, population-related factors that affect external provision of military capabilities or wealth affect war power.

Fourth, population-related factors that affect the mobilizational capacity of government institutions affect war power. Population composition in relation to political cadre and elite composition matter here. Also the economic stakes of the contributing population in war power relative to a currently or potentially hostile population come into play.

Finally, population-related factors of a more substantive kind can shape the degree of political commitment to expand or at least risk war assets in a particular conflict. Casualty expectations and their distribution across population segments affect political decision making. Memories of war losses in World War I certainly affected the French and British reaction to the rise of the Nazis. Images of the consequences of nuclear attack on dense urban populations do enter into U.S., Soviet, Japanese, and Israeli judgments about weapon acquisition and military strategy. Judgments about the fairness of the military service and casualty burden across age grades and racial segments affected elite judgments about the costs to the United States of conducting the war in Vietnam (for example, Fligstein 1980). Even more basic, beliefs about the fate of a segment of a population at the hands of another if it avoids fighting or losses in a war can reflect historical experiences at the hands of its enemies.

POLITICAL LEADERSHIP AND PUBLIC POLICY

The previous section treated political elites and leaders almost as if they were objective, neutral observers of the interplay between population-related factors and conflict, military capability, and war power. The realities are far different. Political elites and their policy agendas are shaped by, and in turn help determine, population-related factors.

Population Images and Conflict

Political leaders do not come to population-related factors with a clean slate, but rather with a set of memories and images. These memories and images affect their policy priorities and attentiveness to and interpretation of information about population-related factors. Given our topic, particularly relevant memories and images are those that characterize populations in terms of enmity, capacity, vulnerability, and loyalty. They induce a political climate in which particular "demographic fears" and "demographic hopes" provide a foundation for numerous specific decisions. The perceived balance between hopes and fears and trends in that balance has much to do with the policy priority accorded to issues that have clear import for population-related factors. Low priority to such issues only indicates that the perceived balance is a comfortable one, not that political leaders have no pertinent images.

Images of enmity or hostility loom large when historic relationships feature overt conflict between populations whose leaders advance incompatible claims. The claims may be for economic, political, or sociocultural matters of value. For example, they may be for land or water, autonomy or dominance, state enforcement of or a laissez-faire stance toward religious practices. All have in common the premise that population group interests are fundamentally antagonistic. When the matters of value at stake are hard to divide and thus to negotiate in an incremental way, the relationship between populations seems to preclude compromise. Should a political leader believe that the actions of his own population warrant the enmity of another, it will seem almost inconceivable that relationships can take any form other than the pursuit of revenge and vigorous steps to block vengeance. Population-related enmity images are not the monopoly of the historically oppressed or vanquished. They can be equally salient for political leaders whose own group history is one of successful conflict and domination.

Images of capability take on special importance in a climate of enmity. They engender expectations about what different populations *can do* to each other. In a context of hate they appear to indicate what different populations *will do* to each other. Capability, in the sense of what populations are "capable of" by way of collective action, has a multifaceted image. In relation to conflict it surely involves military effectiveness, brutality, deception, and obsessive action insensitive to the associated costs. Political elites attribute to their own population and that of their national or group opponents rather stereotyped characteristics in each of these respects. For military effectiveness these attributions include relative technical skill, discipline, initiative, decisiveness. For brutality they refer to readiness to kill, maim, and torture combatants and noncombatants. For deception they contain proclivities to lie and pretend to induce a false sense of confidence or mask implacable hostility. For obsessive action we can note beliefs about the willingness of enemies to commit what amounts to individual or collective suicide in order to damage or destroy enemies. Enemies are alleged to place no value on human lives. At an extreme, obsessiveness implies that no rational calculus is governing enemy behavior, and thus deterrence cannot work.

Images of vulnerability held by political leaders follow in part from views of the relative capabilities of their own population to that of its enemies. However, they are highly colored by two other perceptions. The first involves demographically related experiences. When political leaders themselves, or their cohort, vividly remember being the targets of genocide which was largely successful in terms of drastically reducing the size of their population group, elimination in biological and cultural as well as political terms remains a haunting concern. Compared to that possibility, all courses of action that make it less likely, "never again," are acceptable. The horror of forced migration is only slightly less influential in political elite mindsets. When the vulnerable population is objectively small relative to its enemies, political leaders can well imagine that these experiences can be repeated. When that population seems to political leaders to be essentially without friends to help balance its manifest enemies, these experiences are always imminent. Less dramatically, but surely more frequently, political leaders see their regimes and political systems as vulnerable to particular domestic population subgroups. These are groups thought to be in a position to bring down a government or fracture a nation. Vulnerability images of this sort portray particular population groups as especially able to undermine the economy, physically disrupt the political order, or determine what the organs of state power will or will not do.

Images of loyalty relate to this last sort of vulnerability. Observation and anecdotes suggest that several types of loyalty images are held by political leaders. These include the loyalty of particular population subgroups to the leader and his clique, of other population subgroups to the subgroup to which the leader and his associates belong, and of population subgroups to the nation relative to foreign populations. The interest of political elites in the loyalties of others depends on their vulnerability to their disloyalty. As noted earlier, loyalty images enter into the choice of military participation and training policies. They also enter into conflict expectations in terms of likely hostilities and the viability of maintaining the support required to conduct internal and external war successfully.

Unfortunately, we do not have systematic, comparative studies of political elite images in population-related terms. Rather we have a great deal of illustrative case knowledge that underscores their importance. Without recognizing their role, it is extraordinarily difficult to understand the behavior of political leaders and activists (see Eberstadt and Breindel 1979; Hewitt 1977; Hlophe 1977). Elite images about population in relation to conflict often feature the factors that we found important for conflict. These are the pressure of population numbers on resources, spatial location of population groups in relation to natural resources, population movements, segmental divisions, and levels of knowledge and skills. The preceding discussion adds to this list interpretations based on historical experience and special sensitivities among political elites of relatively small populations.

The demographic hopes and fears of political leaders and the images discussed here obviously affect elite approaches to politics. Political leaders tend to assume that their images are accurate and widely shared rather than idiosyncratic. Accordingly, elite images shape what leaders conclude they ought to know and do, and also affect leaders' expectations about the actions and responses of others. That is, they shape elite judgments about effective rhetoric and packaging of issues and about the bases of political support and opposition.

Population and Politics

The decision problem for political elites is how to act effectively on the basis of their images of population-conflict relations within an inherited setting of precedents and institutional arrangements, of political precedents and institutions that often explicitly relate to population.

At an extreme, elite images, precedents, and institutions converge to emphasize conflict along population-related lines. This is most obvious in politics when the politically participating population overwhelmingly agrees that it faces a vengeful, capable enemy to which it is vulnerable and against whom no other populations will be loyal. In such situations the political priorities of leaders and followers become focused on the conflict with an enemy defined in population terms. Most if not all public policy is formulated, assessed, and promulgated in terms of a conflict along population lines. Political elites rise and fall as their public concludes that they are or are not best qualified to provide security against "them."

More frequently, precedents and institutions emphasize conflicts along population lines over the costs and benefits of state policy. Sometimes the lines relate to population distribution when subpopulations are concentrated in different localities; sometimes, to population segments when state policies provide them with differing degrees of autonomy and resources and extract a different share of their labor and wealth. Under some patterns of precedents and institutions, especially when distribution and segmentation overlap, affected persons perceive a common interest which is relatively easy to mobilize for conflict. Arrangements that organize political authority relative to the central government along regional or communal lines foster these properties. Familiar cases include Eritreans in Ethiopia, Walloons in Belgium, French and English speakers in Canada, and blacks in the United States (for example, Spillerman 1976; McRoberts 1977).

Expulsion involves either forced relocation or the removal of barriers to exit. The point is to neuter the suspect subgroup in political terms either through departure from the polity altogether, or removal to a region of little economic, political, or military significance. Assimilation involves dissolving socioeconomic and cultural boundaries that distinguish one subgroup from others viewed as more loyal. State policies about language and family law feature assimilation strategies, as do programs to mix previously separate populations in terms of place of residence, work, or education. Co-optation centers

on measures to provide potentially or currently hostile subgroups with particular stakes in the current political regime or nation state. Incentives can be
economic (preferential investment, employment, and subsidy measures) as well
as ones of status and access to the political system. Co-optation only seems
promising when enmity has shallow roots.

Splitting strategies can take two forms. The first involves political
rhetoric and action to divide disloyal or hostile subpopulations by developing an awareness of conflicts of interest among them and then making the
dominant order seem compatible with satisfaction for one side. Policies that
aid the rich or the poor, the traditional or the modern within population subgroups are illustrative. The second form tries to fractionate subgroups so that
none has the resources to wage conflict successfully or expects to be supported
by others. When successful, each subgroup comes to depend on the political
elite and state organs for protection against all the others. This last strategy
for conflict management makes sense only when political elites need very little from their citizens. It is incompatible with mustering national capacity for
external conflict.

Finally, a coercive domination strategy treats some population
subgroup (or groups) essentially as colonials or serfs. They are denied any prospect for successful conflict with the ruling order. Other parts of the population acquire a vested interest in their continuing subjugation. When political
precedents and institutions structure policy choices along population-related
lines, political elites have no choice but to pursue some mix of these strategies to manage conflict.

Precedents and institutions for dealing with the population-conflict
nexus may of course become out of date in the face of population changes.
Formerly successful conflict-management strategies can lose their efficacy.
Whether there will then be an upsurge in population-related conflict depends
both on the nature of population changes and on the extent to which established precedents and institutions are conducive to changes in strategy.

In multi-ethnic societies, a "one man, one vote" system mechanisti-
cally but rather automatically reallocates political representation in accordance
with different population growth rates and locational shifts. Substantial precedents support assimilation strategies, whatever the imperfections of their workings and consequences. Not only is it relatively easy for political leaders to
adapt to population changes; they also have clear incentives and grounds for
taking a public stance which at least permits, even if it does not accelerate,
assimilation, co-optation, and splitting.

Yet these strategies are very general. The specifics of likely public
policy—how much of a particular kind of action, at what point in time—
involve still another set of considerations. Political leaders favor policies, including resource allocations, that involve matters they can clearly control or

manipulate. Among those they favor are ones that will have a desirable impact in the immediate future (months and years versus decades). While long-term costs may dissuade them from pursuing courses of action that offer short-term benefits, the prospect of long-term benefits will rarely compensate for short-term costs. Indeed, for all practical purposes, political elites, overwhelmed by images of vulnerability and enemies capable of anything, deny the existence of the long term. With regard to policies affecting the population-conflict nexus, we should then expect political elites to concentrate on what they believe can be readily influenced within existing precedents and institutions to achieve visible results quickly. Of course, they may not say that is what they are doing.

Though population-related statements and actions may seem to conflict with these rules, careful examination will usually show that they do not really do so. Family allowances and other incentives to increase birth rates are illustrative. Faced with a comparatively more rapid growth of population on the part of a traditional enemy, political elites often support incentives to raise their own constituents' birth rate (tax credits, transfer payments, housing preferences, child care). Such steps can do little to increase the military population for more than a decade. Examination of the political economy in which such policies are adopted will usually reveal important short-term benefits to the political elite. In the family incentives case they often involve immediate income benefits for the less well-off, bonding them to the political order. The poor tend to have a greater propensity for bearing children, and the marginal value of newly conferred economic benefits will be higher for them. Child-bearing incentives also evidence concern for security, thus bolstering the elite's reputation against criticism on that score. To the extent that they bear on conflict, the connection is more to internal conflict than to international conflict.

The importance of manipulability and short-term benefits suggests that the population-related actions of governments depend on the scope and degree of state authority. We expect measures that conflict with established precedents for government action to fail and be abandoned before very long. With respect to distribution, migration incentives and disincentives can often be varied and have a quick impact (Nelson, 1976). Most governments already have institutions for limiting or facilitating emigration and immigration across national boundaries. Most governments already pursue policies that make some locations more or less economically attractive. Examples include investment, tax and labor policy, settlement incentives, and the provision of economic and social infrastructure. Segmental divisions are open to short-term manipulation by government actions raising or lowering barriers to entry to particular economic, military, and bureaucratic positions. Especially when the state is a large employer in a nation, these measures can be put into effect rapidly. Many of the measures to diminish or heighten segmental differences need pose no overt threat to the continued existence of the segments concerned. Most are more feasible for political elites in a context of growing political and economic participation opportunities. In sum, the political elites most able to pursue relevant measures are those already possessing the greatest state power operating in situations of substantial economic and political development. Stagnant or shrinking political economies have little capacity to alter population-related factors through deliberate action, even if they have special needs to do so.

SOME MODEST CONCLUSIONS

The implications of population for conflict cannot be generalized apart from particular settings that themselves differ in social organization, economic development, technology, and political arrangements. These do not change with population development in any neat fashion. The considerations reviewed do not then provide clear advice to most political leaders about specific actions to optimize population factors relative to objectives for conflict and war. Context differences will determine those specifics, and the relevant objectives vary tremendously. What does emerge is a set of recommendations about how to pursue a more realistic understanding of the population-conflict nexus and the capacity to shape it.

First, understanding the population-conflict nexus involves comprehending population-related images in the minds of political elites and those to whom they listen. Historical memories may be inaccurate, incomplete, or poor guides to future events. None of that gainsays their importance for the decisions high officials will make or the problems they will address.

Second, our discussion of war power, policy precedents, and political institutions suggests the need to examine the capacity of political arrangements to make use of human capital, to represent and affect population distribution and segmentation, and to adapt to changes in population-related factors. The need for understanding political resources and population constraints applies to responsible persons and groups in nations and international organizations working with national governments.

Third, population-related factors have a clear bearing on conflict, military capability, and war power only when related in terms of current and emerging patterns of social, economic, and political development. Policies and events that change any of these facets of development need to be examined for their impacts on the population-conflict nexus. Governments need the capacity to make those assessments and secure international assistance in doing so.

Fourth, as the previous recommendation implies, the population-conflict nexus and the public policies pertinent to it lie, in major respects, outside of the mission and means of ministries, departments, and bureaus concerned with population size policy. Governments need the capacity to inject a population dimension into most major decisions about social and economic policy, national security policy, and political institutions.

Finally, in order to overcome familiar patterns for the bureaucratic division of labor, two conditions have to be met. Senior national political figures will have to invest their effort and political capital to overcome bureaucratic inertia and parochialism, and, given the difficulty of the task and the burdens already on national planners, international organizations will have to provide skills, resources, and possibly direct incentives. Population as an important dimension of development policy, and, in turn, conflict, military capability, and war power, must be given a more central place in national policy.

REFERENCES

Adekson, J. B. "Army in a Multi-Ethnic Society." *Armed Forces and Society* 2 (1976): 251–72.

Chamie, J. "The Lebanese Civil War: An Investigation into the Causes." *World Affairs* 139 (1976): 171–88.

Choucri, N. *Population Dynamics and International Violence: Propositions, Insights, and Evidence.* Lexington, Ma.: Lexington Books, 1974.

————, and R. North. *Nations in Conflict: National Growth and International Violence.* San Francisco, Ca.: Freeman, 1975.

Cline, R. *World Power Assessment.* Washington, D.C.: Center for Strategic and International Studies, 1975.

Dominguez, J. I. "Racial and Ethnic Relations in the Cuban Armed Forces." *Armed Forces and Society* 2 (1976): 273–90.

Eberstadt, N., and E. Breindel. "Commentary: The Population Factor in the Middle East." *International Security* 3 (1979): 190–96.

Enloe, C. H. *State Security in Divided Societies.* Athens: University of Georgia Press, 1980.

Erickson, J. "Soviet Military Manpower Policies." *Armed Forces and Society* 1 (1974): 29–47.

Fligstein, N. D. "Who Served in the Military, 1940–73." *Armed Forces and Society* 6 (1980): 297–312.

Foot, M. R. D. *Men in Uniform.* London: Institute for Strategic Studies, 1961.

Grundy, K. W. "Racial and Ethnic Relations in the Armed Forces." *Armed Forces and Society* 2 (1976): 227–32.

Guyot, J. I. "Efficiency, Responsibility, and Equality in Military Staffing." *Armed Forces and Society* 2 (1976): 291–304.

Hewitt, C. "Majorities and Minorities: A Comparative Survey of Ethnic Violence." *Annals of the American Academy of Political and Social Science* 433 (1977): 150–60.

Hlophe, S. S. "The Crisis of Urban Living under Apartheid Conditions: A Socio-Economic Analysis of Soweto." *Journal of Southern African Affairs* 2 (1977): 343–54.

Janowitz, M., and C. C. Moskos, Jr. "Five Years of the All-Volunteer Force." *Armed Forces and Society* 5 (1979): 171–218.

Khuri, F. I. "The Social Dynamics of the 1975–1977 War in Lebanon." *Armed Forces and Society* 7 (Spring 1981): 393–408.

Knorr, K. *The War Potential of Nations.* Princeton, N.J.: Princeton University Press, 1956.

_____. *Military Power and Potential.* Lexington, Ma.: Lexington Books, 1970.

Mazrui, A. *Soldiers and Kinsmen in Uganda.* Beverly Hills, Ca.: Sage, 1975.

McCarthy, J. D., O. R. Galle, and W. Zimmern. "Population Density, Social Structure, and Interpersonal Violence." *American Behavioral Scientist* 18 (1975): 771–91.

McNown, R. F., B. Udis, and C. Ash. "Economic Analysis of the All-Volunteer Force." *Armed Forces and Society* 7 (1980): 113–32.

McRoberts, K. "Quebec and the Canadian Political Crisis." *The Annals of the American Academy of Political and Social Science* 433 (1977): 19–31.

Morgenthau, H. *Politics among Nations.* New York: Knopf, 1960.

Nelson, J. M. "Sojourners versus New Urbanites: Causes and Consequences of Temporary versus Permanent Cityward Migration in Developing Countries." *Economic Development and Cultural Change* 24 (1976): 721–57.

Organski, A. F. K. *World Politics.* New York: Knopf, 1968.

_____, and J. Kugler. *The War Ledger.* Chicago: University of Chicago Press, 1980.

Rosen, S. "War Power and the Willingness to Suffer." In *Peace, War, and Numbers,* edited by B. M. Russett. Beverly Hills, Ca.: Sage, 1972, pp. 167–83.

Singer, J. D., S. Bremer, J. Stuckey. "Capability Distribution, Uncertainty, and Major Power War, 1820–1965." In *Peace, War, and Numbers,* edited by B. M. Russett. Beverly Hills, Ca.: Sage, 1972, pp. 19–48.

Specter, P. E. "Population Density and Unemployment: The Effects on the Incidence of Violent Crime in the American City." *Criminology* 12 (1975): 399–401.

Spillerman, S. "Structural Characteristics of Cities and the Severity of Racial Disorders." *American Sociological Review* 41 (1976): 771–93.

Stein, A. A. *The Nation at War.* Baltimore, Md.: Johns Hopkins University Press, 1980.

Wheeler, D. L. "African Elements in Portugal's Armies in Africa." *Armed Forces and Society* 2 (1976)233–50.

Wright, Q. *A Study of War,* abridged ed. Chicago: University of Chicago Press, 1964.

"Women as New 'Manpower.'" *Armed Forces and Society* 4 (1978): 555–716.

Wool, H. *The Military Specialist.* Baltimore, Md.: Johns Hopkins University Press, 1968.

8

Integrating the Perspectives
From Population to Conflict and War

ROBERT C. NORTH

FROM THE INDIVIDUAL TO THE NATION-STATE

THE PURPOSE OF THIS CHAPTER is to consider ways in which population growth may affect the disposition toward conflict and also the ability of a country to undertake conflict and wage war successfully—when combined with other critical variables. We shall start with the basic needs, wants, desires, and demands of individual human beings and show how these may contribute to effective organizations (states and alliances of states), on the one hand, and international conflict and war, on the other.

Every human being has needs, wants, and desires—for biological survival, security, affiliation, self-respect and so forth (Maslow 1970). To ensure minimal survival, he or she requires food, water, air, and living space. As a population grows, the need for these basic resources increases. Whatever the minimal amount of basic resources needed to keep a single person alive, a thousand people will require about a thousand times as much, a million people a million times as much, and so on. In addition people have wants and desires above and beyond physiological basics. Although these are to a large extent psychological, they tend to be intensely interactive with somatic (biological) requirements. In the attempt to achieve satisfaction people formulate demands partly on themselves, partly on the physical environment, and partly on other people (the social environment) (Easton 1965, pp. 38–39).

To obtain and use resources effectively, people rely upon technology (applied knowledge and skills). Technology may refer to knowledge and skills that are mechanical (technical, engineering) or organizational (managerial, administrative, social, behavioral). Technology enables people to obtain new resources and to develop new uses for old resources. The development, maintenance, and use of technology also require resources (energy; materials for tools, machines, and other structures; and resources to be processed and transformed into useful goods and the maintenance of services). Generally the more advanced the technology, the greater the amount and the wider the range of resources required. In addition advances in technology tend to have social outcomes: people come to expect and demand a greater amount and a wider range of resources, goods, and services, and the organizations and institutions of the society are likely to become more complex (Choucri and North 1975, p. 15).

To satisfy particular requirements, people develop specialized capabilities in two ways: by developing and applying technical knowledge and skills, or by cooperating with others and organizing. Central to cooperative effort and the establishment and management of economic and political organizations is the bargaining process. Demands can be envisaged as combining with capabilities multiplicatively to produce activities or behavior. Central activities in the political process on all levels of organization are bargaining and leverage.

Bargaining and the exercise of leverage provide a wide range of modes for determining who does what, when, and how; who gets what, when, and how; and who pays for what, when, and how. Thomas Schelling (1960) has referred to a bargaining situation as one in which "the ability of one participant to gain his ends is dependent to an important degree on the choices or decisions that the other participant will make" (p. 5). Bargaining itself can be defined as a process of negotiating over the terms of a purchase, agreement, contract, division of effort, responsibility, cost, advantage, or other outcome; access to resources, privilege, status; authority to make and enforce decisions, and so forth.

Recently developed theories have treated organizations as the outcome of continuous bargaining (and adaptive learning) and coalition-formation processes. Fundamental to this approach is the idea that most political processes and organizational developments are not only the outcome of pursuing common goals (or separate but interdependent goals), but also of allocating costs and benefits (Cyert and March 1963, p. 27).

Bargaining can be accommodative (positive, rewarding, "the carrot") or coercive (penalizing, punishing, "the stick"). Whether a particular sequence of bargaining moves is accommodative or penalizing depends in considerable part upon the type of leverage that is applied. Leverage may consist of rewards of various kinds (or promises), exactions of penalty, or applications of force (or threats) (Snyder and Diesing 1977, pp. 232–34).

Formal bargaining theory has commonly emphasized highly rational, strategic skills — possibilities for bluff and for a shrewd calculation of possible alternate outcomes through particular moves or sequences of moves (as in chess or poker) — rather than the leverages that are available in political, organizational, and conflict bargaining (poker as played in bar rooms of the old wild west when each player in addition to his gold and his poker skills had a six-gun on his belt). In human history people making demands on others have commonly drawn upon whatever capabilities they have possessed in order to mobilize leverage potentials. Again, they have sought to enhance such capabilities in two basic ways: by adding to or reorganizing their personal knowledge, skills, or resources in order to deal more effectively with others; or by bargaining, cooperating, joining with others in a coalition, momentary or longer lasting, in order to accomplish collectively what they would have found difficult, costly, or impossible to accomplish alone. Coalition formation occurs, then, because some individual (or group) induces others to join in a collective effort to accomplish some task (or set of tasks) (Pfeffer and Salancik 1968, pp. 24–27). With the historical development of state-level organizations, massive armies, and powerful weapons, the relative capabilities and leverage potentials of bargainers have become increasingly important.

The successful formation and maintenance of a coalition may be expected to depend upon some means of distributing — or redistributing — gains and costs. If coalition members are to sustain their participation, they must feel that they gain more than they lose, or at least conclude that the penalties of participation are preferable to the penalties of withdrawal (Schelling 1960, p. 31). The leader of a protocoalition builds up a coalition piecemeal by bargaining with other leaders, coalition representatives et al., offering some payment or other inducement for joining the coalition or threatening a penalty when it appears necessary (Snyder and Diesing 1977, p. 349). He or she operates on credit, "promising rewards with the understanding that he will honor his promises only if he is successful," or issuing threats on the basis of whatever credibility can be drawn upon (Riker 1962, p. 106).

Symmetry and asymmetry in organizational processes can be identified in terms of the capabilities and leverage potentials of participants in a bargaining process, in terms of their respective concerns for or commitments to the outcome, the costs they bear, the advantages they seek, and so forth. The concept of asymmetry implies allometry — a tendency toward dominance or control and compliance, submission or dependence — resulting from differential growth or other processes of change. State-level organizations are characterized by asymmetry and allometry — classes, elites, bureaucratic hierarchies, and the like. Allometry in bargaining relationships, coalition formation and coalition maintenance can result from differences in physical strength, knowledge, skill, status, and access to resources.

In bargaining among themselves, applying leverage, and forming coalitions in support of particular issues and policies, national leaders, their advisors, bureaucratic chiefs, and others are presumably influenced by their personal needs, desires, values, goals, and demands as well as by their perceptions of what the national interest requires. Among national leaders — and also to a considerable extent among the rank-and-file of the populace — these needs, values, and goals (basic sustenance, security, affiliation, self-development) tend to be intensely interactive. These assertions should apply to authoritarian and totalitarian states as well as to democratic ones (Dallin 1981, pp. 343, 371–72, 376, 381, 383–85).

State-level societies — coalitions of coalitions — are maintained through extractive, distributive (allocation), and other regulatory arrangements commonly referred to as governments or regimes and through at least minimal compliance of component coalitions, their members, and the rank and file of the population. Coalitions on all "higher" levels of organization are sensitive to — and tend to change with — increases and decreases in membership (population), with advances in technology, and with changes in the demands and relative capabilities of component coalitions and their members. The allocation of rewards (often referred to as side-payments) and of costs (penalties, negative side-payments) are among the leverages available to regimes (and regime leaderships) for the maintenance of law and order (and often also for the perpetuation of their own tenure). Not only is access to resources a *sine qua non* for sustaining the basic needs and demands of a society; sustained access is a prerequisite for meeting the psychologically generated requirements of people on all levels of society, as well as for the maintenance of capabilities and leverage potentials of individuals, groups, and the state itself.

POPULATION, DEMANDS, AND CAPABILITIES

Demands combine multiplicatively with capabilities to yield activity or behavior such that if either demand or capability is zero no activity can be expected to take place. If either demand or capability is extremely high, however, it is possible that the strength of one may compensate for the weakness of the other. Conversely, action tends to be constrained by demand and capability, which can be defined as a function of technology (knowledge and skills) combined with appropriate resources. As previously indicated, population growth can contribute to demand and capability, but — depending upon resources and technology — it can also constrain capability.

A growing population, especially when combined with advancing technology and industrialization, "cannot be supplied with indefinitely increasing quantities of materials and food from a limited area of land. It may be compared to a tree which must throw out roots over a sufficient area of soil to provide itself with nourishment. As the tree grows bigger, the roots extend over a greater and greater distance" (Hawtrey 1930, p. 63). This is not a new observation. As its population grows, Plato asserted, a country "which was large enough to support the original inhabitants will now be too small. If we are to have enough pasture and plough land, we shall have to cut off a slice of our neighbors' territory; and if they are not content with necessaries, but give themselves up to getting unlimited wealth, they will want a slice of ours." Similarly, Thucydides (trans. B. Jowett, p. 574) recorded how the early Greeks attacked and subjugated nearby islands—"especially when the pressure of population was felt by them."

As resources are depleted in the domestic environment (or in a particular sector of it), the costs tend to rise. The gap widens between resources demanded and the resources locally available. In principle there are then five possibilities: (1) outside territories may be discovered, explored, conquered, purchased, or otherwise obtained; (2) some members of the society may emigrate—move into a new resource environment (as the English colonists settled in the thirteen Colonies or Irish, Italians, Central Europeans, and others migrated to the United States generations later); (3) trade may be established with other societies; (4) further technologies may be developed (but not without adding to existing demands); or (5) any two or more of these alternatives may be combined. Throughout recorded history, all five alternatives have been employed many times.

With rising demands, national leaderships, special interest groups, and many of the rank-and-file may be expected to reach out—directly and indirectly—for resources beyond home borders and to demand some degree of security for the maintenance of trade routes and the protection of a wide range of associated activities and interests. This process of outward expansion has often taken the form of territorial aggrandizement but is commonly manifested in many other forms as well (Kuznets 1966, pp. 334–48).

A society with a growing population and insufficient resources within its own territory will be seriously constrained in its activities unless it finds some way of acquiring the resources it demands. "When the demands of a society are unmet and existing capabilities are insufficient to satisfy them, new capabilities may have to be developed" (Choucri and North 1975, p. 16). These will differ according to the means of expanding access to resources that are pursued.

Whether—and how (by trade, conquest, purchase of territory)—a society reaches for resources beyond its sovereignty is conditioned by location, the levels of population and technology, and the resources, technology, needs, power, and friendliness of neighboring states.

PROFILES OF STATES

Depending upon how it relates to other key variables, population can affect the demands that a country generates and increase or decrease its capabili-

ties in major ways. In general, a large (and growing) population with a com-
mensurately advanced (and advancing) technology can contribute both to rising demands and increasing capabilities—especially if adequate resources
are available. By contrast, a large (and growing) population coupled with an
underdeveloped and lagging economy, while generating demands for food
and other basic materials, can seriously constrain capabilities and access to
resources. Suppose we consider four types of countries—A, B, C, and D—
according to their population-technology-resource profiles (North, Ike, and
Triska 1981):

Country A: High Population, Low Technology, Low Access to Resources

These dimensions have characterized many colonialized areas of the
world, such as India in the past century, and several "semi-colonies," such as
China in the late nineteenth and early twentieth centuries, as well as various
"developing" countries since World War II. In the past they were commonly
penetrated and often occupied and governed by other, stronger states. Famine
has often been endemic in such countries, and there has been some tendency—
especially if the national territory has been extensive—for some enclaves to
"fracture off" and seek local autonomy, as the warlord regimes in China after
the collapse of the Chinese Empire in 1911–1912.

Country B: High Population, High Technology, Inadequate Access to Resources

The home territory of a B-type society is characterized by an insufficient "carrying capacity," and hence, unless the country can trade freely and
maintain high levels of production and marketing, strong tendencies toward
militarization and coercive expansion are likely to eventuate. Historically,
Japan was an almost classic example. If they are to survive and aspire to significant power and influence, B-profile countries have few options: if their
access to raw materials and markets is seriously impaired, or if they are constrained in any way from developing a strong trade network with balanced
imports and exports, a disposition toward coercive expansion is likely to develop. Whether capabilities can be achieved for effectively carrying out such
a policy is often problematical.

Country C: High Population, High Technology, Adequate Access to Resources

A C-profile country is likely to have strong possibilities for the expansion of its activities and interests. Historically, many C-profile countries

such as England, France, Belgium, and the Netherlands have started out small but have steadily expanded their territories to imperial proportions. If a C-profile country commands a large population and an expansive territory, it is likely to become a great power or superpower. In the past this pattern has been characteristic of many exceedingly powerful states and empires, for example, ancient Egypt, Assyria, Persia, China during certain centuries, Alexandrian Greece, the Muslim regimes of the Middle Ages, and the French and British empires in the nineteenth and early twentieth centuries.

Country D: Low Population, Advanced Technology, Adequate Access to Resources

Societies characterized by pattern D may obtain resources domestically and/or through extensive and efficient trade networks. In either case, the relatively low population can facilitate comparatively high levels of per capita production at relatively low absolute levels of resource acquisition and processed goods. Over much of the period since the Napoleonic wars, Sweden has tended toward a D-profile. It may or may not be significant that a number of modern states that are thought of as "peaceful" seem to fit the D pattern.

The word *relative* is critical to this discussion: the significance of each profile derives from the *relative* levels and rates of growth of the population, technology, and resource variables — both domestically, within states, and externally across and between states.

LATERAL PRESSURE

We have referred to any tendency on the part of people to extend external activities, either violently or peaceably, from home territory (or from a core area within home territory) as lateral pressure (Choucri and North 1975, p. 16) — a concept similar to economist Simon Kuznets' (1966) idea of outward expansion. Lateral pressure has been expressed variously, in both peaceful and violent activities, as exploration and peaceful settlement, as conquest, often as trade and financial influence. Whatever the mode, the consequences may be expected to depend upon the capabilities of the expansionist country relative to the capabilities of its neighbors. B-profile countries are likely to generate powerful dispositions toward territorial expansion, although they may be constrained by the superior capabilities of other states. Countries with C-profiles such as some states of Western Europe during the late nineteenth and early twentieth centuries, the superpowers — with the advantage of an extensive frontier — were lateral pressure states *par excellence*. A-profile societies, often characterized by rapid population growth, lack the technological advancement and economic growth for sustained external expansion. With low population levels relative to their technological development, states with D-profiles have developed capabilities and patterns of activity (trade networks, high *per capita* production and the like) which make territorial expansion appear expensive, risky, and generally unnecessary. Such societies tend to become masters of commercial and diplomatic (largely accommodative) bargaining.

Commonly, the initial disposition of a high-capability, high-lateral pressure society has been to extend its efforts into regions of low capability — often the sparsely inhabited areas of indigenous bands, tribes, or chiefdoms. Such people have often been pushed aside, confined to reservations, killed, or wholly overcome and absorbed. The command of wealth obtained externally (as well as domestically), Thucydides wrote of ancient Greece, "enabled the more powerful to subjugate the lesser cities" (p. 570). The greater the disparity in technology and specialized capabilities between the conquerors and the conquered, the more ruthless and devastating the outcome has tended to be. Even for the conquest of peasant communities, "the natural way" has been "to take the land directly and to wipe out its settled population" (Weber 1968, II, p. 916). In each historical case the expansion of a society's activities and interests into far places has been an indicator of its domestic vigor, capabilities, and power. Similarly, each substantial contraction or withdrawal has tended to mark the diminution — relative if not absolute — of the society's capability on critical dimensions.

Neither the external activities of a society nor the foreign policies of its government are necessarily the direct outcome solely of a demand for resources, markets, services, or other economic considerations. In the course of its foreign activities a society may pursue security, prestige, status, religious or political converts, or some other outcome. The motivations of any society are almost certain to be mixed: some interest groups support a policy with one value in mind, others support the same policy as a means of achieving something else. Most of these considerations, however, tend to be interdependent. The sustained access of a society to basic resources may depend upon security capabilities, for example, which may depend, in turn, upon access to oil and metals, and both sets of capabilities depend upon successful affiliation (organization and administration). In sum, most major goals of a society require not only sustained access to energy and other resources, but also the sustained interactivity of a range of specialized capabilities, all tending to generate further demands, bargaining, applications of leverage, coalition formation, competitions and other adversarial activities — both domestically and externally.

In general the external activities of a society tend to derive from domestically generated demands and activities that cannot be met or successfully carried out without some reference to the external environment. International competition and conflict are thus closely linked to the domestic growth of countries in the system, with the result that the domestic and foreign activities of any given country are likely to be intensely — although not always obviously — interdependent. Just as domestic growth may contribute to a country's foreign activities, so its foreign activities, in alliance, competition, or conflict with those of other countries, may generate further domestic demands and growth. In general the stronger the tendency of rival countries toward expansion of their activities and interests, the stronger is likely to be the feeling by each country that its "national interests" ought to be protected and the stronger is the probability that competition or conflict over territory, resources, markets, political or diplomatic influence, military or naval power, status, or prestige will be intensified.

NATIONAL INTERESTS

National interests may be private or corporate rather than governmental. They become national interests when governmental leaders decide for one reason or another to define them as such. This behavior tends to be especially characteristic of the international relations of powerful states and empires, although countries of lesser capabilities may undertake similar patterns of activity within a regional context. During the late nineteenth and early twentieth centuries, the metropolitan powers of Europe engaged in such activities throughout much of Africa and Asia. "The critical factor in determining the importance to a nation of an interest is not the kind of interest, but the existence of the feeling that it must be defended (and then the intensity of this feeling is measured by the costs that a nation is willing to incur in the defense of this interest" (Choucri and North 1975, p. 19).

With respect to specialized capabilities and overall power, states and empires do not stand still relative to one another. Some are growing while others are declining, and thus the condition of the international system is in continuous flux. A-profile countries may compete with others, and some may develop faster than their neighbors. Wars may be fought between them. A few may narrow the gap between themselves and B, C, and D profile countries. Under such circumstances "a rapidly growing society — one whose mounting military preparations are commensurate with its outwardly expanding interests and commitments—can pose a threat of preponderance in the system" (Ashley 1980, p. 36). When two societies are mutual rivals and a military gap between them is wide or widening, "the lagging actor can come to feel that its interests, perhaps its survival, are threatened" (Ashley 1980, p. 35). Such a country may feel itself at a relative disadvantage in the world competition for resources, markets, prestige, or strategic superiority. Efforts to catch up may be undertaken, not only in diverse adjustments, but across a wide spectrum of capabilities including technology, industrialization, agriculture, standard of living, culture, and the exploration of outer space.

Differences in capabilities between powerful countries are likely to have meanings that are quite distinct from those that distinguish a potential colony or a client state from a major, dominating power. In confrontation with a major C-profile power, a weak A-profile state has limited possibilities for bargaining and leverage, whereas the less strong of two major powers normally has the possibility of increasing its specialized capabilities including its military forces. This option often leads to intensified competition between states. Of course there are ways a highly motivated, relatively low-capability A-profile state—especially in a client relationship with a more powerful state—can hold a C-profile state at bay or even defeat it (commonly in part by attrition).

We have indicated above two main ways a country can increase its capabilities. One way is to increase its domestic technology and specialized capabilities (production, organizational, military); another is by coalition formation—the negotiation of favorable alliances. Such bonds normally imply the pooling of some capabilities for the maintenance of shared interests. A leading power may seek an alliance to prevent a growing power from overtaking it in some area, or a growing power may seek an alliance in order to overtake a stronger power. Such alternatives can have their own costs, however, since each state may be expected to have demands and leverage potentials of its own.

In general we would expect high-capability, major powers to influence, dominate, possibly exploit and on occasion overrun societies of significantly lower capabilities. There have been many spectacular reversals. Pre-state societies—especially tribes and chiefdoms of nomadic horsemen from plains or steppes and Nordic seamen—have often overrun states with substantially larger populations and more advanced technologies—usually when the latter had been in stages of decline. In a long succession of outflows Indo-European, Turkish, Mongolian, Tungusic, and other peoples flowed outward from northern forests and Eurasian steppes south to the Mediterranean littoral in ancient and medieval times, westward from the steppes into Europe, through the Middle East as far as Egypt, deep into India and China, and so forth (McNeill 1963, pp. 484–506).

FROM OUTWARD EXPANSION
TO ESTABLISHING SPHERES OF INTEREST

When two countries extend their respective interests outward, there is a strong probability that such interests will be opposing, and the activities of these nations may collide. These activities may be governmental or private — diplomatic, commercial, military, and so forth — and they may involve quite different interests, levels of intensity, and implications for other countries.

When the expanding activities and interests of a nation — especially a domestically growing nation — so intersect or collide, the more likely the possibilities for conflict (as well as for cooperation). The deeper roots of major power confrontations are usually to be found in "mutual antagonisms engendered, even institutionalized, by bilateral competition" and coercive leverages emerging from such collisions (Ashley 1980, p. 35). National leaders, assuming and making claims for the sovereignty of their respective states in line with coalition and adversary bargaining concepts, tend to perceive other states automatically as rivals. Indeed, societies "which refuse to submit to common laws cannot but regard one another with suspicion" (Aron 1959, p. 7).

As an intersection intensifies, the resulting possible outcomes are almost boundless. "Indeed, much of the generative quality of history — the tendencies of enduring historical trends and structures to converge, recombine, and produce a rich new set of relationships seemingly marking the opening of a new epoch — can be attributed to the emergent combinatorial possibilities that such intersections afford" (Ashley 1980, p. 29). Often such collisions bear implications for coalition formation as well as for intensified conflict: bargaining — both coercive and accommodative — commonly attracts supporters even as it creates adversaries. Collisions of activities and interests can lead to the withdrawal of one (or both) of the parties, an agreement between them, or continuing conflict (Choucri and North 1975, p. 9)

Here an important theoretical caveat needs to be put forward. Rarely, if ever, are population growth, advancement in technology, rising demands, increases in military capabilities, expansion of national activities and interests, and like phenomena the proximate explanations of war (Choucri and North 1975, p. 9). Such phenomena are normally located near the base or throughout what might be envisaged as the midsections of a means-end hierarchy of *mixed motives* leading to war. They generate demands, constrain capabilities, set the stage, arm the players, contribute to critical issues, and deploy the forces, but they seldom join the antagonists in combat. The more proximate explanations are likely to include a confrontation or provocation and the bargaining and leverage moves that are made by the contestants in the course of seeking a resolution.

To a large extent active conflict and various phenomena related to it (coercive diplomacy, deterrence, escalation, arms races, crises, limited war, and even all-out war) can be explained in terms of the concepts and processes discussed so far — differential growth and development (population, technology, access to resources), demands, differential capabilities, coalition formation, adversarial bargaining, leverage (rewards), coercive leverage (penalties), and outward expansion or lateral pressure. Coercive diplomacy lies at the base of many interactions between states: "a coercive move puts pressure on the adversary to accept one's demand or bargaining 'position,' perhaps by threatening punishment if he fails to comply, or by a variety of other techniques" (Snyder 1961, p. 222). Anyone seeking to understand large-scale violence and war might begin by focusing on this proposition.

FROM COMPETITION TO COERCION

Much bargaining, negotiating, competitive bidding, and so forth can be implicit in the actions undertaken by the two sides, rather than explicit. Under such circumstances, it is always possible that one country, A, may misinterpret the intention behind an action taken by its opponent, B — thus reading into B's move (undertaken for whatever purpose, even inadvertence or sheer meanness) a level of coercion that was never contemplated. If A retaliates, then, with a coercive response, B, whatever its original intention, may be expected to respond with a coercive move of its own. Every move undertaken by one nation and seen by another nation as affecting it adversely thus has the possibility of being interpreted as a signal conveying information about subsequent moves or outcomes and thereby initiating an exchange of coercive leverages.

Usually the more salient coercive leverages (penalizing moves or threats) — and those likely to be more proximate to confrontations, crises, escalations, and war are political, diplomatic, and military, but they may also be economic. Of course, all political, diplomatic, and military moves involve economics in so far as their implementation depends upon energy, capital, labor, industrial processes, transportation, and so forth, but factors also can be used as leverage directed against an opponent. Just prior to and during World War II, states used foreign trade as instruments in their policies of power and international control (Hirschman 1945). With respect to the supply effect of foreign trade, Germany concentrated on imports needed for the war machine; accumulated large stocks of strategic materials; redirected trade to politically friendly or subject nations; and sought control of oceanic trade routes. Certain smaller countries became dependent on German trade.

The supply effect involves the securing of access to strategic materials. It results from (1) policies that secure gains from trade, particularly the importation of strategic goods; (2) trade directed to countries from which there is minimal danger of being cut off; and (3) the control of trade routes. These aspects of national trade policy lead to a direct increase in the preparedness of the country for war and provide protection in the event of trade interruptions. Just as war or the threat of war can be construed as a direct means of obtaining a particular result, so the supply effect may serve as an indirect instrument of power. Therefore, the final result of the supply effect of foreign trade implies at least the possibility of war (Hirschman 1945, p. 14).

The influence effect provides leverage which a particular country can exert over its trading partners to make them dependent upon their trade with that country. The influence effect can be accomplished by (1) developing a monopoly of exports and directing trade to countries requiring these articles; (2) directing trade to smaller, poorer countries and those with low mobility of resources; (3) creating vested interests in a trading partner's power groups; and (4) exporting highly differentiated goods to create dependent consumption and production habits. The influence effect is thus achieved by encouraging the dependence of a trading partner on one's own trade without becoming dependent on the trade of the opponent. As a result the threat of interrupting or withholding trade becomes a potentially powerful economic weapon in international relations.

Every nation has at least minimal influence of this kind, but some have vastly more than others. Through the control of its frontiers and the power over its citizens, such a country "can at any time interrupt its own export and import trade, which is at the same time the import and export trade of some other countries. The stoppage of this trade obliges the other countries to find alternative markets and sources of supply and, should this prove impossible, it forces upon them economic adjustments and lasting impoverishment" (Hirschman 1945, pp. 15–16). Superior financial capabilities can also be used as a form of coercion leverage.

It is a characteristic of human affairs that a threatening, penalizing, coercive, or otherwise potentially injurious move by one party in an interactive situation often evokes a comparable, but possibly more threatening or punishing, response from the other party (Pruitt 1969, pp. 392–93). Such a response may be forthcoming regardless of whether or not his purpose was to threaten or inflict an injury. This phenomenon is variously referred to as escalation, schismogenesis (Bateson 1972, pp. 64–72, 108–11), an action-reaction process, the conflict spiral — even a vicious circle. In affairs of state it often happens that a move undertaken by A in the interests of self-defense may evoke a comparable response from B. Similarly, a move made by A to deter a threatening or damaging move by B may, in fact, evoke from B not the submissive response expected by A but a counter-measure of greater magnitude than B might otherwise have contemplated. An escalation, the conflict spiral, or action-reaction process takes place when two parties, caught up in "negative bargaining," trade coercive leverages back and forth—each action by A being an increase in threat or actual violence over the preceding leverage applied by B, and vice-versa.

Between countries, the course of an escalation may be constrained by various types of relationships internal to one or both participants (Pruitt 1969, p. 402). When two countries are in confrontation, for example, there may be a tendency for ethnic or other special interest groups with severe grievances in one country to seek—or anticipate seeking—support from fellow ethnic or other interest groups within the opposing country and hence resist the escalation effort of the country in which they are located. Something similar can occur when domestic coalitions (rival political parties, for example) are in bitter dispute over foreign policy.

The phenomenon of escalation, schismogenesis, action-reaction process or conflict spiral stands in contradiction to deterrence theory, which theoreticians and national leaders commonly use to rationalize and justify efforts at influencing the behavior of rival nations. The purpose of deterrence is to "control" the behavior of another country in spheres of activity wherein particular moves are unwanted. History provides many examples of successful deterrence—and many that were unsuccessful. The reason for this inconsistency is that as a form of bargaining and application of leverages, deterrence is highly plastic: whatever the deterrence measure applied, the decision about response lies with the respondent and not with those who have applied the measure. To be effective, according to theorists, a deterrent must be stable and credible. The critical question, however, is whether or not a threat by country A can be relied upon to deter an aggressive or other potentially threatening activity by B. How can a nation's leaders be sure that a deterrent move will not induce the opponent to take some threatening countermove of its own?

CONFLICT ESCALATION AND ARMS RACE

The arms race can be identified as a special type of escalation process wherein an increase in A's military capabilities—whether undertaken as a form of deterrence or merely as a routine defense measure—is viewed by the leadership of rival state B as a threat to its security. When the military capabilities of B are increased in order to reduce or close the gap, A's leaders—perceiving the increase as a threat to their country's security—act to increase A's capabilities, and so the competition spirals. As the tendencies of A and B to respond in this way become more "intense and reciprocated," the bilateral competitive processes tend to "interlock," thus yielding the action-reaction, schismogenic, or escalation process (Ashley 1980, p. 35). In such a competition suspicion and fear may be expected to multiply with the armaments (Huntington 1971, p. 531).

The arms race has been referred to as "a form of reciprocal interaction between two states or coalitions" or, more specifically, "a progressive, competitive peacetime increase in armaments by two states or coalitions of states resulting from conflicting purposes or mutual fears" (Huntington 1971, p. 499). Arms races have also been identified as involving "simultaneous abnormal rates of growth in the military outlays of two or more nations" (Wallace 1979, p. 242).

The action-reaction explanation for the arms race phenomenon has been postulated in a mathematical model that countries increase their armaments primarily in response to the increasing arms expenditures of a rival nation (Hollist 1977, p. 504; Bateson 1972, p. 110). As in any other escalating process, once an arms race is underway the participants are likely to find themselves locked into a relationship from which it is difficult for either to withdraw: to the extent that A's leaders perceive their country overtaken by B's rising capabilities, they may see no reasonable alternative other than to increase their own capabilities. Conversely, however, as B's leaders perceive their country falling behind in the competition, they are likely to see no reasonable alternative to a redoubling of effort. This type of action and reaction has been commonplace in superpower relations since World War II.

Studies of the arms race phenomenon are generally classifiable into two groups: those emphasizing competitive international action-reaction processes; and those emphasizing domestic factors such as technology and bureaucratic or interest group pressures. Which perspective is closer to reality has become a debatable issue. Arms race studies emphasizing internal factors have tended to play down but not totally dismiss the effects of competition between rivals.

> This genre of explanation hypothesizes that — in addition to genuine defense concerns among people on all levels of society — the military build-up of either country — or of both — may be attributable in considerable part to domestic growth factors — the development of (and desire to sell) new military technology and weapons systems and the consequent development of special interest groups among all those who invent, develop, build and distribute armaments (and their components and replacement parts) — including technical personnel, labor, suppliers, entrepreneurs, and contractors as well as managers and stockholders. Presumably, such special-interest activities can help fuel the action-reaction competition once it is set in motion. (Hollist 1977, p. 505)

It appears self-evident, however, that the domestic factor and action-reaction process approaches to the arms race phenomenon are not necessarily antithetical. "Indeed, the explanation having the closest match with empirical observations may incorporate components from each" (Hollist 1977, p. 505). It is also possible that the action-reaction process may be the dominant explanation of a particular race at one stage, whereas domestic factors may dominate at some other stage. It would not be surprising to find such variability taking place within the same countries through time as well as across a considerable number of countries at the same time.

FROM ESCALATION TO INTERNATIONAL CRISIS

However the phenomenon of international crisis is defined, it almost always meets the criteria for an escalatory or action-reaction process. Thus, in an international crisis situation escalatory interactions come about in part because the leaders of one country, A, perceiving an action of country B as aggressive or threatening, undertake counter-leverage in one form or another, which is then perceived as a threat by the leaders of B. B's response is perceived by the leadership of A as threatening, whereupon they undertake further coercive action which they hope will deter B and thus bring relief. Or they may expect early changes in the crisis situation to be punishing but necessary enabling steps toward a more rewarding situation in the future. "Often the expectation of 'reward' thus involves the avoidance or elimination of a punishing situation rather than an outcome which might be viewed as intrinsically rewarding" (Nomikos and North 1976, p. 258). Under the pressure of intense interchange, each response is likely to be "automatic and mindless," each moves so swiftly that it can scarcely be distinguished from a "reflex." It is under such circumstances that statesmen start saying, "We have no alternative" (Deutsch 1968, p. 113).

For every crisis that escalates into war, there are many others that "cool down" or de-escalate. What is the difference? In response to threat, coercion, injury or other penalizing activity from country B, country A's leaders may develop the intention of responding with an equivalent or higher level of threat or coercion. After consultation with their advisers, however, they may decide that A does not have the capability to respond at such a level — or that the response they are contemplating may trigger an outcome that would be unacceptable, perhaps disastrous for their own interests and well-being. A's leaders may decide to back down, and then the leaders of B may conclude that A has been deterred (Nomikos and North 1976, pp. 258–59).

Alternatively, as targets of what they perceive as a threatening, coercive or otherwise punishing action by A, the leaders of B may at the start decide upon a conciliatory response which they expect (or hope) will induce A to lower its level of coercive activity. Then the question is, how will A's leaders perceive, evaluate and respond to this move? Will they reciprocate with a conciliatory move, or will they take advantage of the situation by an increase in aggressiveness? Since B's leaders cannot be certain of the outcome, they may decide against conciliatory action and either take precautionary action (order an alert, mobilize or position troops, for example) or strike back at a higher level of threat and violence. Alternatively, B's leaders may try to play safe: they may couple a conciliatory move with a precautionary move—with the possibility that A's leaders may overlook or choose to ignore the former and retaliate against the latter with an aggressive move of their own (Nomikos and North 1976, p. 258).

FROM CRISIS TO WAR

Clausewitz has been remembered primarily for his assertion that war amounts to a continuation of politics by other means. Thus whenever war breaks out, "policy has created the war" (Clausewitz 1943, p. 698). Such a perspective is not substantially different from the view that war occurs at the point where the issue of who gets what, when, and how is no longer to be decided by accommodative bargaining, peaceful negotiation, or even the exchange of coercive threats, but rather by the application of active military intervention as the major form of leverage. From this perspective, "to eliminate the possibility of war is to deprive states of the right to be the ultimate judges of what the defense of their interests or their honor demands" (Aron 1959, p. 8).

Often favored by military theorists, the strategy of quick, decisive use of force attempts to alter an opponent's will by destroying a significant portion of his military capability. This strategy largely dispenses with threats, diplomacy, or subtle modes of persuasion to alter the opponent's policy. Underlying this option is the assumption that "if ample force is used quickly and in a militarily efficient manner, i.e., unhobbled by too many political constraints, it offers the possibility of terminating the conflict before it spreads or develops into a prolonged war of attrition" (George, Hall, and Simons 1971, pp. 16–17).

Another way in which force may be used as an instrument of foreign policy is one that both of the strategies already discussed seek to avoid. This is the alternative of attrition—the strategy of waging "prolonged warfare under a set of conditions or limitations on military operations that give neither side a clear advantage" (George, Hall, and Simons 1971, p. 19). Under special conditions a strategy of attrition may be favored: a weaker state, for example, may pursue a strategy of attrition against a stronger state with the expectation that time will allow an enhancement of its own capabilities. Not uncommonly, especially in developing nations, guerrilla forms of attrition strategy have been used.

Theoreticians who have applied bargaining theory to international conflict have tended to draw a sharp line between limited war — wherein armed force is used as a form of coercive diplomacy (in order to achieve a specific goal) — and "all-out war" or "brute force." Fundamental to the concept of limited warfare is the notion of limits as identified by parties to the conflict.

Is there a qualitative difference between limited war and all-out war, or is the difference essentially a matter of scale? It has been emphasized that if limited war is taken to mean any war at a level less than all out, "then we may say that the concept of limited war and the concept of escalation mutually imply, and intermesh with, each other" (Smoke 1977, p. 17). This means that escalation is the process whereby "the previous limits of a war are crossed and new ones established (or, in the end, the last limits crossed). Conversely, the (expanding) limits of a war are the barriers or thresholds or stages of the escalation process. From this point of view, limited war and escalation are coextensive: neither is 'larger' as an idea, or encountered more frequently in reality, than the other" (Smoke 1977, p. 17).

The difference between coercion and "brute force," according to one perspective, often lies as much in the intent as in the instrument. Brute force tries to overcome an opponent's strength, whereas the threat of pain or destruction tries to structure his motives and behavior (Schelling 1960, 1966).

There may have been episodes in history where superior forces razed villages, cities or even whole nations and did their best to exterminate the inhabitants — all without any purpose other than the meanness of it and the joy of large-scale slaughter. Often it looked that way to the victims of Attila and other "scourges" of the past, and readers of history have frequently accepted the attribution. In many, if not most cases, however, the perpetrator of "brute force" *did* have a purpose (however ill-defined or nefarious it may have appeared to others) — some end, the achievement of which depended on the choices or decisions that the other participants (the opponent, enemy, threat, or victim) would make. In such cases, "brute force" amounts to the additional coercive leverage which one party or the other has available and *decides* to use in order to accomplish his purposes. "War in its most extreme forms is the pure, ultimate form of coercion — the raw, physical clash of armed forces — in a context where the pursuit of objectives in conflict greatly predominates over the pursuit of common interests" (Snyder 1972, p. 218).

Drawing the line between limited warfare and "all-out war" or "brute force" is partly a matter of preference, depending as well on the definition of the bargaining process. Certainly, there are differing degrees of communications according to the context and mode of bargaining. Limited warfare is likely to involve significantly less explicit communication than across-the-table negotiation and diplomacy, for example, and all-out war tends to reduce explicit communications to a minimum or exclude it altogether. A bargaining situation is defined by the assumption that "the ability of one participant to gain his ends is dependent to an important degree on the choices or decisions that the other participant will make" (Schelling 1960, p. 5) — admittedly a broad definition. Within such a context communications between "bargainers" can vary from direct and explicit to indirect (even inferential) and implicit, the latter being characteristic of many all-out war situations (the winner of the "bargain" often being determined on the occasion of unconditional surrender or at the treaty table).

CONCLUSION: THE CONFLICT SPIRAL

From a demand, capability, bargaining and leverage perspective it can be inferred that conflict and war are seldom, if ever, explained from population alone. On the contrary, we may envisage a hierarchy or "pyramid" of dynamic and interconnected variables (population included) which are often contributory, with action-reaction processes (with strong psychological components) being among the more proximate. All these variables originate with human beings and their preoccupations, however, and over the medium to long run differences in population levels and rates of change — combined with differences in levels and rates of change of technology and access to basic resources — can be expected to condition the demands, capabilities, bargaining and leverage potentials and behavioral outcomes of state-level societies interacting with each other.

REFERENCES

Aron, R. *On War.* Garden City, N.Y.: Doubleday, 1959.

Ashley, R. K. *The Political Economy of War and Peace: The Sino-Soviet-American Triangle and the Modern Security Problematique.* New York: Nichols, 1980.

Bateson, G. *Steps to an Ecology of the Mind.* New York: Ballantine, 1972.

Brecher, M. *Decisions in Crisis: Israel, 1967 and 1973.* Berkeley, Ca.: University of California Press, 1980.

Choucri, N., and R. C. North. *Nations in Conflict: National Growth and International Violence*. San Francisco, Ca.: Freeman, 1975.

Clausewitz, K. von. *On War,* trans. O. J. M. Jolles. New York: Modern Library, 1943.

Cyert, R. M., and J. G. March. *A Behavioral Theory of the Firm*. Englewood Cliffs, N.J.: Prentice-Hall, 1963.

Dallin, A. "The Domestic Sources of Soviet Foreign Policy." In *The Domestic Context of Soviet Foreign Policy,* edited by Seweryn Bialer. Boulder, Co.: Westview, 1981, pp. 335–408.

Deutsch, K. *The Nerves of Government: Models of Political Communication and Control*. New York: Free Press, 1963.

Easton, D. *A Systems Analysis of Political Life*. New York: Wiley, 1965.

George, A., D. K. Hall, and W. E. Simons. *The Limits of Coercive Diplomacy: Laos, Cuba, Vietnam*. Boston: Little, Brown, 1971.

George, A. L., and R. Smoke. *Deterrence in American Foreign Policy: Theory and Practice*. New York: Columbia University Press, 1974.

Hawtrey, R. G. *Economic Aspects of Sovereignty*. London: Longmans, Green, 1930.

Hermann, C. F. *Crises in Foreign Policy: A Simulation Analysis*. Indianapolis, In.: Bobbs-Merrill, 1969.

Hirschman, A. O. *National Power and the Structure of Foreign Trade*. Berkeley, Ca.: University of California Press, 1945.

Hollist, W. L. "An Analysis of Arms Processes in the United States and the Soviet Union." *International Studies Quarterly* 21 (1977): 503–28.

Holsti, O. R. *Crisis, Escalation, War*. Montreal: McGill-Queen's University Press, 1972.

Huntington, S. P. "Arms Races: Prerequisites and Results." In *Power, Action, and Interaction: Readings on International Politics,* edited by G. H. Quester. Boston: Little, Brown, 1971, pp. 299–541.

Ikle, F. C. *How Nations Negotiate*. New York: Harper and Row, 1964.

Jervis, R. *Perception and Misperception in International Politics*. Princeton, N.J.: Princeton University Press, 1976.

Kahn, H. *On Escalation, Metaphors, and Scenarios,* rev. ed. Baltimore, Md.: Penguin, 1968.

Kuznets, S. *Modern Economic Growth: Rate, Structure, and Spread*. New Haven, Ct.: Yale University Press, 1966.

Maslow, A. *Motivation and Personality,* rev. ed. New York: Harper and Row, 1970.

McNeill, W. H. *The Rise of the West: A History of the Human Community*. Chicago: University of Chicago Press, 1963.

Morse, E. "Crisis Diplomacy, Interdependence, and the Politics of International Economic Relations." In *Theory and Policy in International Relations,* edited by R. Tanter and R. H. Ullman. Princeton, N.J.: Princeton University Press, 1972, pp. 123–50.

Nomikos, E. and R. C. North. *International Crisis: The Outbreak of World War I.* Montreal: McGill-Queen's University Press, 1976.

North, R. C., N. Ike, and J. Triska. *The World of the Superpowers.* Stanford, Ca.: Notrik Press, 1981.

Pfeffer, J. and G. Salancik. *The External Control of Organizations: A Resource Dependent Perspective.* New York: Harper and Row, 1978.

Pruitt, D. G. "Stability and Sudden Change in Interpersonal and International Affairs." In *International Politics and Foreign Policy: A Reader in Research and Theory,* rev. ed., edited by J. N. Rosenau. New York: Free Press, 1969, pp. 392–408.

Riker, W. *The Theory of Political Coalitions.* New Haven, Ct.: Yale University Press, 1962.

Rosenau, J. N., ed. *Linkage Politics.* New York: Free Press, 1969.

Schelling, T. C. *Arms and Influence.* New Haven, Ct.: Yale University Press, 1966.

_____. *The Strategy of Conflict.* Cambridge, Ma.: Harvard University Press, 1960.

Smoke, R. *War: Controlling Escalation.* Cambridge, Ma.: Harvard University Press, 1977.

Snyder, G. H. "Crisis Bargaining." In *International Crises: Insights from Behavioral Research,* edited by Charles F. Hermann. New York: Free Press, 1972, pp. 217–56.

_____. *Deterrence and Defense: Toward a Theory of National Security.* Princeton, N.J.: Princeton University Press, 1961.

_____, and P. Diesing. *Conflict Among Nations: Bargaining, Decision Making, and System Structure in International Crises.* Princeton, N.J.: Princeton University Press, 1977.

Thucydides. "The Peloponnesian War," trans. B. Jowett. In *The Greek Historians,* vol. 1, edited by F. I. B. Godolphin. New York: Random House, 1942, pp. 567–1001.

Wallace, M. D. "Arms Races and Escalation: Some New Evidence." In *Explaining War: Selected Papers from the Correlates of War Project,* edited by J. David Singer. Beverly Hills, Ca.: Sage, 1979, pp. 240–52.

Weber, M. *Economy and Society: An Outline of Interpretive Sociology,* vol. 2. New York: Bedminister, 1968.

Wright. Q. *A Study of War,* 2nd ed. Chicago: University of Chicago Press, 1965.

Zartman, I. W. *The Fifty Percent Solution: How to Bargain Successfully with Hijackers, Strikers, Bosses, Oil Magnates, Arabs, Russians, and Other Worthy Opponents in the Modern World.* Garden City, N.Y.: Anchor, 1976.

INDEX

MULTIDISCIPLINARY PERSPECTIVES ON POPULATION AND CONFLICT

was composed in 10-point Digital Compugraphic Times Roman and leaded two points,
with display type also in Times Roman, by Metricomp;
printed by sheet-fed offset on 55-pound, acid-free Glatfelter Antique Cream,
Smythe-sewn and bound over binder's boards in Joanna Arrestox B,
also adhesive-bound with paper covers,
by Maple-Vail Book Manufacturing Group, Inc.;
and published by

SYRACUSE UNIVERSITY PRESS

SYRACUSE, NEW YORK 13210